ANARCHAEOLOGIES

Sara Guyer and Brian McGrath, series editors

Lit Z embraces models of criticism uncontained by conventional notions of history, periodicity, and culture, and committed to the work of reading. Books in the series may seem untimely, anachronistic, or out of touch with contemporary trends because they have arrived too early or too late. Lit Z creates a space for books that exceed and challenge the tendencies of our field and in doing so reflect on the concerns of literary studies here and abroad.

At least since Friedrich Schlegel, thinking that affirms literature's own untimeliness has been named romanticism. Recalling this history, Lit Z exemplifies the survival of romanticism as a mode of contemporary criticism, as well as forms of contemporary criticism that demonstrate the unfulfilled possibilities of romanticism. Whether or not they focus on the romantic period, books in this series epitomize romanticism as a way of thinking that compels another relation to the present. Lit Z is the first book series to take seriously this capacious sense of romanticism.

In 1977, Paul de Man and Geoffrey Hartman, two scholars of romanticism, team-taught a course called Literature Z that aimed to make an intervention into the fundamentals of literary study. Hartman and de Man invited students to read a series of increasingly difficult texts and through attention to language and rhetoric compelled them to encounter "the bewildering variety of ways such texts could be read." The series' conceptual resonances with that class register the importance of recollection, reinvention, and reading to contemporary criticism. Its books explore the creative potential of reading's untimeliness and history's enigmatic force.

ANARCHAEOLOGIES

Reading as Misreading

Erin Graff Zivin

Fordham University Press

New York   2020

Fordham University Press gratefully acknowledges financial assistance and support provided for the publication of this book by the University of Southern California.

Visit us online at www.fordhampress.com.

Library of Congress Cataloging-in-Publication Data available online at https://catalog.loc.gov.

Printed in the United States of America

22 21 20   5 4 3 2 1

First edition

for Erin

Contents

ANARCHAEOLOGIES

Introduction: Ethical and Political Thinking after Literature

> To break with the religious myth of reading.
> —Louis Althusser[1]

> If the body's most archaic instinctual reactions are caught up in an encounter with what it does not immediately recognize in the real, how could thought really claim to apprehend the other, the wholly other, without astonishment?
> —Anne Dufourmantelle[2]

Reading gets a bad rap these days.

If you'll humor me, I'd like to share an anecdote from a recent lecture at my university by a junior scholar in the field of Latin American literary studies, in order to provide you with a sense of what I mean. In the lecture, he'd just carried out an elegant and original close reading of a passage of a contemporary novel. In response to a question about the passage during the Q&A, he began by apologizing, confessing, asking for forgiveness from the author of the novel (with whom, he explained, he was personally acquainted) for reading it "irresponsibly." He felt guilty, irresponsible, because he'd approached the passage as a pretext to speak about a theoretical problem that might not be immediately apparent to most readers of the novel, rather than treading the well-worn path, both within and outside of Latin American literary studies, of providing a comprehensive, totalizing interpretation or theory of the novel in question. He spoke of a passage in order to make a larger theoretical argument, rather than "faithfully" and "authoritatively" accounting for the novel as a whole.

He felt guilty. He hoped the author would forgive his betrayal.

Yet guilt, and modesty, work in mysterious ways. He confessed, yet he simultaneously made an accusation. In his refusal to participate in the discipline-constituting, canon-building work that many literary scholars have carried out before him, he took aim at the institutional politics of literary studies. Latin American literature, by no means the only field in which this takes place, has been created through such readings, and this scholar—an assistant professor not in the tenure stream at their home institution—wanted none of it. (I mention this faculty member's rank and tenure status because we might expect such a risk to be taken by a tenured, senior scholar, whose position and professional legitimacy within the profession would be less likely to be called into question.) What would happen if we were to return to reading in this transgressive way, not in order to be "faithful" to the intentions or desires of a work's author, or to the totality of a text, or a generation, or a nation, and certainly not to recuperate or conserve a dying discipline, but rather to entertain the possibility of interpretation in and through its most radical possibilities, that is to say, through betrayal?

This little anecdote illustrates even more than I've described. If the scholar in question rebelled against an elitist, conservative, humanist approach to reading and to literary studies, what about the "other side" of this elitism? What John Beverley called "neo-Arielism" in his book *Latinamericanism after 9/11*—referring to what he understood as a return to the lettered practice of constituting and consolidating a cultural elite through intellectual labor, as the Uruguayan writer José Enrique Rodó advocated in his 1900 book *Ariel*—stands in opposition to a "committed" intellectual practice, an army of academics in solidarity with progressive or revolutionary causes, with armed resistance, and with "the people" in general. Beverley's book, a fascinating if flawed map of the field after the events of September 11, 2001, paints a picture in which the demise of the global and Latin American Left in the wake of the collapse of the Soviet Union in 1989, as well as the subalternism that followed in the 1990s, left only one possible avenue for politically engaged work that would seek to dismantle hegemonic and elite systems. This avenue, which must exclude the possibility of ethics (a cousin of neo-Arielism, according to Beverley) and deconstruction (insufficiently political), involves the unconditional support of "pink tide" (*marea rosada*) governments during the first decade of the new millennium: a tide that has once again turned in the intervening years.

Yet if we acknowledge that the opposition between elitist literary studies and politically committed cultural studies no longer holds,[3] that ethics might be understood not as a substitute for a more "legitimate" pursuit of social and economic justice but rather as residing at the very heart of that struggle, if we acknowledge that, historically, Latinamericanism has depended upon these oppositions for its very existence, then I believe it is fair to say that the present book emerges out of the *ruins* of Latinamericanism. Yes, nearly all of its "objects" of study hail from Argentina. Yet *Anarchaeologies* rejects the identitarian practices of Latinamericanism past (Beverley acknowledges that Latinamericanism is by definition "a form of identity politics" [*Latinamericanism*, 5]), arguing instead for an interpretative practice that would guard a kernel of nonidentity at the core of any identitarian claim. Moreover, it rejects the regionalist conceit that a "proper" Latin American studies would eschew European thinkers, that an engagement with, among other things, continental philosophy, would amount to a betrayal.

Anarchaeologies betrays this sense of betrayal, or rather, it *embraces* betrayal, impropriety, and transgressions not unrelated to the transgression confessed in the opening anecdote. This book advances a reading practice *not* in the reactionary, conservative sense I have just described but rather as a practice that would guard the errors, blind spots, and misunderstandings that I argue, following the work of Jacques Derrida, Paul de Man, and others, comprise the most potent aspects of literary texts. It rejects the notion that attending to textuality, to literariness, constitutes a betrayal of ethics or politics, just as it denies the reductive idea, advanced by some, that literary texts would exhibit ethical or political import or meaning only through a readable, translatable ideological message. No: Anarchaeological reading opens the way for a more elusive, opaque—yet not for that reason any less radical—ethico-political path. *Anarchaeologies* argues, finally, for the pursuit of an undeconstructible notion of justice that may not be recognizable as either ethical or political.

This book emerges at a particular crossroads, historically, geopolitically, and disciplinarily. It is of, and exceeds, the early twenty-first century: It responds to contemporary ethical and political questions while making an argument that it is only by deconstructing history, by acknowledging the intempestive or untimely nature of the present, that we can attend to its most radical demands. It is of, and exceeds, Argentina: Argentine narrative, film, and art-activism comprise the book's central corpus, if only to make the case for an anti-identitarian (national, regional, or otherwise) method of reading. It is of, and exceeds, Latin American studies: It proposes a Latinamericanism-after-deconstruction (or perhaps a deconstruction-after-Latinamericanism), one that engages with and pushes past the dominant disciplinary modes of allegory and representation, identity and difference. It intervenes in and moves beyond antagonisms and deadlocks between deconstruction and Marxism, ethics "versus" politics, between a conservative humanism that would seek to revindicate the institutions of literature and literary studies, on the one hand, and those who would reject literary texts as a possible source of thought: ethical, political, or otherwise.

Anarchaeological reading—engaging with the blind spots, errors, anarchic and anachronic qualities of a text—should therefore be understood within a broader disciplinary intervention that I am calling *indisciplinary exposure*. Rather than opposing literary study to ethical and political thought, Latin American studies to continental philosophy, *Anarchaeologies* makes the case for a constant and relentless exposure of one discipline to another, one genre or medium to another, one regional practice to another. Exposure is a variation of relation: By exposing one to the other, we do not arrive at a complementary or synthetic/dialectical harmony. Rather, each discipline—or text, or genre, or concept, or regional identity—is revealed to be constitutively defective. At the same time, paradoxically, a discipline's most radical possibilities are marshaled at this very point of weakness, error, failure. The limits of philosophy and comparative literature are made evident when exposed to Latin American studies, and the insular quality of area studies is made evident through its exposure to continental philosophy and critical theory. (A similar effect, differently shaped and with different consequences, will result from *exposing*, say, "German Romanticism" to philosophy written in Chile by Deleuzian thinkers, or Gramscian engagement with populism to the contemporary African novel.) Most significantly, exposure makes impossible the very separation between "theory" and "practice," "thought" and "object of thought," which historically has been distributed unevenly across geopolitical regions.[4]

Reading after the Last Reader

> But look where sadly the poor wretch comes reading.
> William Shakespeare, *Hamlet*

What kind of readings, or misreadings, will I advance in the pages that follow? Let me begin with a recent example from the (since deceased) Argentine writer Ricardo Piglia.

Poised on the border between two political and literary epochs, in the interregnum between social and cultural orders, Piglia's 2005 book *El último lector* (The last reader) details modern literary representations of readers and reading, with the hope of signaling some possible avenues for life after the so-called death of reading. Almost despite himself, Piglia sketches out what a postmortem form of "reading" might look like. *El último lector* provides, in its argument's blind spots, a theory of anachronic reading and a corresponding anachronic literary history that help fashion this "new regime for relating to the past" (Rancière, *The Politics of Aesthetics*, 25).

Piglia begins *El último lector* by describing a photograph of Borges trying to decipher the words of a book he has pressed against his face: "Ésta podría ser la primera imagen del último lector, el que ha pasado la vida leyendo, el que ha quemado sus ojos en la luz de la lámpara. 'Yo soy ahora un lector de páginas que mis ojos ya no ven.' . . . Un lector es también el que lee mal, distorsiona, percibe confusamente. En la clínica del arte de leer, no siempre el que tiene mejor vista lee mejor" (This could be the first image of the last reader, he who has spent his life reading, he who has burned his eyes by the light of the lamp. "I am now a reader of pages that my eyes no longer see." . . . A reader is also he who reads badly, distorts, perceives confusedly. In the clinic of the art of reading, he who has the clearest vision is not always he who reads most clearly) (19, translation mine). We recall that, in "El etnógrafo," Borges's narrator describes two types of protagonist, one visible, one invisible ("Cuenta con un solo protagonista, salvo que en toda historia los protagonistas son miles, visibles e invisibles, vivos y muertos" [It has a single protagonist (though in every story there are thousands of protagonists, visible and invisible, alive and dead)], 59/334), an invitation, a call to close reading. The blind reader, then, might be that reader who— desperately close to the text—is attuned to its marks of invisibility, to those elements of unreadability that serve as a demand for *more* reading.

Most of what follows dwells within the bounds of European modernism (Joyce, Kafka, Poe), but—not unlike the modernists and *vanguardistas*

Jorge Luis Borges in the National Library

themselves—Piglia makes a secondary, albeit significant, gesture toward a kind of primal scene of reading set in the period of early modernity in Cervantes and Shakespeare. These two moments—broadly understood— serve as an odd couple of bookends that bracket and hold together a period we might call "modern" in a sort of anachronistic, contradictory organization of literary history. I want to read, with you, Piglia's curiously partial readings of these early modern scenes of reading and suggest that Piglia's own blind spots serve as a guide to reading *as* and *after* the last reader.

Describing James Joyce's *Finnegans Wake* as "un río, un torrente múltiple" (a river, a multiple torrent), of which we read "restos, trozos sueltos, fragmentos, la unidad del sentido es ilusoria" (remains, loose pieces, fragments, the unity of meaning is illusory) (20), Piglia asserts that such a representation of spatially scattered pages is already anticipated by Cervantes, who writes, in *Don Quijote*, that his narrator (distraught at finding the text of the Knight's story incomplete) "leía incluso los papeles rotos que encontraba en la calle" (would even read the torn papers he found in the street). The characterization of reading as involving scattered, torn, even rejected materials at what is arguably literary modernity's founding moment marks, from that primary scene, reading's possible, even necessary, departure from the task of achieving totality or of gathering these torn materials back into a pristine prior meaning. We erroneously associate this alternative, discrepant, fragmenting and fragmentary path with late modernity, or modernity's breakdown. Here, where the path opens before us, it is also—if we return to the well-studied original, misquoted in Piglia— linked to the task of translation:

> Estando yo un día en el Alcaná de Toledo, llegó un muchacho a vender unos cartapacios y papeles viejos a un sedero; y como soy aficionado a leer, aunque sean los papeles rotos de las calles, llevado de esta mi natural inclinación tomé un cartapacio de los que el muchacho vendía; vile con caracteres que conocí ser arábigos, y puesto que, aunque los conocía, no los sabía leer, anduve mirando si parecía por allí algún morisco aljamiado que los leyese . . .

> (One day when I was in the Alcaná market in Toledo, a boy came by to sell some notebooks and old papers to a silk merchant; as I am very fond of reading, even torn papers in the streets, I was moved by my natural inclinations to pick up one of the volumes the boy was selling, and I saw that it was written in characters I knew to be Arabic. And since I recognized but could not read it, I looked around to see if some Morisco who knew Castilian, and could read it for me, was in the vicinity) (68)

I won't tackle all of the provocative elements in this rich, oft-cited passage, but I want briefly to highlight two: the relation between reading and translation and the link between reading/translation and conversion. Eric Graf, Antonio Medina Molera, María Rosa Menocal, and Jacques Lezra have sought to unravel the densely complex web of humor and cultural critique inherent to this scene, which both veils and exposes the ethnic politics of seventeenth-century Spain (when the curiously dubbed "morisco aljamiado" translator begins to read the found manuscript, he begins to laugh at a bit of marginalia identifying Dulcinea as the best pork-salter in town). We see, from this humorous encounter, that texts appear to readers not only as coded artifacts demanding translation but that such readings, such translations, carry with them a return of the repressed: *restos*, here, of the violent processes of religious conversion in Inquisitional Spain, inextricably linked to the founding moments of literary *and* political modernity. These traces surface nowhere in Piglia's account of the scene: The blindness that *El último lector* displays requires his readers to return to the scene he reads in order to ask after that blindness, from within the doubled scene, Cervantes and Piglia, Cervantes's work reading Piglia's symptomatic misreading of his text, Piglia returning to Cervantes's in order to provide a future for reading out of reading's original scene, or one of them. If Cervantes's work is the event announcing Piglia's work and Piglia's is the announcement of the end and afterlife of reading as a reading of Cervantes's work, then Piglia's misreading of Cervantes's work is also an event, repetitive and nonrepetitive at once, a reading whose blindness to the eventhood of the text it reads and seeks to repeat constitutes it as a genuinely modern event.

A similar demand to read the repressed, residual ghosts of the past takes place in the other scene of early modern reading cited by Piglia, this one from *Hamlet*. In one of Shakespeare's few stage directions, the eponymous hero appears, or is directed to appear, reading a book: "Enter Hamlet, reading on a book" (2.2). We learn, upon returning to the play following Piglia's invitation, that Hamlet is greeted by the Queen with pity: "But look where sadly the poor wretch comes reading," she observes. Piglia does not consider *either* the context of this act of reading (the conveyance to Horatio of letters of state from Norway for the king's reading and the public reading of Hamlet's letters to Ophelia) *or* the Queen's reaction to Hamlet's reading.

The first provides a broad scope for the act of reading—it is a political act, and it is the expression of a subjective passion. The second bears

Laurence Olivier, *Hamlet* (1948)

mentioning for its ambiguity: Gertrude's comment asks us, in what respect is Hamlet a poor wretch? Does he come "sadly" because he is reading or because he is in mourning for his father? Or is he reading because he is in mourning or, more precisely, because this, that is, that Hamlet *read* the situation before him and *act upon* that reading, is precisely what his father's ghost has demanded of him? Some of us have perhaps most recently thought through the king's spectral demand from Derrida's treatment of it in *Specters of Marx*, in which haunting is understood as an ethico-political demand that must itself be read ("Read me, will you ever be able to do so?"). These political, emotive, ambiguating traces surface nowhere in Piglia's account of the scene: As in his reading of *Don Quijote*, the blindness that *El último lector* displays requires his readers to return to Shakespeare's scene in order to ask after that blindness, from within the doubled scene, now Shakespeare and Piglia, *Hamlet* reading Piglia's symptomatic nonreading of his text, Piglia returning to *Hamlet* in order to provide a future for reading out of reading's original scene, or one of them.[5]

El último lector, I want to suggest as a point of departure for this book, can be understood as a kind of manual for reading after the so-called *end* of reading: a blind-leading-the-blind guidebook for the twenty-first century. When we read after Piglia's blind spots, when we *ourselves* read blindly, we read for the gaps produced by the untimely. "Hay un anacronismo esencial en don Quijote que define su modo de leer," Piglia tells us, "y a la vez su vida surge de la distorsión de esa lectura. . . . El último lector responde implícitamente a ese programa. Su lectura siempre es inactual, está siempre en el límite" (There is an essential anachronism in don Quixote that defines his mode of reading . . . and at the same time his life emerges out of the distortion of that reading. . . . The last reader responds implicitly to that program. His reading is always untimely, it is always on the limit) (189). In this sense, the so-called death of reading becomes a productive concept *not* when we understand such a death as a *punctual* event, a rupture that marks a before and an after, but when we view reading as always already dying, a practice haunted by its own untimeliness.

—|—

No book is autonomous. Every book is open, exposed to the books that have preceded it (those written by its own author as well as by others) and the books that will follow it. *This* book begins by responding to questions I posed in my last book on Inquisitional logic and *marranismo*, and it ends by posing new questions that may lead to another book, or to something else, still undefined, on the politics of truth and error in the so-called post-truth era. To close it off as independent, sovereign, self-sufficient is a necessary fiction. The front and back covers embrace something unfinished.

When I began to write this book, which wasn't yet a book, the *marea rosada* was in full swing in many Latin American countries, the Arab Spring had swept the Middle East, the Occupy movement had shifted US conversations about class for the first time in decades, and Obama was president of the United States. The political challenges of the time flowed from neoliberalism and, in particular, its seemingly irresistible absorption of every aspect of life, including university life. I urgently wanted to find language to articulate ethical and political demands that spoke to this late-capitalist moment, after certain ethico-political concepts—subjectivity, sovereignty, decision, recognition, identity, difference—had apparently been exhausted yet still seemed to pervade our vocabularies, on the street and in the classroom. I wanted to see how, in an age ostensibly marked by the "end" of literature, we might breathe new life into certain reading practices, deconstructive reading practices, that could help destabilize the closure of the relation between ethics and politics as well as point a way forward. I discovered in a number of literary and cultural works from the last half-century in Argentina unwitting ethical and political philosophical texts that, through their particular and peculiar engagement with and response to globalization and neoliberalism from the South, offered unexpected insights into problems raised by thinkers such as Levinas, Derrida, de Man, Badiou, and Rancière.

As I drafted the final chapters, right-wing governments returned to power in Argentina and Brazil, Venezuela tumbled into crisis, the Brexit referendum passed, and a new president was elected, somehow, in the United States. These events did not mark a paradigm shift in the political climate and the concepts that seek to describe and transform this climate but rather stood as symptoms of a number of the battles that had been playing out across Europe and the Americas in response to the globalization of capital.

I began to write *Anarchaeologies* in Southern California in 2012; I composed its final pages in Buenos Aires, Argentina, in 2017. I watched, from afar, as the forty-fifth president of the United States was sworn in, and as the poor and working classes, women, and sexual and ethnic minorities— not to mention the planet—took beating after beating. Meanwhile, neoliberal and neofascist policies took hold in the first year of Argentine president Mauricio Macri's administration; union members and families of the disappeared once again took to the streets; and a nascent, nonidentitarian feminist movement, Ni Una Menos, gained momentum. In this last collective endeavor, women and trans activists came together first to shed light upon the epidemic of femicides in their country (one woman murdered every eighteen hours) and soon joined forces with workers, Mapuche activists, and others fighting the latest stage in the neoliberal laboratory we call Latin America.

As a US-based Latinamericanist, I began to view the challenge of this book in a slightly different light. At the same time that these events, which brought to the surface many of the latent forms of violence in the Americas, Europe, and beyond—made *more* pressing the need to articulate certain ethical and political demands (even when these demands are, as I'll argue, by definition inarticulable, opaque, secret, untranslatable)—they also added a new, or newly evident, dimension to these urgent questions. It is not enough to argue, as this book does, against identitarian scholarship and identity-based politics. We are living a new chapter in the ongoing struggle against racial, sexual, and economic injustice, a struggle that haunts the pages that follow. At the same time, the intensification of violence and repression calls for more refined approaches to ethical and political thinking. What if our ethical and political demands were not reduced to the demand for recognition? What if our demands were *unreadable* but not, for their illegible quality, any less radical? The task of thinking is ever more urgent; the task of reading is more difficult and more compelling than ever.

We have been told that literature is "dead." *Anarchaeologies* is a critical appraisal of aesthetics, ethics, and politics in an ostensibly "postliterary" epoch. It brings together works in continental philosophy and critical theory and literary and visual works from Latin America to practice and to formalize *anarchaeological reading*: reading for the blind spots, errors, points of opacity or untranslatability in works of philosophy and art. How *do* we read after the so-called death of literature? For we do continue to read—both on- and offline, both digital and print media, "high" and "low" culture, more and more—yet we do so, surely, conditioned by what the Latin American literary critic Patrick Dove calls "the suspension or exhaustion of key principles of aesthetic and political modernity," a result of neoliberal-driven forms of globalization that have been particularly devastating for Latin America. Let us agree with Dove that we have reached the limits of certain aesthetic, ethical, and political concepts— sovereignty, subjectivity, autonomy, to name only a few. This book argues in favor of a reading practice that would guard *and* unsettle the most radically ethico-political demands of literature.

Taking as its point of departure Jacques Rancière's concept of literary misunderstanding (*malentendu littéraire*), which underscores the "nonrelationship constitutive of the very faculty of producing and interpreting signs," *Anarchaeologies* exposes twentieth-and twenty-first-century literary works by Jorge Luis Borges, Ricardo Piglia, Juán José Saer, and César Aira; films by Albertina Carri; art activism by the collective Internacional Errorista; and musical lyrics by Leonard Cohen to works in continental philosophy and critical theory. This practice of exposing extraneous frames and languages to each other helps *Anarchaeologies* advance a theory of reading-as-misreading as a way to reevaluate not only aesthetics but also those forms of ethics and politics rooted in logics of identification, recognition, and comprehension. An original and far-reaching account of literature, of reading, and of the ethico-political possibilities of both is to be found in the encounter of the postmodern Argentine aesthetic field and the corpus of continental philosophers and critics who bring to the fore the violent ethics of the act of reading.

Anarchaeologies reads Saer through Rancière; Aira with Badiou; the work of the avant-garde collective Internacional Errorista against de Man; and Cohen's music with Kierkegaard, Levinas, and Derrida to show how ethical and political concepts are thought and unthought through and from the literary: indeed, through the act of reading itself. When the act of interpretation—and here I refer to an interpretative practice that *reads after* and *guards* the blind spots, errors, and equivocations of the text—is transferred to the task of ethical and political thinking, classical concepts such as sovereignty, will, decision, and responsibility are shown to be constitutively defective.[6] Rather than weakening either ethics or politics, however, the anarchaeological reading these works stage and demand *opens up* and *radicalizes* the possibility of justice (in the Derridean sense).

The book is divided into five parts: "Anarchaeologies," "The Ethical Turn," "Violent Ethics," "Political Thinking after Literature," and "Exposure and Indisciplinarity." Each part attempts to unsettle and rework classical ethical and political concepts through anarchaeological reading. While a specific literary, ethical, or political concept may be at the center of any one of the parts, it is always in a relation of tension with—and exposure to—the "same" concept seen from the vantage point of an ostensibly exterior discourse or discipline. Thus, to give one example, the idea of "divisible sovereignty" that we encounter in the philosophical work of Jacques Derrida will be approached in and through César Aira's 2006 short story "Picasso." Yet at the same time, this performative exposure reveals the identity of each discourse (genre, discipline) as a nonidentity: the secret flaw or defect that resides at the core of *every* genre, every discipline, every concept, but that also stands as its single and singular condition of possibility.

Part I ("Anarchaeologies") introduces the two central methodological and conceptual terms of the book: misunderstanding and anarchaeological reading. In the first section, "Misunderstanding Literature," I draw upon Jacques Rancière's notion of literary misunderstanding—*malentendu littéraire*, which bears a formal compatibility to *mésentente politique*, or political dissensus or disagreement—in order to develop the first concept that structures this book as well as the relation between literature, ethics, and politics. Here I propose a mode of reading that would expose the misunderstanding that is constitutive of both the literary *and* the political. I then turn to an understudied scene from Juan José Saer's widely read 1983 novel *El entenado* in order to consider a literary practice that performatively and constatively bears witness to the misunderstanding that constitutes, exposes, and unsettles the modern subject. The motif of misunderstanding recurs throughout *Anarchaeologies* vis-à-vis a cluster of concepts—blindness, error, equivocation—to which I will turn in order to imagine new interpretative possibilities not only within literary criticism but within ethical and political thinking as well. I call such thinking "anarchaeological" thinking.

In the second section, "Toward an Anarchaeological Latinamericanism," I develop the idea that serves as the book's title. Here I argue against a mode of reading—of the text, of the archive—that would employ archeological means to uncover a buried truth (the moving links between truth [*alêtheia*]; archaeology, the origin or archē [ἀρχή]; and reason, sense or phrase, logos [λόγος] are a sort of map of Western philosophy from its inception): against, that is, an excavational mode of thought, a cousin of a certain conservative philological tendency, that has as its foundation or ground that which hides beneath it, an identifiable and revealable truth. Instead, I propose the notion of anarchaeological reading, an interpretative practice that would expose itself to or register the secret, incalculable qualities of the archive or the text. After reviewing several examples of archaeological and anarchaeological engagements with the archive of the student-popular movement in 1968 Mexico, I analyze Albertina Carri's troubled relation to the inheritance of her murdered militant parents in the documentary films *Los rubios* (2003) and *Cuatreros* (2016). Literature or literariness is central to this methodological and theoretical argument, which understands a reader's *response* to the literary, or (less intuitively) his or her response to a nonliterary object *as if it were* a literary object, as a demand for reading that opens, rather than forecloses, the multiple and contradictory possibilities of interpretation.

Part II of *Anarchaeologies* is a critical engagement with the so-called ethical turn in critical studies of literature, culture, and philosophy. "The Ethical Turn" takes the reader through the tense articulation of ethics and politics in current criticism and political philosophy via the geopolitical context of Latin America and of Latin American studies. In its first section, titled "Ethics against Politics," I show how the notion of an ethical "turn" tends to place ethics and politics in a relation of antagonism or substitution (ethics or politics, but not both). What if the two terms were to be thought instead as operating *against* each other? Here "against" would indicate both antagonism (ethics versus politics) and correlation, even support: Ethics stands or leans against the backdrop of politics and vice versa, an arrangement in which ethics and politics would be mutually dependent.

In "Levinas in Latin America," I focus on four types of ethical philosophy in Latin American and Latinamericanist thought: *theological*, *literary*, *political*, and *deconstructive*. First, I evaluate the theologian Enrique Dussel's overly literal reading of Emmanuel Levinas, which he absorbs into a philosophy of Latin American liberation. Next, I juxtapose Dussel's Levinasianism with Doris Sommer's "ethical" approach to literary studies in her essay "The Talker Turns," which analyzes Mario Vargas Llosa's 1987 novel *El hablador*. While on the surface these two approaches to ethics appear divergent or even contradictory, I argue that both turn on the logic of identification and recognition that has dominated Latin American studies and that has framed our discussions of both subjectivity *and* alterity. I then unpack the debate over the relation between ethics and political militancy that surfaces in Argentina following the publication of the philosopher Oscar Del Barco's 2007 letter "No matarás" (Thou shalt not kill). Here I suggest, in response to the philosopher Diego Tatián, the cultural critic Alejandro Kaufman, and the literary critic Patrick Dove, that the opposition between ethics and politics obscures or overlooks what could be most promising in ethical and political thinking. I conclude by turning to several recent, more deconstructive approaches to ethics that refuse the logic of recognition-identification, questioning our understanding of ethics, politics, and the relation between the two and proposing, finally, that misreading, misunderstanding, and untranslatability guide our thinking moving forward.

Part III, "Violent Ethics," pursues untimely, unorthodox readings of what I call Levinas-after-Derrida, a thinking of ethical responsibility that has already been subjected to the work of deconstruction. My analysis, which moves from the account of the binding of Isaac to Jorge Luis Borges's parable "Kafka and His Precursors," argues that we should imagine ethics as guarding an intempestive, violent secret at its core. An "anarchaeology" of ethical decision provides us with this imaginary reconstruction of the field of ethics; the timing of this "anarchaeology" is always paradoxical, even preposterous.

In the first section, "Abraham's Double Bind," I explore the undecidable, *violent* nature of the ethical scene by considering philosophical and quasi-philosophical responses to the binding of Isaac (Kierkegaard's *Fear and Trembling*, Levinas's *Proper Names*, Derrida's *Gift of Death*, Leonard Cohen's "Story of Isaac"). My approach stresses the ways these works dwell on misunderstanding, undecidability, and intempestivity. While Kierkegaard underscores the impossibility of understanding Abraham, both Kierkegaard and Levinas pursue (from opposing perspectives) the dilemma posed by the necessary choice between duty to God and ethical responsibility to Isaac. Derrida will show such a choice to be impossible, linking the ethical to the nonethical (a gesture that echoes his early work on ethics and violence in "Violence of the Letter"). I conclude with Cohen in order to demonstrate the way in which, through poetic language, it becomes possible to confront the aporetic ethics that Derrida aims to describe through philosophical language. This poetic aporia (Cohen's Isaac, in an indirect reference to his father, recalls, "Thought I saw an eagle / But it might have been a vulture, / I never could decide") exposes the terrifying fact that ethics does not banish violence but rather guards it and may reproduce it as its continuing condition.

The second section, "Untimely Ethics: Deconstruction and Its Precursors," takes up Borges's notion that literary precursors are retroactively determined in order to examine the preposterous timing of this "anarchaeology" of violent ethics. Here, I consider two possible "precursors" of deconstruction, from two quite different traditions, Levinas and Borges himself. First I trace the concept of the illegible demand (for reading) in the thought of Levinas and Derrida, suggesting that the most significant consequences of Levinas's work can only begin to be traced "after" Derrida. I then argue, through an analysis of Borges's short essay "Kafka y sus precursores," that if literary and philosophical precursors can be determined retroactively and anachronically (Borges "after" Derrida), then intempestive reading—reading after whatever is untimely in the work before it—might serve as the condition of possibility for indisciplinary, *marrano* thinking.

Part IV of this book, "Political Thinking after Literature," places violent ethics "against" politics by revisiting classical political concepts such as sovereignty and decision from the vantage point of literature, literary criticism, and art-activism. The first section, "The Metapolitics of Allegory," focuses on what has been the most obviously political of literary devices: allegory. Latin American literary studies, I suggest, has been haunted by Fredric Jameson's (in)famous claim that "all third world texts are . . . national allegories," which hatched a critical countertradition in Latin-americanism that rejected Jameson's argument without pursuing alternative readings of allegory. I trace the link between allegory and intention, or will, in the "masters" of Latin American literary criticism (Sommer, González Echevarría, Alonso), who fashioned their own authoritative voices in the 1980s "against" and according to a non–, even anti–de Manian conception of allegoresis that excluded the possibility of unreadability and instead grounded their analyses in unexamined concepts of sovereignty, will, and intentionality. The result, I take it, is not only to bolster the authority of the (sovereign, deciding) critic but to make that bolstering into literary allegory's primary function. By way of contrast, I then propose a reading of César Aira's 1997 novella *El congreso de literatura*, in which the *impossibility* of politics understood as entailing sovereign decisionism, or the intentional fidelity to an event (Badiou), is articulated allegorically, showing that allegory *itself*, in addition to politics, does not have to obey the logic of sovereign decisionism.

In the second section, "The Aesthetics and Politics of Error," I propose "error" as a weak, or *erroneous*, political concept. I ask how literature (taking as my example Aira's 2010 novel *El error*), critical theory (Paul de Man's *Blindness and Insight*), and poetic-political discourse (the theatrical actions of the Internacional Errorista) can work against, with, and through one another to offer a working definition of error. I don't suggest that "error" is the same for each, nor do I argue that we can arrive at a consolidated definition of "error." Rather, I demonstrate that the concept "error"—and in a sense *every* concept—can be thought *only* at the point of mutual exposure, or encounter, between discourses, disciplines, fields. An encounter between literature and philosophy (to give one example) would expose the constitutive flaw or lack in each (one could say, the "error" of each).

Part V of *Anarchaeologies*, "Exposure and Indisciplinarity," asks whether and how anarchaeology, misunderstanding, error, and the violence of ethics-against-politics may be thought to provide a critique of the very institution that seems to make them possible as ways of thinking: the university. I approach the matter through the lens of what Derrida calls "university responsibility." In "Mochlos; or, The Conflict of the Faculties," Derrida likens "the discourse of responsibility" in Immanuel Kant's 1798 *Der Streit der Fakultäten* to "a pure ethico-juridical agency, to pure practical reason, to a pure idea of the law, and correlatively to the decision of a pure egological subject, of a consciousness, of an intention that has to respond, in *decidable* terms, from and before the law" (11). Derrida is interested, by contrast, in imagining a responsible university as an institution within which interpretations of texts would be ventured not as decisions offered by an "egological subject" in "decidable terms" but as readings that would guard the text's *undecidable* qualities. Such decisions, such interpretations, would still be subject to an injunction (read me, translate me, inherit from me), and the interpreter, according to Derrida, should not be understood as "subjected passively to this injunction." Over a decade later, in *The Politics of Friendship*, Derrida proposes the concept of passive decision as "the decision of the other-in-me," a strikingly Levinasian idea, detailed in several parts of this book, that brings together decision and undecidability as necessarily bound. Here, what at first seemed to be a "pure egological subject"—a subject that decides and, in doing so, obeys the law—is now seen to be a subject haunted by an other that decides in, and for, her. The autonomous subject's obedience to the Kantian moral law can now be read somewhat differently, as emanating from the "alterity of the other" (Nancy). I return, once again, to the narrative of César Aira ("Picasso" and *Triano*), in order to consider the possibility of anarchaeological reading as *exposure*: the exposure of literature to painting, painting to literature, philosophy to literature, literature to philosophy.

The book closes, however provisionally, by offering the outlines of an institution whose foundation is passive, exposed responsibility—that is, anarchaeological reading: an "exposed" university. The university so imagined is exposed not only to other institutions or to other ethico-political demands, apparently external to the university, but also to *internal*, unsettling demands. The exposure of one discipline to another would reveal in this case the wounded quality of the sovereignty or autonomy of each, the "points of untranslatability" (Derrida) that provide the basis for *and* unsettle disciplinary thinking. I invite the reader to imagine an indisciplined or indisciplinary university, in which literary studies, moribund, would find, in anarchaeological readings, an afterlife through its exposure to other practices and discourses, such as philosophical discourse, and philosophy, moribund, would find an afterlife through its exposure to aesthetic discourse. In the book's Afterword, I consider the role of the university and the broader politics of truth and error in the so-called post-truth era, or the age of Trump.

Throughout the book, I employ a series of terms that are related to but not synonymous with anarchaeological reading: blindness, misunderstanding, *marranismo*, violent ethics, error, passivity, exposure, indisciplinary thinking, deconstruction. "Anarchaeologies" is the name I'm giving to this cluster of terms that, as a result of their powers to unsettle—as well as the unsettling relation *among* the terms—may suggest a way out of the ethico-political impasse in which we find ourselves. It is my hope that *Anarchaeologies* will offer, through a revitalized (but not romanticized or religious) reading practice, a practice of reading-as-misreading, a way to maneuver within and beyond the closure of ethical and political thinking under neoliberalism.

Part I. Anarchaeologies

Misunderstanding Literature

Listen, I have sobbed from pleasure. And I've cackled / over my
own tombstone, carved with: *Understanding*.
—Robin Coste Lewis

Literature I could, fundamentally do without, in fact, rather easily.
. . . But if, without liking literature in general and for its own
sake, I like something *about it*, which above all cannot be reduced
to some aesthetic quality, to some source of formal pleasure
[*jouissance*], this would be *in place of the secret*. In place of an absolute
secret. There would be the passion. There is no passion without
secret, this very secret, indeed no secret without this passion.
—Jacques Derrida, "Passions: An Oblique Offering"

In his invitation to contribute to a special issue of *CR: The New Centennial
Review* on the topic of "Literature and the Secret of the World," David
Johnson referred to John Beverley's provocative 2011 book *Latinamericanism
after 9/11*, in particular to the conclusion of the chapter that diagnoses a
"neoconservative turn" in Latin American literary and cultural studies.
There Beverley states, decisively, that "Borges *is* literature, and literature
is, finally, what those of us who work in the field of literary and cultural
criticism do as intellectuals" (94). Like Johnson, I too felt a certain interpellation in Beverley's words when I first read the book, even as I wondered
about the relation of equivalence established between "Borges" and "literature" and between "literature" and "us." Who, or what, is Borges? What
is literature? Who are we? What, exactly, do we do? In what way are these
productive questions, and to what extent do they reinforce the identitary
logic that underscores Beverley's argument, that is, a logic that stands on
and has as its goal the reproduction of ethnic, national, linguistic, and
political identities? What if, instead of trying to identify Borges, literature,
and ourselves, or our work, we were to turn our attention elsewhere, upon
the places where those identities (and projects) fail or prove impossible? In
that sense, I would rather read Beverley's statement (which, like Althusser's
allegorical example of ideological interpellation, is also an accusation, an
indictment) as an interpellative statement that produces a failed subject, that
*mis*recognizes Borges, literature, us. The question then becomes, for me,
this: Can literature (or literary discourse) allow us to articulate such failures
more precisely, or, if not, can literary discourse bear witness to the impossibility of such an articulation? Is "literature" misunderstood, or, on the

contrary, can literary discourse create the conditions of possibility for a theory of misunderstanding, indeed, of misunderstanding as the constitutive quality of literature itself?

To take up the question of misunderstanding, I want to turn to a 2003 essay by Jacques Rancière, "Le *malentendu* littéraire," in which the philosopher asks whether literature has a particular relationship with misunderstanding.[1] He opens the essay by engaging in a close reading of the *Trésor de la langue française* dictionary's entry for "misunderstanding," which gives two possible definitions: "a divergence of interpretation regarding the meaning of words or acts leading to disagreement" and "a disagreement brought about by such a divergence" (31), both of which imply an elusive yet proper interpretation of words, the deviation from or quarrel over which leads to problems.[2] Yet the same entry betrays an internal contradiction when it turns to literary examples to illustrate the definition. "Inevitably," he quotes Martin du Gard as having written, "at the bottom of all passionate love, there is a misunderstanding, a generous illusion, an error of judgment, a false idea each has of the other," while in Zola we find the affirmation that "Their disharmony only grew, aggravated by one of those peculiar misunderstandings of the flesh that chill the most ardent heart: he adored his wife, she had all the sensuality of a sensuous blonde, yet already they were sleeping apart, ill at ease, easily hurt" (32). Rather than corroborating the definition (of misunderstanding, but also of words, of acts, of signification), the passages end up subverting it by exposing the gap at the heart of love, the misunderstanding that resides at the core of language itself, "a non-relationship constitutive of the very faculty of producing and interpreting signs" (33).

The essay then traces a genealogy of literature as misunderstanding, turning to Sartre's *What Is Literature?*, in which the philosopher claims that writers, after 1848, "don't want to be understood," refusing "to serve the ends the bourgeois public assigns to literature" (33). Yet this too is a misunderstanding, a misunderstanding of literature and of misunderstanding itself: "Misunderstanding . . . is fictitious," Rancière claims, "it is the fiction that seals the tacit contract between the literary elite and the dominant class at the expense of . . . the people" (34). Among the reasons why such a relationship is fictitious or impossible is the problematic assumption that "the elite agree on what they are doing" (34). On the contrary, it is *disagreement* that characterizes the political and that stands as the correlative of literary misunderstanding. The idea of *malentendu littéraire*, then, bears a formal compatibility to *mésentente politique*: "This is the ground on which political disagreement arises. It is also the ground on which we can theorize the relationship between politics and literature, between political dis-agreement and literary 'misunderstanding'" (41).[3] Despite the structural affinity, however, politics and literature do very different things, particu-larly in relation to the concepts of *partage* (partition or distribution) and counting:

> Political disagreement and literary misunderstanding each attack one aspect of [the] consensual paradigm of proportion between words and things. Dis-agreement invents names, utterances, arguments and demonstrations that set up new collectives where anyone can get themselves counted in the count of the uncounted. Misunderstanding works on the relationship and the count from another angle, by suspending the forms of individuality through which consensual logic binds bodies to meanings. Politics works on the whole, lit-erature works on the units. (41)[4]

Both politics and literature challenge the idea of "what counts" by intro-ducing a language (and for Rancière language resides at the core of each) that would derail any count deemed to be total, whole. Yet they do so in radically different ways, so much so that literary misunderstanding "tends to steer away from serving political misunderstanding," which is why Rancière opts to speak about the metapolitics of literature rather than the politics of literature (or "content-based commitment").[5] At the same time, literary misunderstanding—or literature understood as misunderstanding—might act as a condition of possibility (although certainly not the only condition of possibility) for a radical rethinking of the political along Rancièrian lines. That is, while literary language might not "serve" politics in an explicitly ideological or strategic way (as the bearer of a translatable message or position, as a means to a particular end), misunderstanding literature, or reading the misunderstanding quality that is constitutive of the literary, might call our attention to the misunderstanding that resides at the heart of the political—at least of a notion of the political that poses a radical demand grounded in dissensus (rather than, for example, Rancière's idea of "police," which, in contrast to politics, would merely preserve the status quo).

Here I take a first step toward outlining a mode of reading that exposes the misunderstanding constitutive of both the literary *and* the political. By this I do not mean an exposure that would seek to remedy, resolve, or clear up such a misunderstanding: misunderstandings that can be cleared up through exposure or analysis or clarification are precisely *not* what Rancière, or I, have in mind. Rather than appealing to what Rancière describes as a common fantasy of "a form of communication that would be *devoid* of misunderstandings" (2, italics my own), I am interested in a reading praxis that would point to the *gaps* in processes of signification and subjectivation, whether these gaps are understood as textual gaps (Pierre Macherey's discussion of the gaps and silences in literary texts), misrecognition (Judith Butler's Lacanian reading of Althusserian inter-pellation),[6] or the posthegemonic (as in Jon Beasley-Murray's take on Gramsci's and Laclau's theories of hegemony). Responding to a conventional misreading of literature (the conflation of "literature" as a historically—and geographically—specific institution with "the literary," or that which would exceed such an institution),[7] I want to introduce a logic that would subvert identitarian thinking (the "is" in "Borges is literature," in "literature is what we do"). At work in the literature and in the political scenes I study we find instead a sort of secret that is not susceptible to archaeological disclosure; I will call it the marrano secret. I refer here—as I have detailed in other published work—to a secret not necessarily evident to the person or the work that holds it (as the crypto-Jew or marrano is not perhaps aware of the ties that bind him or her secretly to Spain, to Sepharad: He or she is, *and is not*, Jewish, Spanish, Christian, self-aware, acting or desiring intentionally, and so on). If in previous work I examine concrete representations of the figure of the marrano in literature, here I take this figure "figuratively," dwelling upon the idea of the marrano-as-metonym, the notion of a universal marrano subject that bears witness not to a secret that he keeps but rather to the secret that keeps him: a subject, in short, that refuses a logic of revelation, self-reflexivity, intelligibility. I then turn to an understudied scene from Juan José Saer's 1983 novel *El entenado* (*The Witness*) in order to consider a literary practice that performatively and constatively addresses the idea of misunderstanding and, in doing so, bears witness to the subject's failure to understand. We will come to see the idea of misunderstanding as constitutive of a wounded or equivocal subjectivity, that is, constitutive of the condition of marranismo as that which exposes the impossibility of subjectivity.

What is the relationship between the secret, or the marrano secret, and misunderstanding, or literary misunderstanding? Is it possible to trace a formal link between the marrano secret, literary misunderstanding, and disagreement or dissensus, over and above any thematic compatibility? Let us recall the marrano as an early modern figure that the Argentine philosopher Ricardo Forster has described as the alter ego of the nascent modern subject:

Leer al marrano, en parte, significa leer la incompletitud del hombre en la modernidad, o comenzar a comprender la imposibilidad de esa estrategia colosal montada por el cartesianismo, que supuso proyectar un sujeto autosuficiente, en términos racionales, capaz de ordenar, en términos de completitud, su lugar en el mundo. Mientras que, en el caso del marrano, nos encontramos desde el comienzo con la falla, con la grieta, con el lado oscuro, con la incompletitud. (155)

(To read the marrano, in part, implies a reading of the incompleteness of man within modernity, a beginning to understand the impossibility of the colossal strategy mounted by Cartesianism, which aimed to project a self-sufficient subject, in rational terms, capable of ordering, in terms of completeness, his place in the world. Meanwhile, in the case of the marrano, we are confronted from the beginning with a flaw, a fissure, a dark side: with incompleteness.)

The fractured, incomplete marrano does not offer an "alternative" to the Cartesian subject's wholeness or autonomy but rather exposes "la imposibilidad de *toda* identidad," the impossibility of *all* identity (156, italics my own). The faultline, void, or gap that traverses the marrano alludes to her constitutive guilt: The marrano is always already a subject-at-fault, a flawed, or failed, subject. For Forster, the marrano's significance lies in the exposure of this faultline, of the mistaken or faulty quality of the modern autonomous subject: Such exposure, moreover, takes place through the act of *reading*. Jacques Derrida, for his part, links marranismo to absolute secrecy, locating "in the metonymic and generalized figure of the Marrano, the right to secrecy as right to resistance against and beyond the order of the political" ("History," 64).[8] In what follows, I turn to Saer's *El entenado* in order to consider misunderstanding as both trope and performative utterance, asking what the literary might have to tell us about subjectivity, truth, or the failure of both.

A fictionalized account of the arrival of Juan Díaz de Solís and his crew to the Río de la Plata in 1516, *El entenado* (translated into English as *The Witness*) is narrated from the perspective of an orphan or bastard (*entenado*) who has accompanied the crew as cabin boy and who is taken captive by the Colastiné Indians, with whom he lives for ten years, bearing witness to, among other things, the killing and eating of his crewmates.[9] The novel has been read by literary scholars as a metafictional account of the Spanish arrival to the New World (de Grandis), as a rewriting of the colonial *relación* or *crónica* (Gnutzmann, Romano Thuesen), as a theorization of the impotence of language (Miller), as a decentering of the subject of the conquest (Copertari), as "speculative anthropology" (Riera), as an ethical response to the call of the other (Legrás), as a deconstruction of cannibalism (González), and, finally, as a register of the crisis of literature in the wake of dictatorship and transition to neoliberalism (Gollnick). While a majority of the criticism dwells upon the ten years the protagonist and narrator spends living among the Colastiné, as well as the ensuing decades after his return to Spain, at the end of which time he sits down to compose the story as an old man—that is, while most critics are concerned primarily with the colonial (protoethnographic) "encounter" with the other and the related problem of representation—I want to turn to an earlier moment, a relatively understudied scene that is narrated in the opening pages of the short novel and that concerns itself not with the question of the other but with the problem of the subject.

After having spent several months at sea, during which time boredom, heat, sexual desperation, and madness begin to overtake the claustrophobic crew (a period represented in a few short pages of the novel), the three ships finally catch sight of dry land, at which time some of the sailors dive into the sea even before they dock, others wait until reaching shore to run onto the sand and jump up and down in place or jog in circles, others joyfully urinate into the ocean, while still others opt to remain on board, observing this new land from a safe distance. They spend the first evening singing, farting, and laughing around a campfire and, the next day, come to realize that they have reached an unknown place, rather than their expected destination of the Indies, at which point the crew begins to argue among themselves over whether to stay or continue to the south. Their shouting is interrupted by the appearance of the captain, whose disembarkment provokes fear, awe, and respect in the contentious crew as they await what they imagine must be an official speech claiming the new land. The speech never comes, however, and the narrator relates the surprise and horror of what takes its place:

> La expectativa aunaba a los marinos, inmovilizados por la misma estupefacción solidaria. Por fin, después de esos minutos de espera casi insoportable, ocurrió algo: el capitán, dándonos todavía la espalda, emitió un suspiro ruidoso, profundo y prolongado, que resonó nítido en la mañana silenciosa y que estremeció un poco su cuerpo tieso y macizo. Han pasado, más o menos, sesenta años desde aquella mañana y puedo decir, sin exagerar en lo más mínimo, que el carácter único de ese suspiro, en cuanto a la profundidad y duración se refiere, ha dejado en mí una impresión definitiva, que me

acompañará hasta la muerte. En la expresión de los marinos, ese suspiro, por otra parte, borró la estupefacción para dar paso a un principio de pánico. El más inconcebible de los monstruos de esa tierra desconocida hubiese sido recibido con menor conmoción que esa expiración melancólica. (20–21)

(Expectation united the sailors who stood immobilized by the same shared sense of stupefaction. At last, after the almost unbearable waiting, something happened: the captain, still with his back turned to us, let out a long, deep, heartfelt sigh that could be clearly heard in the silent morning and that sent a slight tremor through his solid, upright frame. Some sixty years have passed since that morning yet I can say without the slightest exaggeration that something about the depth of that long-drawn-out sigh so impressed me that it will remain with me till I die. The effect on the sailors, however, was to replace the look of amazement on their faces with the beginnings of panic. The most incredible of monsters inhabiting that unknown land would have been greeted with less horror than that melancholic sigh.) (19)

"Something happened"—"ocurrió algo"—but what? The mystery of what experience, thought, emotion has provoked the sigh—and the subsequent reaction of dread displayed by its witnesses—is left unsaid here. As he does in a number of the most dramatic scenes of *El entenado*, Saer inserts the voice of the narrator, writing more than a half-century after this unforgettable day on the beach, so that the captain's sigh is not only observed by the panicked sailors but also recalled six decades later and then witnessed a *third* time by the reader, who is only implied here through the narrator's address. It is not until several pages after the "event" that founds the novel, or that which has triggered the event—the "ocurrió algo"—that the reader is offered a theory of what might have provoked such terror.

El capitán parecía despavorido—si se puede hablar de pavor en el caso de una verificación intolerable de la que sin embargo el miedo está ausente. Las pocas palabras que pronunciaba le salían con una voz quebrada, débil, cercana al llanto. Y el sudor que le atravesaba la frente y las mejillas y que se perdía en el matorral negro de la barba, le dejaba alrededor de los ojos estelas húmedas y sucias que evocaban espontáneamente las lágrimas. Ahora que soy un viejo, que han pasado tantos años desde aquella mañana luminosa, creo entender que los sentimientos del capitán en ese trance de inminencia provenían de la comprobación de un error de apreciación que había venido cometiendo, a lo largo de toda su vida, acerca de su propia condición. En la mañana vacía, su propio ser se desnudaba, como el ser de la liebre ha de desnudarse, sin duda, para su propia comprensión diminuta, cuando se topa, en algún rincón del campo, con la trampa del cazador. (25–26)

(The captain seemed utterly terrified—if one can use that word to describe the state of mind of a man possessed of unbearable knowledge from which nevertheless all fear is absent. The few words he uttered came out in a weak, broken, almost grief-stricken voice; the sweat running down his forehead and cheeks into the dense black scrub of his beard left damp, muddy trails around his eyes that immediately made one think of tears. Now that I am an old man and many years have passed since that shining morning, I can begin to understand that what lay behind the captain's feelings in that precise moment was the realization that all his life he had been mistaken about the kind of man he was. In that empty morning, his very being was laid bare as no doubt (within the capabilities of its limited understanding) is the soul of the hare when in the corner of some field it encounters the hunter's trap.) (24–25)

In this passage, the perspiration, tears, and trance of the captain are described as stemming from the apprehension of a terrible fact that has quite literally broken his voice, interrupting or making impossible the traditional speech-act, anticipated by the sailors, claiming the newly discovered land.[10] The narrator signals an aporia at the heart of this knowledge by employing discourse that lies somewhere between the literary and the legal or scientific, between the language of testimony and the language of proof. "La comprobación de un error"—the proof of an error—evokes a legal or scientific logic in its ostensible allusion to a provable truth. Yet no such truth ever enters the narrative: There is no narrated identity said to have been shattered by the event. Rather, the rhetoric is conditioned by the experience of radical exposure (which conditions all rhetoric, according to Moreiras).[11] It is the laying bare of the captain's being, metaphorically linked to the hare that encounters the hunter's trap, that has most jolted the captain and, by extension, the onlookers. But this is not an exposure to an anthropomorphic other, not to the "other" of the West (who will shortly appear), but to the heteronomous, equivocal condition of the subject itself. The experience of exposure, or shattering, eclipses any possible "firmness" of either new world or old, the latter of which ultimately escapes narration in Saer. The traumatic moment is not narrated in the chronological or causal mode that often dominates such readings: There is no before and after; the event has always already happened, and the exposure merely represents the moment in which it becomes clear that what resides at the core of the captain, laid bare before an equally barren land, is nothing more than an error. Put another way, the realization by the captain that he has been wrong about himself does not so much replace a previously whole subject with a new, broken subject but rather confirms that the subject was broken, fractured, equivocal to begin with. At the same time, this moment departs from the tradition of literary-religious epiphany in its refusal to name that which came before or what shall follow. This is not an epiphany that unveils a hidden or forgotten "truth" (*anamnesis*) but instead the exposure of a constitutive error, the affirmation of a terrible secret: the secret that it is misunderstanding or equivocation that founds the subject, a "proof" that the captain has been "disproven," a proof that resists the logic of proof altogether.

Almost immediately following this scene, the captain is shot by arrows and killed in the very place in which his being is laid bare. In fact, all of this happens before the "real" action even begins: before the dramatic kidnapping of the narrator; before his decade of captivity; before his witnessing of the annual orgy of incest, anthropophagy, and disorder that nearly unravels and at the very same time constitutes the community in which he is living; before—perhaps most significantly—his return to Spain to be "adopted" once again, this time by Father Quesada; before his travel with a popular theatrical troupe; and before, finally, at the end of his days, he sits down to compose the story we are reading. So why is this early scene significant, and what work does it do for the narrative that follows?

First of all, the fact that this traumatic scene stands as one of the first scenes of the novel allows for the event to interrupt something that nevertheless remains outside the narrative. Just as the protagonist's attempt to recall the events of his ten years in the Río de la Plata repeatedly calls attention to the *impossibility* of representing the Colastiné tribe, their language, the past, experience itself, the past *before* the past—the moment that would ostensibly signify a status quo about to be disrupted, a situation before-the-event, also remains elusive, outside the scope of this narrative as well as the order of representation. At the same time, the cancelling out of the subject through the captain's realization that he has been wrong about himself, through his self-exposure, refocuses the reader's attention away from the constative or cognitive "content" of the captain's hypothetical previous identity (here shown to be irrelevant) and onto the performative act of exposure. This is why it is significant that Saer stages this moment before the encounter with the Colastiné Indians. This encounter with the other will also take place, and it will also be traumatic—although, as the narrator is careful to point out, not nearly as terrifying as the melancholic sigh of the captain that anticipates it. This is the melancholic sigh of the marrano subject, if not of the historical crypto-Jew, then of the marrano-as-metonym, the spectral secret that haunts the Spanish imperial subject from its very inception.

Why do we need literature to alert us to this secret, especially if we are to consider the idea of the secret as that which can neither be revealed nor concealed? Couldn't we just as well "do without" literature, as Derrida suggests in the epigraph, or might Saer's novel offer the possibility of a literary discourse that would bear witness to that which "exceeds the play of veiling/unveiling . . . forgetting/anamnesis"? If so, then the premature event on which *El entenado* opens performs, exposes, the constitutive error of the modern subject and shows (or is witness to) the way that error is relayed through literary discourse, through a discourse that alludes to its own failure to recall. Does that event then serve as the condition of possibility of the narrative, or does the narrative serve as the condition of possibility of the event? What subject, or nonsubject, what equivocal sovereign subject, does the novel make possible? What kind of politics does literature condition, if it does anything at all?

Finally, what relationship do reading, criticism, theory, and philosophy have with such a literary event, if we can even claim that something has indeed happened? Imagine an intellectual endeavor—say, a book—that responds to a demand (it could be a literary demand; it could be an ethical or a political demand) that is impossible to fulfill. Imagine a critical practice that would be relentless in its pursuit of this impossible event, a reading that would bear witness to the "wrong" that, to return to Rancière, lies at the heart of the political. This would be a critical practice performed not by an authoritative, sovereign subject who dominates a "field" or "discipline" or "corpus" but a thinker constituted in her fidelity to an event of reading as misunderstanding, who (in Lacanian terms) never gives way on her desire to pursue the "passion" that marks literature and its impossibility, "in place of the secret," in the secret's place: by a thinker, finally, who does not disavow but guards the constitutive error of her own thought.

Toward an Anarchaeological Latinamericanism

In a 2012 issue of the *New Left Review*, the art historian and essayist T. J. Clark published an essay entitled "For a Left with No Future," a manifesto of sorts—or, as Susan Watkins contends, a "counter manifesto" (79)—in which he insists that the European Left should renounce any sort of utopian orientation in favor of a "politics in a tragic key" (59), what he calls, following a kind of nihilist-punk slogan, a politics of "no future." His critique of the vision of an alternative, utopian future on the part of the revolutionary Left (defined here as "root-and-branch opposition to capitalism") has substantial consequences for the present not only of the European Left but of the Latin American Left as well, despite the fact that they currently find themselves in radically disparate situations. "Is this pessimism?" asks Clark, responding:

> Well, yes. But what other tonality seems possible in the face of the past ten years? How are we meant to understand the arrival of real ruination in the order of global finance . . . and the almost complete failure of left responses to it to resonate beyond the ranks of the faithful? Or to put the question another way: if the past decade is not proof that there are *no* circumstances capable of reviving the left in its nineteenth and twentieth-century form, then what would proof be like? (54–55)

Clark's words—published eight years ago, a political lifetime—seem even more apt today, his "pessimism" more on point. Nevertheless, the problem with this argument, in my view, has to do with the establishment of an opposition between a utopian future and a tragic future. If for Clark it is vital to take a critical distance from the utopian in favor of a somewhat pessimistic "presentism" (Watkins, "Presentism?" 79), there remains a crucial blind spot in his logic: The tragic does not present an alternative to the utopian (nor can the utopian offer a way out of the tragic), because both utopian and tragic thought fall under the same sign of the future as calculable or predetermined. In the utopian version of the future, we know what it is that we desire, and it is only a question of whether this future will come about or not. In the tragic version of the future, or the tragic version *without* future, we know what we want, and we know that our desires will *not* come to fruition.

These two alternative futures, utopian and tragic, are in fact closer than they may appear: a prescriptive politics, on the one hand, and a politics that would eliminate agency or action, that is, the very possibility of politics. As Gabriela Basterra argues in *Seductions of Fate*, when we choose to employ the adjective "tragic" to characterize catastrophic events, we "occlude our own involvement in the decision-making process that led to so much suffering, as well as our own responsibility for its outcome" (1): We abandon, simultaneously, the possibility of ethics *and* the possibility of politics. Both the utopian *and* the tragic keys, then, represent a politics of no future in their exclusion of the possibility of the unforeseen or unforeseeable, the incalculable, the very possibility of an event. In *The Politics of Friendship* (2005), Jacques Derrida writes of the future as the absolute other, the *arrivant* that we do not expect and for whom we are never prepared, not (or not only) because of the catastrophic nature of the arrival but also because we lack a vocabulary, a lexicon, to think such a future: It exceeds the limits of representation (and, by extension, of politics).

If we are interested in, and committed to, the possibility of democracy—not the extant forms of democracy that are on offer under the discontinuous regime of global capital, nor any other version of democracy that we could fathom, but a democracy-to-come, that is, incalculable—it is worth asking: What are the conditions of possibility for the thinking of democracy (as movement, as change itself, as event) or for reflecting upon that which is unthinkable? How can we trace different genealogies of thought, of possible avenues of thinking, that would at once take into account the violence of Inquisitional logic, or identitarian thinking, while creating the conditions of possibility for the deconstruction of such violence, knowing full well that such deconstruction is ultimately inseparable from violence? Can we propose, finally, a relation with the past that does not annihilate futurity, which rejects both utopian and tragic registers, and in doing so carves a space in political thinking for the incalculable?

To respond to these questions, I want to explore two genealogies of Latinamericanist political thought. The first could be called, to borrow from Alberto Moreiras, the "identitarian register" ("Common Political Democracy," 178), which I would link to Inquisitional logic. The second genealogy could be characterized as a "marrano register" (178–79). Morei-ras understands the second as an intellectual countertradition to Spanish Imperial reason, but I am interested in pursuing marranismo as a decon-structive reading practice, a *thinking* that exposes the contours of Inquisi-tional (or identitary) logic and demands a reconsideration of politics relation to ethics, the aporetic conjugation of which would open a space in which, *from* which, to begin to think an unforeseeable, future, democracy-to-come, or to think what is *unthinkable* about such a future.[1]

Inquisitional Logic

To read Inquisitional logic as identitarian logic, let us recall Page duBois's *Torture and Truth*, in which she traces the etymological trajectory of the word *basanos* in classical Athenian culture, where it referred to a touchstone that tested the purity of gold. The meaning of *basanos* then changed to signify a test of loyalty and then shifted again to refer to the violent evo-cation of the "truth" from the body of the slave. DuBois demonstrates the way in which the practice of torture in Western culture is intimately tied to classical notions of truth as *alêtheia*, a buried truth brought to light (5). Within the context of literary exegesis, we might understand *alêtheia* as related to what Althusser called the "religious myth of reading," that is, a myth of reading for a discoverable, transparent, unmediated truth.

Does the marrano conceal a secret, an identity, a truth that the right techniques, the correctly applied pain, can disclose? In my research on literary representations of the Inquisition and marranismo, I found the marrano to be an aporetic figure.[2] On the one hand, representations of the marrano tend to underscore her crypto-Jewishness, and Inquisitorial inter-rogation is shown to extract the clandestine truth duBois describes in her work. The marrano is interrogated in order to bring to light her Jewish-ness, the hidden heretical impulse, as if it were possible to preserve it intact despite the process of conversion and, in some cases, despite the years, the generations that have passed since the conversion of the marra-no's ancestors (and, in any case, what precisely was "there" to begin with?). In nineteenth- and twentieth-century narrative, theater, and film, the marrano bears a symbolic weight or, more precisely, an allegorical weight, a mode of signification that shares the secret form, or formal secret, of the crypto-Jew. Written during or in the wake of dictatorship, such depictions of the interrogated marrano allegorize the tortured political prisoner under totalitarian state violence. Yet the majority of these works end up repro-ducing the Inquisitional logic they aim to resist by remaining bound to an *identitarian* reading of the marrano. Despite a political or ideological opposition to repressive state violence, these works maintain the violent bond between torture and truth, missing altogether the deconstructive potential of marranismo.

There are, of course, alternative readings of the marrano.[3] For Derrida, the marrano guards and is guarded by a secret, but that secret is not based upon the hiding or revelation (through confession) of *alêtheia*: "It would not be a question of a secret as a representation dissimulated by a conscious subject, nor, moreover, of the content of an unconscious representation, some secret or mysterious motive that the moralist or the psychoanalyst might have the skill to detect, or, as they say, to de-mystify" ("Passions," 24). The Derridean secret exceeds the play of burying and unburying; that is, it subverts the notion of *alêtheia* that is constitutive of Inquisitional logic. *This* is the distinction I consider vital to a discussion of marrano thinking: By exposing the limits of Inquisitional logic, the deconstructive impulse opens more possibilities than it excludes, both in theory and so-called practice.

Yet the notion that there is, in cultures, identities, or works of literature or culture an unburied truth once forgotten and to be brought to light has shaped a strand of Latinamericanist political thought into a tradition compatible, or complicit, with the logic of archaeology and of the Inquisition.[4] This excavational mode of thought, a cousin of a certain conservative philological tendency, has as its foundation or ground—in addition to what is built upon it—that which hides beneath it, an identifiable and revealable truth. One example can be found in the "decolonial turn" of the early twenty-first century, a school or "option" that aims to excavate an authentically indigenous essence from postcolonial Latin America and emancipate it from the Eurocentrism that has kept it prisoner. Yet such *arche-logic* can also be found in less expected sites, where its political and intellectual consequences and commitments are dramatically different from those we find in decolonial studies. I am thinking, for example, of a recent article by Bruno Bosteels, "Una arqueología del porvenir," in which he reads José Revueltas's *Dialéctica de la conciencia* "como una suerte de arqueología del futuro: un rescate de la memoria genérica de la humanidad, sus rebeliones y derrotas, a través de una iluminación profana que no sólo condensa nuestro pasado inmemorial sino que también lo proyecta sobre la utopía de aquello que queda aún por venir" (as a kind of archaeology of the future: a salvaging of the generic memory of humanity, its rebellions and defeats, through a profane illumination that not only condenses our immemorial past but also projects it upon the utopia of that which is still to

come) (162). Bosteels's argument does not stand or fall on a narrowly con-
ceived concept of identity—indeed, the strong use of the pronoun "our"
suggests the weight he places on the normative force of quite a different
sort of universal identity. Bosteels's "archaeology of the future" may be
limited not by its desire to return to the past in order to think the present
or future but rather by its exclusion, from its approach to the present, of a
reading that takes into account the act of reading itself. The logic of archaeology, even in its strongest contemporary versions, suffers from the lack of
auto-critique or exposure of the limits of its own thinking or theorizing,
the inability to call reading *reading*.

A second example, more archaeological still, would be the cover of
Bosteels's 2012 book *Marx and Freud in Latin America*, which shows three

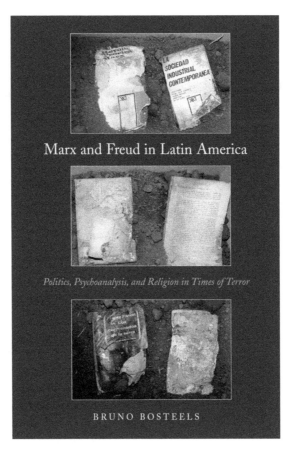

Cover of Bruno Bosteels, *Marx and Freud in Latin
America* (© 2012, Verso Books)

images from the Argentine artist Marcelo Brodsky's installation *Los conde-
nados de la tierra*. The installation includes boxes of books that had been
buried during the dictatorship in the 1970s and 1980s by a leftist couple and
excavated several decades later by their children after hearing that they
were hidden in their backyard in La Plata.

These highly suggestive images metonymically signal the project of the
book—and, one could deduce, Bosteels's larger project of actualizing com-
munism through a kind of revindication of a repressed militancy from the
1960s and 1970s. Bosteels explains that the studies in his book, like the
images from Brodsky's installation, "consist in an effort to dig similar holes
and tell the story of what happened with those works and others like them
that were censored, forgotten, buried, or destroyed since the mid-1970s"
(21). This work in countermemory concerns not only books that were
literally buried or censored and later disinterred but also "the ideas, dreams
and projects that were otherwise forced to find a more figurative hiding
place in the inner recesses of the psychic apparatus of their original readers
and proponents" (21). Such an approach to politics and history, or to
political history, is symptomatic of a ubiquitous desire in Latinamericanist
thought to gain access to the truth of the past, a desire that, in the work of
Bosteels, acquires a sharp and rigorous quality but, I want to insist, does
not allow for a notion of the future that would leave room for the incalculable. Again, my criticism has little to do with the appropriation of Revueltas or Brodsky, whose works in principle open up a number of fascinating
and diverse (and divergent) avenues of interpretation, but rather with the
foreclosure of futures (and of pasts) that cannot be reckoned or thought in
advance or understood, even "figuratively," in their pastness.

If we can understand Inquisitional logic as a kind of archaeological
mode of thought, what I am proposing as marrano thinking would appear
in relation to another logic, anarchaeological, an-archical, a critical reading
practice that would not only insubordinate (in the sense given this verb by
Nelly Richard in *La insubordinación de los signos* [*The Insubordination of Signs*])
but also expose the instability of the principles of identity, originality,
foundation, truth. In contrast to Bosteels's project, recent scholarship by
Susana Draper ("Fragmentos de futuro en los abismos del pasado"), Gareth
Williams (*The Mexican Exception*), and Samuel Steinberg (*Photopoetics at
Tlatelolco*) enacts a decidedly different approach to the past. In all three, it
is possible to detect a gesture of return to the events of Mexico City, 1968,
not in order to "bring to light" the truth of the Mexican student–popular
movement but instead to traverse the fantasy of the movement, together
with its dissolution, without seeking to suture the gaps necessarily produced

in such readings. *This* is marrano thinking: a rejection of the excavation of a buried truth in favor of an anarchaeological approach in which the future of the past remains unaccounted for: that is, the very possibility of reading.

This is not to say that these critics would be in agreement, if asked, on what "marrano" or "anarchaeological thinking" amounts to or on how it proceeds—any more than the critics I have been lining up, brutally, on the "archaeological" side agree. If Williams underscores the impossibility of accounting for "the singular experience of the democratic event called 1968," Draper reads Roberto Bolaño's *Amuleto* as

> una manera de pensar la escritura de la historia que, en tono benjaminiano, exige una prosa diferente—un acto de imaginación que parece recordarnos que todo recuerdo del pasado está siendo un acto de ficcionalización de ese pasado, una traducción casi imposible de voces aniquiladas—una escucha espectral que en el texto respondería quizás a la pregunta de qué tipo de "construcción" del 68 se puede hacer en el 1998, cómo heredar su promesa y repetir su gesto sin intentar calcarlo. (65–66)

> (a way of thinking the writing of history that, in a Benjaminian tone, demands a different kind of prose—an act of imagination that appears to remind us that every memory of the past is a fictionalization of that past, an almost impossible translation of annihilated voices—a spectral rumor that in the text might respond to the question of what type of "construction" of '68 can be made in 1998, how to inherit its promise and repeat its gesture without intending to reproduce it.) (my translation)

Steinberg, for his part, glosses the multiple representations (intellectual, aesthetic, official) of Tlatelolco as both a literal and allegorical crypt of the student-popular movement and its annihilation. But there is no effort by Steinberg to exhume the buried event of '68 as signifier of the failed movement. Rather, he remains preoccupied with the aporetic quality of the revelation of the event, its *photopoiesis*, which hides at the very same time that it reveals: "Each writing of 1968 occupies a double movement, on the one hand standing in reference to and calling forth a larger and more complete archive of that year, and on the other, hoping to silence this endless writing by naming, finally, what event truly occurred then and there" (37).

Despite the differences in approach of these anarchaeological critical endeavors, we witness an oblique, ambivalent relation to the historical-political archive, with the past serving as future. It is for this reason, perhaps, that in each of the three projects we can find the Derridean motifs of passive decision and hauntology: In exposing itself to the past as absolute future, to the illegible event of '68, anarchaeological thinking conditions an unconditional relation to an incalculable future. At the same time, there is something as yet unarticulated in these projects, each of which is indebted to the Derrida of *Specters of Marx* and *The Politics of Friendship*, texts themselves indebted to the ethical philosophy of Levinas, whose influence upon the concepts of passive decision and the spectral injunction, or call, demands a closer look. Anarchaeological, or marrano, thinking cannot be framed as a properly political thought, as I will now suggest, but rather represents a critical reading practice: what Moreiras has characterized as the suspension of the ethical by the political and of the political by the ethical ("Infrapolitical Literature," 186).

Misreading Ethics

One of the limitations of Latinamericanist political thought—or perhaps one of its symptoms—stems from a misreading of the question of the ethical (in particular, in the work of Levinas), together with a partial or total eclipse of the possible (aporetic) relation between the ethics and politics. I say "misreading" not because these readings (for now I will limit myself to those of Enrique Dussel and Bruno Bosteels) are unfaithful to the work of Levinas but because they are *too* faithful—that is, literal—in their incorporation or rejection of a Levinasian ethics. This sort of misreading reduces, rather than expands, the possibilities of interpretation. I propose, instead, to read Levinas against the grain, to offer an equivocal, heterodox reading, a *productive* misreading, a *malentendu* in the Rancièrian sense, that, rather than identifying antagonistic ideological positions, exposes the constitutive equivocation of the political from the vantage point of the ethical: what I was just calling marrano thinking.

Dussel and Bosteels (together with other decolonial thinkers such as Walter Mignolo and Badiouians such as Peter Hallward) define the ethical philosophy of Levinas as an ethics of difference, something that Badiou himself complicates: "For the honour of philosophy, it is first of all necessary to admit that this ideology of a 'right to difference,' the contemporary catechism of goodwill with regard to 'other cultures,' are strikingly distant from Lévinas's actual conception of things" (*Ethics*, 20). Dussel takes up the notion of responsibility toward the other in his postulation of a distinctly Latin American liberation philosophy. Taking issue with what he calls the "Eurocentric" nature of Levinasian thought, Dussel substitutes Levinas's so-called Jewish other with the oppressed others of Latin America, "the fifteen million Indians slaughtered during the conquest of Latin America, and the thirteen million Africans who were made slaves" ("'Sensibility' and 'Otherness,'" 126). He chooses to ignore the fact that the so-called Jewish victim cannot be found on a single page of Levinas's work, save for the dedication of *Otherwise than Being* to "the memory of those who were closest among the six million assassinated by the National Socialists, and of the millions on millions of all confessions and all nations, victims of the same hatred of the other man, the same anti-semitism" (v), which is followed by a *second* dedication in Hebrew that lists the names of Levinas's relatives murdered by the Nazis. That is, Levinas carries out an improper but necessary translation between a numerically "same" multitude of victims and the proper names of the victims "closest" to him, an improper but necessary translation between an abstract construction of the victim— numerical, "millions on millions"—and a highly specific, concrete, even personal acknowledgment of the names of his relatives. Dussel renders abstract again this acknowledgment on Levinas's part in order to compare the "European" numbers to the numbers killed "during the conquest of Latin America" and in the slave trade. (The gesture would surely have been, rather, to list, in the languages of the exterminated Latin American and African peoples, similarly personal, concrete proper names.) Instead Dussel substitutes in place of the proper name—radical, untranslatable singularity—an identitarian logic that annihilates it.

In his essay "The Ethical Superstition," Bosteels reproaches Dussel's reliance, in his articulation of an ethical philosophy of liberation, upon the idea of the other as victim, maintaining that his book *Ética de la liberación* could just have well been called *Política de la liberación*, were it not for "the spirit of our time and its authoritarian consensus regarding the dignity of the ethical over and above all potentially illusory, if not purely voluntaristic political commitments and partisanships" (17). Bosteels identifies a contradiction in Dussel's work: Despite the characterization of the other as victim, ethics and politics are interchangeable for Dussel, according to Bosteels. What's more, Dussel (in his later work) surprisingly refers to a Badiouian notion of subjectivization as central to the process of liberation, says Bosteels: "el devenir-sujeto de la víctima" (the becoming-subject of the victim) (17). This presents a serious problem for Bosteels not because Dussel adopts a Badiouian theory of the subject but because he blurs the distinction (crucial for Bosteels) between ethics and politics, understood here as processes of victimization and subjectivization, respectively.

Why this insistence upon the distinction between ethics and politics as discrete domains without possible relation? In a recent essay on the polemic that surfaces in response to the publication of a letter by the Argentine philosopher Oscar del Barco, "No matarás"—a confession in which del Barco admits to having participated in militant acts of violence and condemns such acts, provoking a heated argument over political memory of the armed Left in Argentina, which I discuss in depth in Part II—Patrick Dove underscores the danger in creating a false opposition between the ethical and the political:

> For many this antagonism takes the form of an either/or: either politics or ethics (either Marx or Freud, Badiou or Levinas, for instance) but not both. The translation of this antagonism into the logic of choice comes with a price: it happens at the expense of thinking what these two spheres might have in common, either despite the antagonism or precisely because of it. By the same token, the either/or has the effect of imputing to each "sphere" a sense of stability and self-consistency that may in fact blind us to what is really at stake in ethical and political thinking. ("Memory between Politics and Ethics," 280)

What Bosteels identifies as a weakness in Dussel's work—the inability to distinguish one thing from the other—ends up exposing the compatibility between ethics (as victimization) and politics (as subjectivization). At the same time, Bosteels's argument obscures the potential force of both the ethical *and* the political ("what is really at stake in ethical and political thinking") by framing the relation between ethics and politics as an opposition or choice.

The dichotomy ethics/politics, Levinas/Badiou depends upon an anthropomorphized other that greatly interests Dussel but whose presence in Levinas is questionable. The other as victim, according to Dussel, is grounded in the notion of the vulnerable other, a concept that can be found in the early Levinas of *Totality and Infinity*—"[God's] very epiphany consists in soliciting us by his destitution in the face of the Stranger, the widow, and the orphan" (78)—but that is completely absent from his later work *Otherwise than Being*, in which the demand of the other is read as the demand of the other within the same: "There is a claim laid on the same by the other in the core of myself, the extreme tension of the command exercised by the other in me over me, a traumatic hold of the other on the same" (141). The idea of the other within the same permits us a retrospective reading, against the grain, of the demand "Thou shalt not kill"—together with the figure of the stranger—as figurative concepts (in this reading, the other is not identifiable as such; there is no articulated or articulable demand). The concept of the other within the same renders impossible, in one blow, both the sovereign subject as well as the other-as-victim: In its place, we witness what we might call (with Moreiras) a *nonsubject* that decides not from his autonomy but from his passivity, the Derridean passive decision that we read in *The Politics of Friendship*: "The passive decision, condition of the event, is always in me, structurally, another event, a rending decision as the decision of the other. Of the absolute other in me, the other as the absolute that decides on me in me" (68). In his discussion of Luis González de Alba's *Los días y los años*, Gareth Williams takes up this idea, this strange and compelling structure of passive decision, arguing that "in [de Alba's] approach to 1968 decision and responsibility are *of the other*; that is, they come back or come down to the other, from the other, even if it is the other 'in me'" (*The Mexican Exception*, 143). The possibility of deciding is what makes a sovereign—a ruler, a sovereign subject. Passive decision, for Williams, is what makes the democratic event of '68 simultaneously possible and impossible (as it makes sovereignty both sovereign and not, both possible and not).

The oblique, absence-presence of Levinas in anarchaeological thinking comes about, once again, through the idea of the spectral and, in particular, of the spectral as demand in the (otherwise very different) projects of Draper and Steinberg. If Draper locates, in Bolaño, the "spectral sound" of "annihilated voices" (translation mine), Steinberg argues that "the demand—for politics, for class struggle, for being-in-common—continues to haunt the cultural discourse of 1968 and every attempt to finally resolve those energies as hegemonic calculation, that is, without politics" (28). Both projects, in my view, are indebted to, heirs of, Derrida's *Specters of Marx*, itself indebted to the legacy of Marx (but also, at the same time, of Levinas). Derrida likens the inheritance of Marx to the appearance of a specter, whose call or injunction is ethico-political. Like the ghost of Hamlet's father, the specter of Marx returns to warn us that "the time is out of joint," a call at once a warning and a demand for justice, a justice that stands in uncomfortable yet urgent relation to a notion of injustice (*adikia*) "against which there is no calculable insurance" (*Specters*, 32). It is the alarming proximity of justice and injustice that leads Derrida to distinguish between the moralism of an identifiable, fulfillable duty and the terrifying unreadability of the ethico-political demand. He writes:

> Otherwise it rests on the good conscience of having done one's duty, it loses the chance of the future, of the promise or the appeal, of the desire also (that is its "own" possibility), of this desert-like messianism (without content and without identifiable messiah), of this *abyssal* desert, "desert in the desert," . . .

one desert signaling toward the other, abyssal and chaotic desert, if chaos describes first of all the immensity, excessiveness, disproportion in the gaping hole of the open mouth—in the waiting or calling for what we have nicknamed here without knowing the messianic: the coming of the other, the absolute and unpredictable singularity of the *arrivant* as justice. We believe that this messianic remains an ineffaceable mark—a mark one neither can nor should efface—of Marx's legacy, and doubtless of inheriting, of the experience of inheritance in general. Otherwise, one would reduce the event-ness of the event, the singularity and the alterity of the other. (33)

Again, the aporetic presence-absence of Levinas, the demand of the other over me in me—a call to which I do not know how to respond except from passivity—suggests that the limit of the ethical is intimately bound to its political valence, or potential, and vice versa. I'll return to this scene of passivity, this Levinasian moment or specter in Derrida, at various moments in this book in order to tease out what I consider to be a vital aspect of anarchaeological thinking.

Anarchaeological thinking: a critical practice, a reading practice, that exhibits a certain compatibility with what Moreiras has called infrapolitical practice:

What if, before ethics, there were another practice that makes of the double suspension of the ethical by the political and of the political by the ethical its very possibility? This practice, which finds its expression in literature, but is not limited to literature, is infrapolitical practice. It exposes us without ulterior purpose, and therefore remains, itself, beyond the double suspension. It remains haunted, and lives in the haunting. ("Infrapolitical Literature," 186)

I take this passage, from one of Moreiras's earlier writings on infrapolitics, to indicate the link to literature—or to reading-as-misreading—that resides at the center of anarchaeological thinking. Although Moreiras and others have since taken strong public stances "against" literature—which I understand to be the institutionalized, disciplinary forms literary studies has taken—I do not see this as a strong disagreement but rather a different orientation. The haunting Moreiras describes here, which "finds its expression in literature, but is not limited to literature," is not synonymous with but exhibits an important compatibility with the specter I describe as residing at the heart of anarchaeological, marrano thinking.

Similarly, the infrapolitical approach to both ethics and politics—which lays stress on their "exhaustion"—does not, to my mind, imply a break from what I am describing as the urgent ethico-political demand (to read) in Derrida. (I will pursue this line of thinking further in Part II, "The Ethical Turn.") The relation to the other—which always and already involves a relation to the third, to the other of the other—implies a demand that Levinas's work cannot account for. There are two reasons for this: first, because the demand itself (as *saying* rather than *said*) is unthematizable, unreadable, and second, because Levinas is not able to make the leap from ethics to politics. It is for this reason that we need—urgently—the translation of the Levinasian ethical demand to the spectral demand in Derrida, a necessarily partial demand, impossible to fulfill (not, or not only, as Simon Critchley suggests, because the demand is infinite but because, like the marrano secret, it exceeds the play of hiding and revelation: We never "discover" the truth of the demand of the other).

We stand, now, before a genealogy of spectral inheritances, multiple inheritances that demand more work, more thinking. For the illegible quality of the other (the *arrivant*, the event) is in fact a call for *more* reading: Recall that Derrida's specter's injunction is double, aporetic: "One always inherits from a secret—which says 'read me, will you ever be able to do so?'" (*Specters*, 18). Anarchaeological, marrano, thinking would respond to a call not from an exhumed past but from the future of this and other unfixed pasts, whose spectral apparition we know not how to read, though read them we must. In the struggle to interpret the uninterpretable demand of the ethical and the political, which is a demand for justice, against the violence of Inquisitional logic, marrano thinking represents a wager, a risk without guarantee that, by rejecting futures both utopian and tragic, guards the only possibility—remote, minor—of democracy.

Anarchic Inheritance

Is it possible to return to Latin America's radical political past in order to confront, simultaneously, both the urgent demands *and* the incalculable secrets of this archive (which is not one) and that would necessarily take into account the mediated, violent nature of such a confrontation? I've just outlined three rather different responses to the question in work by Susana Draper, Gareth Williams, and Samuel Steinberg, whose unique engagements with 1968 Mexico acknowledge not only the inassimilable ghosts of the past but also the unreadable quality of the archive that poses a radical demand to read, the paradoxically anarchic condition of the archive. As a mode of conclusion, I would like to consider an example from recent cinema, Albertina Carri's 2017 film *Cuatreros*, which, in its troubled relation to Argentina's militant and outlaw past, imagines the inheritance of violence as *itself* a violent act.

Albertina Carri—one of the leading figures of New Argentine cinema—explores discourses and debates surrounding animality and sexuality, bourgeois families and bourgeois justice, anger and mourning, political violence and historical memory in her work, which includes short and feature-length films, fiction, animation, and documentaries, performance art and porno. Her international reputation was solidified with the debut of *Los rubios* (2003), a film about her Montonero parents, Roberto Carri and Ana María Caruso, who were disappeared in 1976 and murdered a year later. A metadocumentary with aspects of fiction that calls into question the possibility of memory, truth, and the genre of documentary itself, *Los rubios* articulates, both performatively and constatively, the always-already mediated quality of memory and representation: the representation of history, of identity, of truth. The film, which was met with international acclaim, was denounced by a few critics, such as Beatriz Sarlo and Martín Kohan, for its experimental qualities and for its departure from more testimonial approaches to the history of the civic-military dictatorship and the militant movements it violently suppressed. Rather than investigating what "really" happened to her parents (although that question is still posed in the film), which would have aligned the film with the norms of the documentary genre as well as with the tireless efforts by the families of the disappeared to locate forensic evidence of their murdered relatives (the well-known Madres de la Plaza de Mayo and HIJOS, Hijos por la Identidad y la Justicia contra el Olvido y el Silencio), *Los rubios* instead dwells upon and pursues the blind spots and errors of collective and individual memory. The most prominent example is the one that resulted in the title of the film: When interviewed by the film crew about Roberto, Ana María, and their three daughters, a working-class neighbor incorrectly recalls that they were all blonds ("eran todos rubios," she insists). Her "error," the film shows, reveals the perhaps more significant "truth" that Carri and Caruso, as middle-class intellectuals, stood out in the provincial neighborhood, metonymically signifying the difficult-to-achieve student-worker alliance that plagued by so many leftist movements of the period.

Los rubios is a theoretically sophisticated film by a precocious young director, while Carri's 2017 *Cuatreros* is conceptually mature and formally complex—again, not-quite-documentary and not-quite-fiction—that returns once again to the ghostly archive of Argentina's militant and outlaw past, this time to document the life of the *cuatrero* ("rustler") Isidro Velázquez or, rather, to document Carri's *failure* to make a film about Velázquez. Velázquez had been the subject of a book by Roberto Carri, *Isidro Velázquez: formas prerrevolucionarias de la violencia.* There'd been a film, too—*Los Velázquez,* based upon the research for her father's book—but it had never been completed, and its director, Pablo Szir, was disappeared during the dictatorship as well. "Debería hacerse una película sobre el caso Velázquez," Albertina narrates in a voiceover, "Debería, debería. Lo mismo que dijo mi hermana cuando empecé a estudiar cine: 'deberías hacer la película de los Velázquez.' Como nunca me llevé muy bien con el 'debería,' nunca me interesó el asunto" (Someone should make a film about the Velázquez case . . . should, should. My sister said the same thing when I began to study film: "you should make the film about Velázquez." As I never got on very well with "should's," the matter never interested me). Yet Carri does not simply reverse her attitude toward *deberes* (duties, obligations, debts), enthusiastically embracing a story she'd previously avoided. Rather, *Cuatreros*—a *successful* film about the *failure* to make a film about Velázquez—unsettles the ideas of duty and inheritance, and their relation, that have structured debates surrounding historical memory, as well as the broader rapport between ethical responsibility and aesthetic production. What kind of debt is inherited in this film, and how is this inheritance characterized? What if we were to think about inheritance, paradoxically, as a certain *rejection* of obligations, of duties or debts, one that both assumes *and* refuses to receive passively the ethico-political legacy of the previous generation, even when that generation (here, Carri's own parents) died for their cause?

After multiple frustrated attempts to make a film about Velázquez, Carri has a breakthrough. The turning point—narrated by Carri midway through the film—occurs when Carri discovers the documentary film *Ya es tiempo de violencia* (Enrique Juárez, 1969) in the archive of the ICAIC (Instituto Cubano del Arte e Industria Cinematográficos) while in Cuba to present *Los rubios.* Juárez, who was also disappeared in 1976, had made a film linking the 1969 Cordobazo to other instances of violent uprising around Latin America and the world. The film—which makes a case for the necessity of armed resistance—together with the birth of her son Furio, who appears frolicking with Carri between shadows and light toward the end of the film, "turns" Carri back to her parents, in particular to her father, with whose militancy she can now identify: indirectly, obliquely, romantically.

We begin to see, in *Cuatreros*, that the notion of inheritance bears a rather peculiar relation to violence, in at least three different ways. First, Albertina, as the orphaned daughter of murdered parents, *inherits* violence (here, violence is the *object* of the inheritance, it is the "thing" inherited, although the heir, too, appears in a position of strange passivity). Second, inheritance is shown to be necessarily violent: Albertina—again, ostensibly passive—is *accosted* by such an inheritance. Both of these are disturbing, if not unknown, ways of imagining what it means to receive an inheritance. Carri, though, offers a third possibility as well, albeit a counterintuitive or unexpected one. In *Cuatreros* (as well as in *Los rubios*, although in a different way), the act of inheriting *itself* is shown to be necessarily violent: The heir—here, not merely passive but decidedly active—performs a violent act in her ordering and disordering of archival material and in showing the archive itself to be constitutively anarchic.

In this triple way, then, Carri reflects upon the violent quality of anamnesis and amnesis: One could say that if she forgets, she negates or annihilates the past, yet her survival at times seems to depend upon a *certain* forgetting: "para sobrevivir también hay que olvidar" (in order to survive one must also forget), she narrates irreverently. Moreover, the act of aesthetic representation *itself* (the shooting of scenes, the slicing, cutting, and splicing of cinematic production) can be read as violent, a connection she makes already in *Los rubios*.

ALBERTINA (en *off*): Ella no quiere hablar frente a la cámara. Se niega a que le grabe su testimonio. Me ha dicho cosas como "yo no hablé en la tortura, no testimonié para la CONADEP, tampoco lo voy a hacer ahora frente a una cámara". Me pregunto en qué se parece una cámara a una picana. Quizá me perdí un capítulo en la historia del arte, no sé. Pero en ese caso me pregunto en qué se parecerá su cámara al hacha con que matan a la vaca.

(She doesn't want to speak in front of the camera. She refuses to let me record her testimony. She's said things like "I didn't speak under torture, I didn't give testimony to the CONADEP, I'm not going to do it now before the camera." I ask myself how a camera resembles an electric prod. Maybe I missed a chapter of art history, I don't know. But in that case I wonder how her camera resembles the ax that kills the cow.)

Me pregunto: at once a rhetorical and undecidable question. Does Albertina erase or annihilate her parents by refusing to follow in their footsteps, ideologically speaking? Immediately before her discovery of Juárez's film in the archive of the ICAIC, Albertina relates the reaction of repulsion she experiences in Havana as well as the horror she feels imagining herself meeting her parents in heaven (or hell), when they will inevitably accuse her of abandoning their struggle, of navel gazing rather than carrying on their legacy.

After viewing *Ya es tiempo de violencia*, however, Carri confesses to the viewer that had she been her parents' age at that point in history, she'd have followed the path they travelled, but that she'd been born in different times: "Si hubiese tenido la edad suficiente en esa época, yo hubiese hecho lo mismo que ellos . . . que Juárez, que Szir, que mamá, y que papá. Hubiese pertenecido a una célula subversiva, sin duda. Pero los tiempos son otros, y me tocó éste" (If I'd been the right age in that time, I'd have done the same as they did . . . as Juárez, as Szir, as Mom, as Dad. I'd have belonged to a subversive group, without a doubt. But the times have changed, and these are the times I ended up with).

A simultaneous identification-disidentification, the formal effects of which can be traced in the unorthodox, experimental qualities of the film. The pivot in the film, then, is simultaneously a turning away from and turning toward her political inheritance. On the one hand, she is struck, for the first time, with a strange empathy for her father's passions and political decisions; indeed, it is this affective identification that allows her finally to make the film. Yet the film she ultimately makes does not, on the other hand, recover or recuperate the militant struggle as an ideological position or path that she idealizes or pursues herself: Instead of telling Velázquez's story, which would be a faithful continuation of her father's

Cuatreros, dir. Albertina Carri

intellectual and political legacy, she makes a film that exhibits no coherent ideological program.

The experience of viewing *Cuatreros* can also be characterized as rather violent: The spectator is accosted by images—one, three, five at a time—accompanied by diegetic and extradiegetic sound that often does not conform with the excess of images, as well as Carri's own narration. The images, which Carri has pulled from disordered archives, work to recreate a certain aesthetic of her parents' era, but not through any cohesive narrative: Styles, gestures, news reports, and soft porn mingle with Velázquez's and Carri's stories, narrated in Carri's voice. The narrative voice, too, exhibits an obsessive quality, simultaneously grounding and ungrounding the ostensible anarchy of the images, often in triple or quintuple. (In this sense, it is quite different from *Los rubios*, in which the figure of Carri is divided into two or three characters and in which Carri's is one of many voices.) Horacio González rightly describes the work as exhibiting a formal *cuatrerismo*, which he understands as a particular relation to the archive: "Lo que hizo Albertina Carri ya es una modalidad segunda o adicional del archivo, es decir, en el sentido profundo del archivo, llevar al origen, a la *arjé*, una historia del poder, esto es, una crítica al poder y por lo tanto a los archivos institucionales, con otro archivo destrozado, que extrañamente la memoria torna homogéneo" (What Albertina Carri created is a secondary or supplementary modality of the archive, that is, in the deepest sense of archive: to take to its beginnings, to the archē, a history of power, that is, a critique of power and therefore of institutional archives, with another destroyed archive, which memory strangely makes homogeneous). In addition to taking the history of power to its origin, Carri's film also *destroys* this origin, or shows the origin, the archē, to be always already destroyed, constitutively anarchic.

You may have noticed that, in my analysis of Carri's work, I make no reference to the theoretical and philosophical works that motivate this book. This is because I want to suggest, as a kind of experiment or test, that *Cuatreros* functions as a conceptual work, in its imagining and unsettling of concepts such as inheritance, debt, and violence. Daniel Link ("Hay guerra") is correct to consider the film "pensamiento político," political thought. Yet I might put it somewhat differently: I would say that by exposing the violent, an-archic core of the archive, in its simultaneous refusal and pursuit of a violent inheritance, *Cuatreros* performs a kind of *pensamiento ético violento*, a violent ethical thinking, a thinking of a violent ethics. Carri's "failure" to make a proper documentary, one in which the history of Velázquez would be successfully excavated along with, one presumes, the "truth" of her father's militancy, gives way to an anarchaeological relation to the militant past, to her violent inheritance. Here, ethics (understood as responsibility to this inheritance) takes the form of a faithful betrayal, at once passive and active, a remembering and a forgetting: a violent inheriting.

Part II. The Ethical Turn

When did we, as a field, as a discipline, as a university system, turn "toward" ethics—if we can say that we did—and from what did we turn away? Let's keep our focus on Latin America (always remembering the field's contiguous disciplines and the university setting, to which I will turn in my conclusion). Here, as in literary and philosophical studies more broadly in the past quarter-century, the so-called turn to ethics has *itself* become a trope, a turning, and a symptomatic trope at that. It reveals a profound anxiety about what has been a pervasive disciplinary obsession over the relation between politics and literature and between politics and intellectual and artistic production more broadly: the question of the committed intellectual, el *intelectual comprometido*. The turn to ethics tends to presuppose, both within and outside of Latin American studies,[1] a turn *away* from politics or a substitution of one for the other, a diagnosis that is grounded in the historical, ideological, geopolitical shifts of the 1980s (the Central American civil wars, the Southern Cone dictatorships, the fall of the Berlin Wall and subsequent crisis of the Left). In what follows, I argue that a diagnosis based in substitution results in an overly narrow understanding of both ethics *and* politics, the opposition between which ends up limiting the possibilities of each (see Dove, "Memory between Politics and Ethics"). After considering the way in which Latinamericanism after 9/11 pitted politics against ethics, I'll focus on four types of readings of ethical philosophy in Latin American and Latinamericanist thought that I characterize, loosely, as *theological, literary, political,* and *deconstructive*. To think beyond, or outside of, or unsettlingly within the opposition between ethics and politics, or the substitution of one for the other, requires us to inherit and to forget (Carri: "para sobrevivir también hay que olvidar") violently, from each of these types of reading, an anarchic secret each reading discloses and also hides. This fourfold anarchaeology begins to designate a relation between ethics and politics at work outside, or beyond, or unsettlingly within the logic of identification-recognition.

Ethics against Politics

> The way [from proximity to justice] leads from responsibility to
> problems.
>
> —Emmanuel Levinas, *Otherwise than Being*

> As a slogan, "against literature" could be read two ways: in the
> sense of versus, that is, in an antagonistic relation with literature;
> or, as in a gestalt figure/ground relation, as a performance that
> has as its necessary condition literature.
>
> —John Beverley, *Against Literature*

Latinamericanism since 9/11 has seemed uneventful to many, in contrast
to the contentious (and often painful) debates of the 1990s. For those of us
who were graduate students during the 1990s and were only just beginning
our first academic positions at the turn of the millennium, there is a sense
of Latinamericanism as a potential site for politically infused, theoretically
grounded intellectual work, but this impression is present only as a trace
or specter—not of something that ever was, but of something that might
have been, an as-yet-unfulfilled demand. We have memories of a possible
future of the past that is marked by catastrophe. In my case, I recall the
volatile Latin American cultural studies panels of the September 2001 Latin
American Studies Association congress: I sat on the floor of a packed conference room, not fully grasping the implosion that was happening around
me, just days before the attacks on New York and Washington, DC, would
obliterate far more than a field of debate. (My generation at New York
University was quite literally the 9/11 generation: We watched the towers
burn and fall during the very same semester in which we drafted, or
attempted to draft, our dissertation prospectuses.)

The decade that followed this moment of rupture ushered in significant
political developments in Latin America. The "pink tide" swept Brazil,
Venezuela, Ecuador, Bolivia, Argentina, and Chile, while elsewhere the
Arab Spring erupted and the Occupy movements gathered momentum.
John Beverley's *Latinamericanism after 9/11* emerged at that political crossroads, before left-leaning governments were largely replaced by neoliberal
and neofascist leaders in many of those same countries. His book was a
timely and welcome invitation to discussion, to revisit debates that were

perhaps abandoned prematurely, but also to initiate new conversations at a moment in which the political and cultural landscape—in Latin America as well as more globally—had shifted drastically. I want, here, to take up some of the issues addressed in *Latinamericanism after 9/11*—namely, the relationship between ethics, politics, and aesthetics—in order to suggest that there might be some broad misunderstandings about what each of these concepts might mean and to propose "disagreement" (in the Rancièrian sense we have seen) or "problems" (in the Levinasian sense) as a fruitful point of departure for intellectual engagement in the decades to come.

When I pit "ethics against politics" I am being intentionally ambiguous. The title of this section refers first to Beverley's 1993 book *Against Literature*, which engages with *and* takes a position "against" literature, not "literature in general" but rather the historically specific form it takes during the fifteenth to eighteenth centuries (viii). As we read in the epigraph, *Against Literature* was composed not only in ideological opposition to the institution of literature (dominated by an elite community of *letrados*) but also *against the backdrop of literature*, that is, with literature as its very ground. Beverley thus acknowledges—although perhaps he does not realize the full extent of this disclosure—the necessary interdependence of (or, conversely, the impossibility of isolating) literary and cultural studies, "high" and "low" culture, what is hegemonic and what is subaltern. I do not mean to suggest that these terms end up meaning the same thing but rather that it is only by exploring the thorny, incomprehensible relations between and among these imbricated terms that it might be possible to produce thought that could work against what José Rabasa has called "processes of subalternization" (rather than dwelling, for instance, on who is and who is not subaltern). This is not to say that it is possible to reverse or erase such systems of domination completely (as might be the goal of certain champions of the decolonial option, for example) but rather that if we maintain the facile separation between dichotomous (and extremely reductive) categories, we might actually fall into the trap of reproducing such systems. I therefore use "against" in the first place to signify the impossibility of isolating the political from the ethical.

Second, "ethics against politics" alludes to the sense shared by many critics in the past decades—both within and outside of Latin American studies—that ethics has come to substitute for, and consequently annihilate the possibility of, politics. The so-called ethical turn in literary studies and philosophy was greeted with a justified skepticism, principally from the Left. What did it mean to posit the ethical as a new position from which to approach the literary or the question of the subject? Would so-called politics be obliterated as a productive locus of criticism, not to mention action? Was the "face-to-face" of the ethical encounter to replace the possibility of collective agency, resistance, or revolution? On this *second* reading of "against," I am interested in setting aside the "either/or" of ethics and politics, arguing that the idea of the ethical as always already political and of the political as always already ethical can be fruitfully explored from the space of the literary. Far from proposing aesthetics as an ideal (or exclusive) site of the ethico-political, I instead suggest that Tom Cohen's notion of *allography* or "other writing" as spectral event might open onto an ethics that does not substitute for politics as well as a politics related to but not synonymous with ethics.[1]

Recall the reading of ethical philosophy I associated with Dussel's work. This "ethics of the other" is identified most closely, we saw, with Levinas's early work and holds that ethics is responsibility for the other—a highly anthropomorphized version of the other.[2] The other is the other person, but the term also takes on a decidedly geopolitical meaning in its appropriation by postcolonial theory and liberation philosophy: Dussel asks whether the other might be "the fifteen million Indians slaughtered during the conquest of Latin America, and the thirteen million Africans who were made slaves."[3] Here, we know precisely who the other is (because she is defined by her economic, ethnic, sexual, and geographical coordinates). Our ethical obligation consists just in this: We need to respond to her suffering (and we know precisely how to do so). Beverley associates the turn to ethics with what he calls a neoconservative wave in Latin American literary studies.[4] It is probably more accurate to say, however, that this reading of ethical philosophy is most compatible (structurally if not also thematically) with the decolonial turn (most explicitly in the work of Dussel but also in Walter Mignolo, Aníbal Quijano, and others), an important tendency within post-9/11 Latinamericanism that goes virtually unmentioned in Beverley's book.

The later Levinas, we saw, turns away from these anthropomorphisms[5] and places the weight of ethics on the notion of the other within the same. He now characterizes ethics as an experience of radical interruption (*Otherwise than Being*, 44) and argues that the ethical subject is constituted in response to this violent rupture or break, by acting upon a decision that carries with it no guarantee that one has chosen correctly. This last is the case because the demand of the other is unreadable—we cannot know what the other desires—a circumstance rendered even more unbearable by the fact that we can never properly identify the other.

To be sure, Beverley raises an important point when he argues that the problem of ethics has to do with its reliance upon the decision of an individual. Levinas gestures in this direction when he describes the difficult passage from the ethical to the political in the lines I take as my epigraph, which concern the difficult passage from the relation to the other to the appearance of the third party: "The way [from proximity to justice] leads from responsibility to problems" (161). At the same time, a Levinasian ethics renders obsolete the very notion of the individual: The autonomous, Cartesian subject around which modernity and capitalism have been structured *does not appear* in Levinas, or rather it is precisely the "being" that this mode of thought aims to displace. Instead, the subject comes into existence in relation to heteronomy, the law of the other, which is why the third party will always have to have appeared alongside the other. The way from ethics to politics, for Levinas, is a difficult but necessary problem; the political demand, that is, the double demand posed by the always-already structuring force of the other—"within" and of the third party "alongside"— haunts the ethical demand.

I would therefore define the dilemma of ethics and politics differently from Beverley. Ethics, or a thinking of the ethical, encounters its limit when it is defined as an ethics of the other, as I argued in agreement with Hallward, Bosteels, and others.[6] I'd like to go a little further, however. Ethical interruption sets aside any opposition between self and other: It does away with identitarian logic altogether, a logic into which the interrelated concepts of "self" and "other" fit snugly. But the same could be said of politics or of a thinking of the political.

For Beverley (and if it could be said that the roots of this thinking are already present in his earlier work, it is most salient in his recent book) we know who the subaltern is, just as "we" know who we, metropolitan academic subjects, disciplinary subjects, are.[7] In Bolivia, the subaltern is the "indigenous communities, retirees, coca-growing peasants, unemployed miners or *relocalizados*" that unite under the banner of the Movimiento al Socialismo (119). In Venezuela, it is the various social movements "crystallized" in the service of Chavismo (114). And because we can identify the subaltern, we can (or Beverley can) suggest that the subaltern has (finally) entered the realm of the state. This was of course the goal all along: "What is asked for in identity politics," he explains, "is not so much the *recognition* of difference as the inscription of that difference into the identity of the nation and its history" (83). The subaltern has become hegemonic, and it is now the task of the intellectual (whether she is a Latin American Latinamericanist or a non–Latin American Latinamericanist) to pledge her support, without critique, to this "postsubalternist" state. What's more, as Beverley indicated in a 2012 Latin American Studies Association panel in San Francisco, this state would have no future, as-yet-undefined form (I believe his exact words were "no habrá segunda etapa"). This somewhat surprising declaration echoes Laclau's embrace of Kirchnerismo in Argentina; as Patrick Dove reminds us, Laclau affirmed that "una democracia real en Latinoamérica se basa en la reelección indefinida" (real democracy in Latin America is based upon indefinite reelection) ("Critique of Critique," fn2). Such a thinking of politics, in my mind, carries with it the same pitfalls of an "ethics of the other": In this version of politics, we know who we are, and we know who the other is; we just need to get her into power, and the rest will fall into place (a sort of reverse trickle-down approach, if you like).

What is left, what remains, when the subaltern becomes hegemonic (and thus ceases to "be" subaltern)? What possible future can be pursued in politics, beyond indefinite reelection? I want to consider Alain Badiou's description of ethical and political subjectivity to suggest that the true field of antagonism might lie not *between* ethics and politics but *within* each of them and may emerge when, as, each is *exposed* to the other. Despite the fact that Badiou's book on ethics is (as Bosteels convincingly argues) but a footnote to his political philosophy,[8] the *formal structure* of the ethical in Badiou has a great deal to do with his conception of the political. Both are described as the fidelity of the subject to an event of truth, understood as a radical break from the status quo of the situation.[9] In *Ethics*, Badiou names politics as one the four potential "fields of truth" of which a truth-event might consist, so that one possible instance of ethical subjectivity would be the militant who remains faithful to the "truth event" of the Cultural Revolution.[10]

Even if we are to acknowledge Hallward's and Bosteels's claim that politics (represented metonymically by Badiou) and ethics (represented metonymically by Levinas) are incompatible, we can read these philosophers against themselves (Badiou in his anti-Levinasianism and Levinas in his antiaestheticism) to identify at least one point in common: the centrality of the event as radical break or interruption. It is through a response or fidelity to this event that one becomes an (ethical *or* political) subject. If there is a limit to Badiou's thinking, it has to do with the possible reification of the event (the naming of the unnamable), which may be precisely the dangerous terrain upon which Beverley and Laclau tread. This impasse is addressed best not by Levinas but by Jacques Rancière, whose reading of the political as disagreement seeks to preserve the gap at the heart of the political, or by Claude Lefort or Roberto Esposito, for whom the impossibility of representation resides at the heart of revolution. Here is Esposito, reading Arendt:

> Because of something it does not say—or rather, because of something that cannot be expressed—this text seems to concern every political form. This something is the unrepresentable center of revolution, its originary fire: the coincidence of origin and principle [*principio*] that releases the political's plurality, the political as plurality. It is this plural essence that is utterly unpronounceable in the language of representation. This is because of a dual principle: the language of representation unifies what is plural, and divides what is unitary. Or better, it unifies represented subjects precisely by separating them from their representative. (66)

The plurality to which Esposito refers is the difference *between* and—more importantly—*within* groups of indigenous communities, retirees, coca-growing peasants, unemployed miners, and *relocalizados*, the difference that must be suppressed or annihilated not only to make an initial political demand but also to take (and maintain) power. It is the residue, or remainder, to which Jon Beasley-Murray refers in *Posthegemony*, the impossibility of representation that haunts every political moment because "something always escapes" (132). This "something" is vital: As Beasley-Murray and Benjamin Arditi would argue, it might actually constitute the (non)ground for *another* kind of politics.[11]

What language do we possess that could begin to trace such impossibility? If unrepresentability is not the failure of the political but *constitutive* of the political, if we agree with Rancière that the political subject is necessarily a speaking subject,[12] so that all we have at our disposal to confront the unpronounceable is language itself, where does this leave us? I want to suggest that literary, or aesthetic, discourse that refuses the mimetic in favor of what, again, Tom Cohen has called *allography* or "other writing" might provide a possible point of departure inasmuch as "the allographic may be thought to produce the figure of a spectral event," as Cohen writes in *Hitchcock's Cryptonymies* (280). Events can no longer be substantialized, and the event of an interruption can no longer be converted into an identity, personal or disciplinary or tribal, subaltern or hegemonic; we are now imagining the *figure*, the improper figure, of a *specter*. Specters have no faces, no figures, no substance—but they can be or produce events, just not events that can become identities. I do not want to imply that the literary serves as a privileged site—or as the *only* privileged site—within which the emergence of the figure of such a spectral event might be found.[13] But to place the argument for the emergence of these events in the domain of improper figuration *could* mean, however, that the task of the critic is to be relentless in her pursuit of such an impossible event within literary and other works. Such a notion of intellectual labor would not abandon the political in favor of the apolitical or the antipolitical (whether understood as ethical individualism or aesthetic isolationism): An intellectual in the service of such a politics would merely refuse to give way on her desire. I am imagining, here, a critical endeavor that would clear the space for the incalculable secret that resides at the heart of every political moment.[14]

Levinas in Latin America

I'll turn, now, to four types of readings of ethical philosophy in Latin American and Latinamericanist thought: *theological, literary, political,* and *deconstructive.* For an exemplary case of the "theological" approach to ethics, I'll take up in greater detail Dussel's assimilation of the work of Levinas into his own philosophy of Latin American liberation. I then juxtapose Dussel's Levinasianism with Doris Sommer's ostensibly very different Levinasian approach to literary studies, focusing upon her analysis of Mario Vargas Llosa's *El hablador.* To consider *political* readings of Levinas, I unpack the debate over the relation between ethics and political militancy that surfaces in Argentina following the publication of del Barco's letter "No matarás." I conclude by turning to several recent, more deconstructive approaches to ethics in Latin American studies that refuse the logic of recognition-identification on which one paradigm of substitution turns and that provide new, unfamiliar concepts of ethics, politics, and the relation between the two.

Ethics of Liberation

Dussel finds Levinas's ethical philosophy *formally* useful, but in his 1973 *Liberación latinoamericana y Emmanuel Levinas* he is, as we saw, anxious to fill in what he perceives as a void in Levinas's account of the relation to the other. While the "great philosopher from Nanterre" describes beautifully the face-to-face encounter between self and other, "[el Otro] no logra terminar su discurso": "El Otro interpela, provoca, clama," Dussel acknowledges, "pero nada se dice, no sólo de las condiciones empíricas (sociales, económicas concretas) del saber oír la voz del Otro, sino sobre todo del saber responder por medio de una praxis liberadora" (The Other is not able to complete his demand . . . the Other interpellates, provokes, cries out . . . but nothing is said, not only regarding the empirical (concrete social and economic) conditions of knowing how to hear the voice of the Other but especially pertaining to the knowledge of how to respond through a liberatory praxis).[1] Levinas's great limitation, according to Dussel, is his inability to take the step from ethics to politics, specifically to a politics of liberation, which—on Dussel's account—would entail a full recognition of the other, the comprehension of the other's particular social and economic conditions and, finally, the concrete demands of the other.

I have argued that for Dussel recognition of the other and comprehension of the other's demand require the assignation of a particular identity to the other. This means, first of all, that the other must become the concrete other person, as opposed to Lacan's big Other, or Levinas's other within the Same, or Derrida's other that arrives from an unpredictable future as *l'avenir* and, as such, catches us unaware, off guard. But if on Derrida's (or Levinas's) account the other is precisely that which we cannot anticipate, that for which we cannot prepare, we can, in contrast, anticipate Dussel's other, that other person that we can—indeed, *must*—define as a *victim*, a point I make above. For Dussel, the recognition of the other (in her particular identity *as* other) can and should lead to the "correct" articulation and interpretation of the demand of the other: The demand of the other becomes the concrete demand of a concrete other. Dussel calls this recognition-comprehension pair the passage from ethics to politics. While he concedes to Levinas his likening of politics to war, or war as the true face of politics, in which self and other are always necessarily in a relation of enmity, he calls for a second step, in which a new totality is constructed that takes into account the demand of the other: "Su crítica a la política como la estrategia del estado de guerra es correcta, valiente, clarividente, pero esto no evita las dificultades que tiene el gran pensador judío para reconstruir el sentido positivo y crítico liberador de una nueva política" ("Lo político en Levinas," 115). In effect, Dussel identifies two different political theologies: one "good" and one "bad," bridged by the ethical experience of the face of the other. Here, ethics comes to interrupt "bad" politics (and therefore is not quite "first philosophy") and then replace it with a new, "good" totality, "una nueva totalidad al servicio del Otro" (119).

This new, benevolent totality, a totality "in the service of the Other," a totality of others bound, as Patchen Markell nicely puts it, by recognition, becomes the basis for Dussel's politics of Latin American liberation. Of course, such a politics of recognition has been the object of critique by political thinkers such as Markell. In *Bound by Recognition*, Markell argues

that the compelling ideal of recognition, "for all its democratic good intentions" is ultimately "impossible, even incoherent; and that in pursuing it
we misunderstand certain crucial conditions of social and political life" (4).
He proposes that, rather than remaining tied to the fantasy of knowledge
of oneself or of the other, we turn our attention to a different kind of
justice: a politics of *acknowledgment* rather than of recognition. Such a
democratic justice would not depend on our knowing and respecting who
the other truly is but would instead require "that no one be reduced to any
characterization of his or her identity for the sake of someone else's achieve-
ment of a sense of sovereignty or invulnerability" (7). The liberation theologian, like the well-intentioned democrats mentioned by Markell, pursues
the route of justice grounded in the recognition-comprehension pair I've
been describing. The blind spot of Dussel's argument lies in the fact that
the philosophy or theology of liberation that aims to offer an alternative to
European or Eurocentric models does so—counterintuitively—by grounding itself in the ideals of recognition and sovereignty at the heart of European modernity.[2]

The Talker Turns: The Ethical Turn in Literary Studies

At first glance, Doris Sommer appears to diverge from Dussel's ethics of
recognition in favor of a more deconstructive approach in her essay "About-
Face: The Talker Turns" (1996), in which she uses a loosely Levinasian
framework to analyze the encounter between same and other in Mario
Vargas Llosa's 1987 novel *El hablador*. The essay forms part of a larger trend
in literary criticism in the 1990s, during which time the rise of ethnic
studies and subaltern studies accompanied, in more hegemonic literary
criticism, a new way of reading the "other"—but it need not stand as the
only example of a possible encounter between ethical philosophy and literary criticism. Sommer's mode of critique relies not only upon an implicitly
identifiable privileged reader who may allow herself to be transformed by
minority writing but also on an overdetermined understanding of what
minority writing is (see her 1999 book *Proceed with Caution*, which includes
a version of the Vargas Llosa essay). In the case of *El hablador*, the critic
assumes the task of evaluating whether the subject (here, the privileged
protagonist) properly responds to the (equally fictional) Indian other. Both
models of reading—Dussel's and Sommer's—turn on the interrelated concepts of recognition and comprehension.

Sommer begins by analyzing the opening scene of Vargas Llosa's novel,
in which the semiautobiographical *limeño* protagonist and primary

narrator—whose narrative is interwoven with that of a secondary narrator, a *machiguenga* storyteller—describes his frustrated attempt to escape his troubled homeland during a stint in Italy. "Vine a Firenze para olvidarme por un tiempo del Perú y de los peruanos y he aquí que el malhadado país me salió al encuentro esta mañana de la manera más inesperada," the primary narrator explains, "fueron tres o cuatro fotografías que me devolvieron, de golpe, el sabor de la selva peruana. . . . Naturalmente, entré" (I came to Firenze to forget Peru and the Peruvians for a while, and suddenly my unfortunate country forced itself upon me this morning in the most unexpected way . . . it was three or four photographs that suddenly brought back to me the flavor of the Peruvian jungle. . . . Naturally, I went in) 7/1). Sommer offers up this scene as a model of a Levinasian, asymmetrical encounter between self and other, in which the other demands recognition by the irresponsible writer who has abandoned his country but who now, having been taken hostage by the photographs, must acknowledge the other of his homeland. The foundational call of the other slips between a loosely Levinasian concept of the demand and the well-known Althusserian scene of ideological interpellation, the call of the police toward whom we cannot help but turn. Sommer leaves the vast divide between ethical responsibility to the other and interpellation by an ideological state apparatus (ISA) largely unthought: The Levinas-Althusser coupling stands as a flimsy rhetorical gesture upon which an argument about ethics and politics (not-quite ethics and not-quite politics) will be based.

Even if Vargas Llosa's narrator can be said properly to acknowledge the other who has assaulted him in his expat reverie, Sommer worries that "acknowledging difference . . . would not be the final word but a first step toward enabling ethical negotiations" (108). The idea of acknowledgment (a synonym, here, for what Sommer calls elsewhere "respect" for the other), linked to the equally problematic concept of recognition (of the other as other), is limiting not only if we are to take this moment as the "final word." For even if we are to acknowledge difference as a "first step" toward a second, one would assume, *more* ethical moment (which Sommer curiously terms "negotiations," an activity that would more often be associated with politics in its crudest form), we are caught within the logic of identitarianism, in which otherness is a mere reflection of the same, where identity and difference feed into and constitute one another: a logic Sommer ostensibly seeks to abandon. While the initial "promise of recognition" takes sudden hold of the reader, the problem, as Sommer sees it, is that the subject has only two choices facing the traumatic "grip" of the other:

succumbing to radical alterity, which would translate into a death of the self, or a complete dismissal of the agonist. Sommer goes on to claim, turning to none other than Dussel, that "absolute alterity . . . leaves no room, philosopher Enrique Dussel worries, for the social dynamism that Latin America desperately needs" (95). Why this turn to Dussel, considering that the liberation theologian never, to my knowledge, calls for social dynamism but rather for justice?

Sommer makes a second reference to Dussel—again, in an odd gloss of his early work on Levinas—when she describes a primary "turn" toward the other through speech. "The visions that rush at the halting narrator would soon conjure memories of talk," Sommer writes, with a footnote to Dussel's *Liberación latinoamericana y Emmanuel Levinas*: "What makes a sound is the voice and the eruption of the Other in us; it does not erupt as 'the seen,' but as 'the heard.' We should no longer privilege the seen, but the heard" (Dussel and Guillot, *Liberación latinoamericana*, 25; qtd. in Sommer, "About-Face," 96). Yet the turn to a speech-centered ethics (not quite Levinasian, in any case: Levinas employs the synesthetic figure of the "listening eye" to describe an experience of the other that is not restricted to any one sense or interrupts the economy of sensing more broadly) does not hold in Sommer's argument. If anything, she undermines the claim on the very next page, describing the violent misplacement of the Quechua-inflected Spanish in Vargas Llosa's fictional jungle, far from its Andean home.

Why does Sommer rely upon Dussel, then, in order to carry out a quasi-Levinasian reading of Vargas Llosa's novel? What do the philosopher of liberation and the literary critic share? On both Dussel's and Sommer's accounts, the appearance of the face of the other is an ideal but partial instance of—a necessary but insufficient condition for—an ethical relation to the other. What Dussel's argument states explicitly but Sommer's deconstructive veneer eclipses is the need for *and possibility of* full recognition: If, for Dussel, the subject (who is this subject?) must identify the other and understand her demand, Sommer is interested in an other that interrupts the self. Yet Sommer's work ultimately fetishizes the other as well as, in other work, the secret of the other. This is perhaps most pronounced in her dangerous conflation of *all* minority writing, from Toni Morrison's *Beloved* to Rigoberta Menchú's *testimonio*. Menchú's and Sethe's (*Beloved*'s protagonist) secrets, while never revealed, nevertheless possess positive content: Their secrets are confessable, translatable, but *intentionally* withheld ("It was not a story to pass on," Morrison's nameless narrator says, at the end of the novel and *about* the novel). Likewise, Menchú's and Morrison's protagonists (and Morrison herself) remain relegated to the realm of an identifiable "otherness" that remains beyond the reach of the reader, here presumed to be privileged, white, hailing from the First World, as if the subaltern, or everyone else, not only don't speak but also can't read.[3]

Vargas Llosa—both the author *and* his semiautobiographical narrator—fail to respond to the call of the indigenous other (who, in any case, turns out not to be an ethnic *machiguenga* at all but the half-Jewish *limeño* Saúl Zuratas). Yet because of the novel's turning to *and* away from this other, which mimics the narrator's ambivalent relation to Peru's Indian population, Sommer argues that *El hablador* can be "a source of both concern and hope": Vargas Llosa's narrator turns away from but loves the Indians, "an endless, intimate standoff" (132). Literary criticism, for Sommer, thus becomes a practice of assessing ethical correctness, which treads dangerously in the terrain of moralism. The task of the work's "ethical" reader, here, is to judge whether the narrator or author has properly recognized and responded to the other: The "ethical" reader can be judged to have succeeded, or failed, in herself judging whether the work's author or narrator has indeed properly responded to the other. Caught in a double logic of recognition-identification, the "ethical" critic ends up measured against an *other* she has *created* for judging the response of the author or narrator. The reader thereby constitutes her own authority as ethical reading subject by both placing herself in the position of the other, thus creating that other, and allowing herself to judge the success or failure of literary responses *to* the other/herself. Levinas's description of the traumatic hold of the other on the same through the demand "Thou shalt not kill" is annihilated in such a gesture, a gesture of sovereign judgment or decision that forecloses any possibility of understanding reading as event *even as it warns against such foreclosure.*

Ethics vs. Politics: Oscar del Barco's Letter

Levinas's allegorical "Thou shalt not kill"—the demand of ethical responsibility in the same by the other, the demand that captures the imagination of both Dussel and Sommer—resurfaces in the 2000s as the Argentine Left debated the relationship between ethics and political militancy following the publication of a letter by Oscar del Barco in the psychoanalytic journal *Intemperie*.[4] The letter, which he titles "No matarás," is a response to a 2007 interview with the former Ejército Guerrillero del Pueblo militant Héctor Jouvé—also published in *Intemperie*—in which Jouvé recounts

Ejército Guerrillero del Pueblo (EGP) members Federico Frontini, Oscar del Hoyo, Alberto Castellanos, and Víctor Eduardo Fernández

the assassination of two comrades from the EGP, Adolfo Rotblat and Bernardo Groswald, two young recruits whose physical and psychological decline caused their leaders to view them as a threat to the morale of the group. Del Barco describes the sense he had, reading the interview with Jouvé, that he was reading about the murder of his own son, that it was as if *he* were the one posing the questions. Reflecting upon his unexpected response to the confession, del Barco realizes that he too must assume responsibility for the deaths that took place at the hands of the militant groups he supported, and he goes on to state that *everyone* who supported these groups must share responsibility for the murders. The ensuing debate—in which colleagues and comrades rush to attack or defend the letter—revolves principally around the Levinasian "Thou shalt not kill" and engages with the memory of armed struggle while reevaluating the relation between ethics and politics in post-2001 Argentina.

Del Barco's letter, which the critic Alejandro Kaufman describes not as "argued presentation" but as a gesture or provocation ("The Paradoxical Legacy of a Lost Treasure," 145), turns to Levinas in order to assume responsibility for the killings. "No attempt at justification will make us innocent again," del Barco asserts:

There are no "causes" or "ideals" that will let us off the hook. We have to take on that essentially irredeemable act, the unprecedented responsibility of having intentionally caused the death of a human being. Responsibility before our loved ones, responsibility before other human beings, responsibility without meaning or concept before what we could hesitatingly call "the absolutely other." But beyond everything and everybody, including whatever God there might be, there is the Thou shalt not kill. Faced with a society that kills millions of human beings in wars, genocides, famines, illness and every kind of torture, at the base of each of us can be heard weakly or imperiously the Thou shalt not kill. A commandment that cannot be founded or explained but that nevertheless is there, in me and in everyone, as a presence without presence, as a force without force, as being without being. Not a commandment that comes from outside, from some other place, but which constitutes our inconceivable and unprecedented immanence. (115)

The letter serves as both confession and indictment and, as such, caused an uproar among the Argentine Left, particularly those who, like del Barco, were (and still are) committed to the causes represented by those groups.

Several of del Barco's readers, who continue to be committed, retrospectively, to the resistance to the fascist government against which these groups fought, worry that the letter places the atrocities committed by the government in a relation of equivalence with militant acts of resistance. Jorge Jinkis, a psychoanalyst and founding editor of *Conjetural*, detects in del Barco's letter an ethical universalism in which "the person who took up arms would be as guilty as the person who sympathized with the ideas that were in vogue," arguing that, taken to its ultimate consequences, "this chain of guilt would go back to the insurrectional organizations being complicit with the transnational arms manufacturers" (121). A second member of the *Conjetural* editorial board, Juan Ritvo, is also troubled by the notion that del Barco's letter "is based on perfectly reciprocal reversals" (127). What does it mean for del Barco to establish, rhetorically, a relation of equivalence between different acts of murder, to insist upon the prohibition of murder as a universal principle (and, consequently, upon ethics as "first philosophy")? Is there room in del Barco's provocation—if we are to agree with Kaufman that it is more "gesture" than "argument"—for a politics that is not opposed to or substitutable by ethics?

While it is possible to identify a central debate in the impassioned responses to the letter, there are also a number of reactions that seem to misunderstand del Barco's gesture. The philosopher Diego Tatián points out that this may have to do with the strange presentation of the letter itself, likening del Barco's claim that the letter "is not a reasoned argument" to Marcel Duchamp's famous statement that *Fountain*, his revolutionary inverted urinal, was "not a urinal," that is, not meant to be a receptacle for urine. Tatián suggests that del Barco's letter can be read as a sort of inverted, aestheticized urinal "in which, disconcertingly, all one can see is a place to urinate" (141). Kaufman, too, cites a general "misunderstanding" of del Barco's letter, which he views not as a political or ideological statement but rather as a cry, "un grito." He sees, in the situation described by del Barco, Levinas's opposition of politics as war (Schmitt, speaking for a very long tradition that includes Hobbes) to ethics: "War could be defined as that collective situation, which is dual since it is constituted by two opposing masses, in which there are only two existential possibilities: kill or be killed" (148). What is exceptional about the murder in question is that it was committed not against the military but against two other participants in the armed struggle. "Del Barco's letter," Kaufman reminds his readers, "was provoked by a sordid event in which a friend rather than an enemy was killed" (151). Can we say that a turn to ethics (whether an ethics based on recognition or *mis*recognition, understanding or misunderstanding) is a turn away from *this* (Schmittian, bellicose) notion of politics but perhaps an opening to a *different* conception of politics?

It is in Ritvo's response, curiously, that we can begin to imagine some possible avenues forward: "There is no ethical norm that can avoid the equivocations of interpretation," he writes (129). Are such equivocations obstacles or openings to alternative conceptualizations of ethics and, by extension, politics? Tatián suggests that phrases such as "Thou shalt not kill" (as well as "Bring them back alive" or "Out with the lot of them") should not be understood literally, social-scientifically, but as literary expressions of the impossible. He asks whether the accusations launched at del Barco from members of the traditional Left—many of whom, understandably, want to preserve the legacy of their struggle—open up or foreclose the possibility for thought and proposes, as a mode of conclusion, that we consider a more extensive and expansive idea of "what we call politics" (142). "Perhaps, we can begin to pose new sets of questions," he writes:

> Is it possible to withdraw from the war of interpretations, which is potentially infinite, even though as in any war there are victors and vanquished? Is there a way out of war? On the answer to this question—which is not an epistemological one, or even a solely theoretical one—hangs the possibility of an understanding, both more extensive and more intensive, of the ways in which we act with and against, others—of what we call politics. Perhaps this

transition has already begun to take place, if only very slowly. If I am not mistaken, Oscar del Barco's letter, whether or not we agree with it, points in this direction. (142)

Del Barco echoes this idea in his "Comments on the Articles by Jorge Jinkis, Juan Ritvo, and Eduardo Grüner in *Conjetural*": "It might be thought that the letter is not strung 'on high' but laid out on the 'ground,' in 'politics,' contradicting what you say about my abandonment of politics, which in reality is an abandonment of what you mean by politics" (155). What is at stake in del Barco's letter (as well as the reactions to it), then, is the question of *what we mean by politics*—and therefore, also, of what we mean by ethics, and, finally, what we might mean by the "turn" from one to the other, or the "substitution" of one for the other.

We see, in both Tatián's and del Barco's remarks, that what is being debated, misunderstood, is not (only) ethics and not (only) politics. Instead, we find in Tatián's and del Barco's remarks the beginning of the proposition that disagreement, dissensus, even a differend (in the irreducible sense Lyotard gave the term) over "what we mean by politics" and "what we mean by ethics" is constitutive of both ethics *and* politics and of the relation, if there can be one, *between* ethics and politics. This is a conclusion, or a proposition, that can only be reached, or offered, not only "after" (*post-* in both its chronological and critical senses) the peak of armed resistance in the 1960s and 1970s but also "after" the so-called ethical turn, if we are to understand this turn as a turn away from politics. If, on the other hand, we are to conceive of the turn to ethics as internal to politics, thus erasing the "away from" as well as any kind of exteriority of each domain to the other, we can begin to think about ethics and politics—that is, an ethics *not* grounded in recognition and a politics *not* based on enmity—as at once mutually dependent and mutually suspensive.

Undecidable Ethics

Now that we have examined three responses by Latin American and Latin-americanist philosophers and critics to a Levinasian ethics, we shall turn to three recent writings on ethics (Dove, Biset, Moreiras) that pass through—implicitly, obliquely, or explicitly—the work of Jacques Derrida. For this group of thinkers, the other is not identifiable as such, and the other's demand is untranslatable: This does not mean, of course, that it is not translated, that the other's demand does not solicit and require, but rather that it does so without end, without conveying its sense entirely, or satisfactorily. "Translation," the "secret," and "misunderstanding" are the conceptual levers the deconstructive approach relies on in order to sketch out what I have called a marrano ethics and its relation to a marrano politics. Such an ethics does not rely on recognition or comprehension—it does not depend upon the identity of the other, or upon the (knowable or unknowable) secret of the other, or upon the identity of the concept of ethics itself—but rather guards the possibility of misunderstanding *itself* as residing at the heart of ethical experience and, as such, may open a way to a yet-to-be-determined politics to come.

I considered, briefly, Dove's response to the opposition between ethics and politics that emerges in the debate over del Barco's letter. Dove, we saw, underscores the cost of viewing ethics as a substitute for or alternative to politics. Dove: "either/or: either politics or ethics (either Marx or Freud, Badiou or Levinas, for instance)." By identifying the antagonism present not only in the del Barco debate (he notes an "obligation to take sides") but also in Latin American studies and philosophy more generally, Dove makes the case for a thinking of ethics and politics that would neither oppose nor conflate the two. He points out that while del Barco *appears* to privilege an idea of ethics understood as responsibility for the other over a politics understood as war, his rehearsal of the ethical scene—however unexpectedly—ends up reproducing the sacrificial logic of his version of politics: "The foundational role played by ethics in del Barco's critique of political violence turns out to mirror . . . the sovereign status of the political in militant reason" (289).[5] Del Barco, Dove claims, merely replaces the Schmittian enemy with the Levinasian figure of the absolutely other, in a rhetorical gesture that does nothing to unsettle politics, ethics, or their relation.

Yet Dove is not content to take del Barco at his word. Like Tatián—who, as we recall, opts to pursue the "misunderstood" phrases in del Barco's letter—Dove sets aside and shows the limits of the ethics/politics antagonism through an alternative reading of the controversial letter. If we receive, together with Dove, the Levinasian "Thou shalt not kill" in and through its impossibility, as a Kantian regulative ideal, "something we aim at [while] knowing full well that we must fall short of it," it becomes a kind of "ethical fiction" (293). This fiction is doubly productive: It becomes a structural demand to which we respond "as if" it were true, and it becomes—as fiction—an opening to the possibility of reading. This reading would be necessarily enabled, invited by the demand's fictionality, but also by its constitutive *mis*understandability, its untranslatability. Dove concludes by pointing to a blind spot in the del Barco debate that acquires a fascinating afterlife only in and through its reading, Dove's reading.

Turning to *Otherwise than Being*, Dove reminds us that for Levinas, politics, or justice, always arrives in the figure of the third, a figure that interrupts the face-to-face encounter between same and other. On this reading, ethics always already implies the arrival of politics so that ethics cannot do without politics (and, conversely, politics cannot do without ethics). Politics simultaneously "establishes the urgency of" *and* "ruins" ethics in a kind of Derridean undecidability.[6]

In his 2012 book *El signo y la hiedra: escritos sobre Jacques Derrida*, the Argentine philosopher Emmanuel Biset imagines a "political" Derrida through a discussion of the interrelated tropes of undecidability, institutions, and hospitality. Biset reads Derrida's implicit Levinasianism—his treatment of ethics as unconditional hospitality facing the arrival of the other, or of the event—as the core around which he develops his idea of politics. Justice, for Derrida, is not equated with politics, as it is for Levinas, but with ethics, with the undeconstructible: It is the principle (or beginning, foundation) of deconstruction ("es el principio de su deconstrucción" [37]). "La justicia es hospitalidad, una hospitalidad hacia el acontecimiento y hacia los otros singulares," Biset writes, "el problema es cómo traducir esta ética de la hospitalidad en una política de la hospitalidad" (Justice is hospitality, a hospitality toward the event and toward singular others . . . the problem is how to translate this ethics of hospitality into a politics of hospitality) (39). Yet, according to Biset, this is an unsettled, flawed translation: "Una política de la hospitalidad es la traducción siempre imperfecta en leyes puntuales de una hospitalidad radical que nunca se identifica con sus leyes" (A politics of hospitality is an always imperfect translation into concrete laws of a radical hospitality that can never identify with its laws) (39). It is in these last words that we see a break with the Levinas of Dussel or Sommer: Politics, here, is not understood as opposed to ethics, as war would be opposed to responsibility for the other. Rather than a relation of opposition, we find, in Biset's Derrida, a constitutive flaw, a point of disidentification between the demand for justice and the institutions that might attempt to guarantee or guard the possibility of justice, *una hospitalidad que nunca se identifica con sus leyes*. So we are no longer speaking of politics understood as war, nor of ethics as recognition of the other's demand, as Dussel and Sommer would have it. We are, instead, pursuing what is now appearing to be an alternative genealogy of the ethico-political in Latin American and Latinamericanist thought: an ethics and politics conditioned by misunderstanding, disidentification, and in the nonidentity of institutions (laws, say) with what they are intended to support (hospitality, in this case).

Dove's emphasis on "reading" and Biset's focus on "translation," both of which describe a relation between quite estranged versions of ethics and politics, appear to be compatible with Alberto Moreiras's writing on infrapolitics, which itself deemphasizes the textual figures of reading and translation. I want to conclude in an infrapolitical key, not so much in order to privilege Moreiras's approach but because I believe that its negative radicality adds a crucial element to the discussion that is not articulated directly by either Dove or Biset. In "Infrapolitical Derrida," Moreiras returns to Levinas via Derrida in order to outline a theory of infrapolitics—or shadow politics, as a concept that would stand in opposition to what he calls heliopolitics—by recalling Derrida's "Violence and Metaphysics," the philosopher's first published engagement with the work of Levinas.

Moreiras opens "Infrapolitical Derrida" with an epigraph from Martin Hägglund's book *Radical Atheism*: "The spacing of time," Hägglund writes, "entails that alterity is undecidable. The other can be anything whatsoever or anyone whosoever. The relation to the other is thus the nonethical opening of ethics. This opening is violent because it entails that everything is exposed to what may corrupt and extinguish it" (88).[7] Although Moreiras does not mention it, Hägglund borrows, here, from Derrida's early essay "Violence of the Letter," in which he defines arche-writing as "the origin of morality as of immorality. The nonethical opening to ethics. A violent opening" (140).[8]

The nonethical opening to ethics: What could this be? In previous work, Moreiras has already offered a loose definition of infrapolitics as a kind of mutual suspension of ethics and politics, to which I refer in Part I: "What if, before ethics, there were another practice that makes of the double suspension of the ethical by the political and of the political by the ethical its very possibility? This practice, which finds its expression in literature, but is not limited to literature, is infrapolitical practice" ("Infrapolitical Literature," 186). The "before" is highly suggestive: By "before ethics" does he mean "in the face of ethics" or prior to, perhaps a philosophy prior to ethics as first philosophy, either temporally, logically, or in terms of importance? In Part III, I will discuss in more detail the complexity of "prior" and "past" in Levinas's philosophy. In Moreiras, I believe the undecidable relation between these possibilities is highly suggestive. There is a further undecidable quality to the relation between ethics and politics in Moreiras. While here he refers to the "suspension" of ethics by politics and vice versa, in "Infrapolitical Derrida" (written nearly a decade later) he will phrase this somewhat differently: Here, infrapolitics "is the double *solicitation* of the political by the ethical and of the ethical by the political." Suspension, solicitation, shaking, shuddering (terms that recall Derrida's discussion of the work of deconstruction in *Of Grammatology* and that we will set in motion with regard to the binding of Isaac): Are we to understand that ethics is the condition of possibility for politics (and vice versa) or precisely the place where this possibility encounters its limit, breaks down? Or rather, might we read, in the slippage between suspension and solicitation, a negativity that promises, that opens?

The nonethical opening to ethics: On the one hand, Moreiras refers to the (largely overlooked) sense that the ethical encounter takes place, for Levinas, precisely at the moment of extreme violence; it could be no other way. Imagine the other side to the command "Thou shalt not kill": To whom is such a command directed? Why, to a murderer, of course! Or a potential murderer, which is what we all are, however ethically we may respond to such a command. Ethics and violence tread upon the very same ground, not as opposites but as perverse partners, inseparable. For Moreiras, then, the nonethical is not to be understood as *opposed* to ethics (the unethical would serve this antagonistic role). The grammar that allows for such an aporetic relation is a negative grammar, a grammar of nonidentity: Moreiras, by advancing the concept of infrapolitics in this way, is in effect engaging with an ethics that is not identical to itself (nonethical) in order to imagine a politics that is not identical to itself (infrapolitics). Both, he claims, are implicit in both Derrida and Levinas, or in Levinas read through Derrida, where it becomes possible to identify a "Levinasian infrapolitical perspective, that is, not just of his well-known suspension of the political in the name of ethics, but also, perhaps surprisingly, in the understanding of the necessary suspension of ethics in the name of a certain politicity which will have become no less fundamental, that is, no lesser aspect of first philosophy" ("Infrapolitical Derrida," 125).

I want to suggest, as a mode of conclusion, that it is through reading *itself* that such a perspective becomes possible: Kaufman's or Tatián's or Dove's reading of del Barco, Biset's reading of Derrida, Moreiras's reading of Derrida reading Levinas, our reading of them all, even as we define the labor of reading quite differently. Of course, this is not a reading that promises comprehension. What Moreiras calls infrapolitics, and what I am calling the deconstruction of ethics and politics, a marrano ethics, or a marrano politics, "would be the region of theoretical practice that solicits the constitutive opacity of the ethico-political relation—hence admits, for every practical decision, of no preceding political or ethical light to mark the path" ("Infrapolitical Derrida," 122). (Admittedly, I am once again pushing infrapolitics toward anarchaeology, teasing out those aspects of infrapolitical thinking that are closest to my own.) This is a reading, or misreading, that takes place not *in spite of* but, rather, precisely *because of* the opacity of the ethico-political relation, the secret, marrano quality of the ethico-political relation, the impossibility of properly recognizing and identifying the other, of translating the other's demand into concrete and correct political action: reading as misreading, a kind of reading that disturbs and shakes the neoliberal closure of the relation between ethics and politics and that, finally, might offer the only possibility of an impossible, undeconstructible justice. I turn now to a description of what this anarchaeological reading offers, precisely in place of a "preceding ethical or political light."

Part III. Violent Ethics

Abraham's Double Bind

One philosophizes with a hammer.
—Emmanuel Levinas, *Proper Names*

Once upon a time there was a man who as a child had heard the
beautiful story about how God tempted Abraham, and how he
endured temptation, kept the faith, and a second time received
again a son contrary to expectation. When the child became
older he read the same story with even greater admiration, for
life had separated what was united in the pious simplicity of
the child. The older he became, the more frequently his mind
reverted to that story, his enthusiasm became greater and greater,
and yet he was less and less able to understand the story. At last
in his interest for that he forgot everything else; his soul had only
one wish, to see Abraham, one longing, to have been witness to
that event. His desire was not to behold the beautiful countries
of the Orient, or the earthly glory of the Promised Land, or
that godfearing couple whose old age God had blessed, or the
venerable figure of the aged patriarch, or the vigorous young
manhood of Isaac whom God had bestowed upon Abraham—he
saw no reason why the same thing might not have taken place
on a barren heath in Denmark. His yearning was to accompany
them on the three days' journey when Abraham rode with
sorrow before him and with Isaac by his side. His only wish was
to be present at the time when Abraham lifted up his eyes and
saw Mount Moriah afar off, at the time when he left the asses
behind and went alone with Isaac up unto the mountain; for
what his mind was intent upon was not the ingenious web of
imagination but the shudder of thought.
—Søren Kierkegaard, *Fear and Trembling*

The biblical scene that obsesses Søren Kierkegaard's naïve reader—the
moment in which Abraham takes his only son and prepares to sacrifice
him—has haunted and also obsessed countless readers and writers, thinkers and artists, believers and nonbelievers. In the past few years alone,
the multimedia artist Saskia Boddeke and British film director Peter
Greenaway's 2015 *Gehorsam/Obedience: An Installation in 15 Rooms* and the
American-Jewish novelist Jonathan Safran Foer's 2016 *Here I Am* engage
with the biblical tale. One of Leonard Cohen's very last works takes the
episode as its occasion. In the philosophical tradition, Emmanuel Levinas,
Jacques Derrida, and Bracha Ettinger (whose work I won't discuss here)[1]

have followed Kierkegaard's lead into the kernel of opacity that troubles so many: into that "shudder of thought" that passed through Abraham as he prepared to murder his own son, the shudder that passed through Isaac as he began to see that it would be he, and not a lamb, who would be sacrificed to God. How do we respond from and through our incapacity to understand, naïve or learned as we may be? What is the nature of Abraham's self-positioning before God, and before his son, and how might we—we who are interested in ethical and political thought, in the thinking of violence—proceed from that point of stubborn stupidity, of unthinkable, violent thought?

Fear and Trembling, which Kierkegaard published in 1843 under the pseudonym Johannes de Silentio, represents the first of a series of philosophical meditations on the binding of Isaac that is also, at the same time, a meditation on philosophy and the task of thinking and even, silently, on silence. *Fear and Trembling* will be read and reread by Emmanuel Levinas and Jacques Derrida: It is a text that is about a text that, as I shall argue, is *also* about the act of reading, the demand to read. What's more, *Fear and Trembling* confronts the traumatic kernel of misunderstanding, misreading, that resides at the heart of the act of reading, as well as of the scene of ethics: of reading as ethics and ethics as reading.

The opening passage, or prelude, of *Fear and Trembling* alludes to the longing, and incapacity, of the naïve, unlearned reader—first as a child, then as an adult—to "understand" the story of Abraham and Isaac ("That man was not a learned exegete, he didn't know Hebrew, if he had known Hebrew, he perhaps would easily have understood the story and Abraham"). Likewise, Kierkegaard thematizes Isaac's own desire to comprehend, and difficulty in comprehending, his father. "Abraham's face was fatherliness, his look was mild, his speech encouraging. But Isaac was unable to understand him," Kierkegaard/de Silentio tells us, and then again: "Abraham lifted up the boy, he walked with him by his side, and his talk was full of comfort and exhortation. But Isaac could not understand him." And later: "He climbed Mount Moriah, but Isaac understood him not." Kierkegaard's naïve reader, like Isaac, "sank down with weariness, he folded his hands and said, 'No one is so great as Abraham! Who is capable of understanding him?'" I will return to the question "Who?" in a moment. For now, though: Why, to what end, does Kierkegaard situate misunderstanding, bordering on stupidity, at the center of this story, which is at least two stories?

Let's pause for a moment. Why should those who are interested in political violence also necessarily think about violence and ethics, about ethics as necessarily violent, about the violence of reading and misreading? In the midst of a global shift not only to the neoliberal right but to the neofascist right—we find clear examples in the United States, in Europe, in Argentina, Brazil—why ethics *now*? We have seen how the by now tiresome opposition between politics-as-war (Schmitt's opposition between friend and enemy as the structure of sovereign decisionist politics) and ethics-as-nonviolence persists in distinct schools of Latinamericanist criticism and beyond—theological, aesthetic schools—and we've seen how others seek to displace that constraining opposition. Let us deepen that displacement by addressing the constitutive violence we find repeatedly *within* these primal—allegorical—ethical scenes, such as Abraham's binding of his son, itself a scene, lest we forget, that follows on and in a way repeats another violent scene: the banishment of Ishmael, Abraham's other, first, son.

In *Fear and Trembling*, Kierkegaard returns to the primal scene of (non) sacrifice in order to think about the ethical bind Abraham faces. The patriarch is tested—in later translations within the Christian tradition, *tempted*—by God. One of the many reasons I choose to call this story the *binding* of Isaac, rather than the *sacrifice* of Isaac—because of course, the sacrifice never

Caravaggio, *The Sacrifice of Isaac* (1603)

happens—has to do with the multiple layers of binding and bondage in the story, the ethical bind being perhaps the knottiest. Abraham is caught between two duties: his duty to God, who has commanded him to sacrifice Isaac, and his responsibility to his son, whose life rests in his hands. We know that these two different ethical registers are linked not merely as *conundrum* or *dilemma* but because Abraham uses the same word to respond to, to be responsible before, both God and Isaac. The word *hineni*, as readers of the Hebrew Bible know, signifies a kind of ethical readiness before the other.[2] *Hineni*, here I am, Abraham tells God, expressing a willingness to follow the order to sacrifice his son. Several verses later, he responds in precisely the same way to his son's call (*"Father?" "Here I am."*) and again a third time as an angel of God calls Abraham to stop him from killing Isaac. *Hineni*, he says, here I am: to God, to Isaac, to the angel of God. The Hebrew word *hineni* is only used in very particular scenes in the Hebrew Bible, and it expresses a kind of presence, or readiness, of a different order than, say, geographical location ("Where are you?" "Over here, next to the kitchen table").

Although Kierkegaard, like Levinas and Derrida after him, reads Abraham's bind as competitive ethical demands, he ultimately privileges what he refers to, or imagines to be, Abraham's faith in God over and above his ethical responsibility toward his son: What Kierkegaard calls faith, engaging with the Christian tradition, trumps the ethical order. Levinas characterizes Kierkegaard's gloss of the *Akedah* as a transcendence and therefore an abandonment of ethics, of the command "Thou Shalt Not Kill": "Kierkegaard . . . wants to transcend the ethical stage, which to him is the stage of generality. In his evocation of Abraham, [Kierkegaard] describes the encounter with God at the point where subjectivity rises to the level of the religious, that is to say, above ethics" (*Proper Names*, 77). Kierkegaard takes this stand, in Levinas's view, because he understands ethics as a universal, as that which would annihilate singularity, the "I's secret" (76). Levinas characterizes this thought as a new, violent turn: a turn that Nietzsche would later imagine as philosophizing "with a hammer" and that Levinas criticizes for its "disdain for the ethical," its immorality.[3]

Levinas rejects such a conception, and dismissal, of ethics as that which would eliminate singularity, suggesting that rather than extinguishing the "I's secret," the ethical injunction addresses the "I" precisely *in* its singularity, that the "I" responds *from* and *through* its singularity. He interprets the repetition of Abraham's response *hineni*—first to God, then to Isaac, then to the angel of God—as a *return* to the ethical order: "But one could think the opposite," he responds to Kierkegaard, arguing that "Abraham's attentiveness to the voice that led him back to the ethical order, in forbidding him to perform a human sacrifice, is the highest point in the drama" (77). Moreover, since this return comes about through an encounter with a messenger of God, Levinas does not have to sacrifice God for ethics. (The difference lies, instead, in Abraham's alternating responses—his attitude toward and attachment to—duty. Or: to the event of the ethical demand.) This would seem to indicate a preference for nonviolence over the violence of Kierkegaard's and Nietzsche's philosophizing hammer—and indeed ethics as understood to prefer nonviolence is certainly present in many subsequent readings of Levinas, such as Dussel's, who, as we have seen, calls attention to Levinas's likening of politics to war and ethics to responsibility and nonviolence, in the subjective decision to refrain from *murdering* the other.

Yet if we read this primal scene of ethical responsibility from and through its literary quality, that is, with an openness not only to the possibility of multiple, and contradictory, interpretations but also with an ear to alternative temporalities, then the idea of the ethical decision begins to look quite different. Now, attending with a literary ear to this scene, we mark out the different times in which Abraham will always already have responded to God, to Isaac, *and* to God's angel. We note, in these different time schemes, that the duty to each does not cancel out the other or instantiate a conundrum or dilemma in which the response to one always already includes—impossibly—the response to the other. The scene becomes constitutively violent, defective. Perhaps it is *this* violence that causes us to shudder, to tremble. (It may be what distinguishes readers in the anarchaeological vein from Kierkegaard's "naïve" reader.)

"I tremble at what exceeds my seeing and my knowing [*mon voir et mon savoir*] although it concerns the innermost parts of me, right down to my soul, down to the bone," writes Derrida in the third section of *The Gift of Death* (54), "Whom to Give to (Knowing Not to Give)," a reading of Levinas's reading of Kierkegaard's reading of the biblical scene, which, through the multiplication of readings we can now begin to conceive of as *itself* about reading, or misreading (I will return to this). Trembling, for Derrida, is also intimately tied to the work of deconstruction: the "shaking" or solicitation we find in *Of Grammatology*. Unlike Kierkegaard, who privileges faith in God over ethical responsibility, and unlike Levinas, who privileges the ethical order over the religious, Derrida interprets Abraham's dilemma as an "ethical aporia," as a double bind in which "ethics must be sacrificed in the name of duty" (67). Abrahamic ethics, suggests Derrida, can be understood not as responsibility for the other but rather as "irresponsibilization." How can this be? Surely Derrida is not advancing an ethics that would *refuse* responsibility for the other when he argues that "far from ensuring responsibility, the generality of ethics incites to irresponsibility" (61).

No, Derrida is after something else. Rather than siding with Kierkegaard against Levinas or with Levinas against Kierkegaard, Derrida underscores the necessarily paradoxical quality of ethics, asserting that one behaves responsibly by behaving irresponsibly:

> The absoluteness of duty, or responsibility, and of obligation certainly demands that one transgress ethical duty, although in betraying it one belongs to it and at the same time recognizes it. The contradiction and the paradox must be endured *in the instant itself.* The two duties must contradict one another, one must subordinate (incorporate, repress) the other. Abraham must assume absolute responsibility for sacrificing his son by sacrificing ethics, but in order for there to be a sacrifice, the ethical must retain all its value; the love for his son must remain intact, and the order of human duty must continue to insist on its rights. (66)

Rather than duty to God prevailing over ethical responsibility for the other (Kierkegaard) or responsibility for the other trumping religion (Levinas), Derrida's notion of aporetic ethics requires that both duties, both responses, be held together "in the instant itself." Counterintuitively, one betrays ethics when one behaves ethically.[4]

Such a logic relies on a strange temporality, a concept of time that a deconstructive, or even what I have just called a *literary*, reading of the scene conjures in order to move away from the "moralist" interpretation. Kierkegaard equates "the instant of decision" with "madness," while Derrida refers to an "atemporal temporality . . . a duration that cannot be grasped" (65). I'd put it somewhat differently, building upon both Kierkegaard's "instant" and Derrida's "atemporal temporality." The instant of decision, the madness described by Kierkegaard—the decision *to* sacrifice his son—always already includes the future decision *not* to sacrifice Isaac in a kind of anachronic simultaneity. If a conventional narrative structure, which would rely upon a linear progression in time from duty to God to responsibility for the other, conveys a "moral" from which a "moral reader" can learn, violent anachronism demands a different conception of ethics, one antimoralist and violent. Violence thus characterizes a number of different registers, decisions, and procedures, which the episode of Isaac's binding draws into tight analogy with one another—just in the way that Abraham's repeated *hineni* draws into analogy his relations to his son, to the interrupting angel, and to God. The quick migration of "violence" from level to level in this episode, from place to place, register to register, also means that the episode calls for a cut—that is to say, a critical decision, the drawing of a boundary, an interruption—that keeps this analogic circuit from becoming just a series of substitutions, of level for level, angel for son for God. It also forces us to see that these decisions, acts, cuts, that interrupt the analogic circuit of substitutions are themselves interrupted—though not by a reader's active decision but by something else, other.

Violence moves in and through the episode, and beyond it, in the time of its consequences, anachronically. One behaves unethically by being ethical. Moreover, Derrida continues, one can behave irresponsibly by claiming to comprehend and thereby adhering *too strictly* to a perceived duty. That is, I am more "at risk" of unethical behavior the moment I am confident of my behavior, of the mores I have successfully interpreted and upon which I will act, than I am when I am uncertain, lost, without a universal or a general word or name to stand on. This "unethical" ethicist appears in the figures of the "moralizing moralists and good consciences who preach to us with assurance every morning and every week" (67), while Abraham, as an aporetic ethical figure, remains in the terrain of the unintelligible, the silent, the secret: "If [Abraham] were to speak a common or translatable language, if he were to become intelligible by giving his reasons in a convincing manner, he would be giving in to the temptation of the ethical generality that I have referred to as that which makes one irresponsible. He wouldn't be Abraham any more, the unique Abraham in a singular relation with the unique God" (74). Here Derrida refers to Abraham's enigmatic response to his son—a response that is neither truth nor lie—in two ways: Whether Isaac or the literal lamb is sacrificed, God will provide, and also, Abraham *is* right, right about a future that will be disclosed, he will have been right, God does indeed provide a lamb (ram), when he assures Isaac that God will provide a lamb for the sacrifice. And this can be extended to the multiple layers of address and response in the tale. (Is God's order intelligible? Is Abraham's response? Is a "legible," "correct" reading of the entire scene of misunderstanding possible?)

Is Abraham a hero? Derrida, following Kierkegaard, says no: "He doesn't make us shed tears and doesn't inspire admiration; rather stupefied horror, a terror that is also a secret. For it is a terror that brings us close to the absolute secret" (79). If Abraham cannot be considered an example of ethical "correctness," of what can he be said to serve as a model, if his singular bind can indeed be generalized? Perhaps the text enacts or *performs* the broader problem of ethics, of the ethical demand, that finds a place in *and* exceeds Abraham's decision. If, rather than interpreting the *Akedah* as pure morality tale, as religion, we instead approach it, allow ourselves to inherit from it, in its literariness (remember that for Derrida, literature is also linked to irresponsibility), perhaps we can begin to imagine a new, unorthodox path into ethical thinking, into a violent thinking of ethics, a thinking of violent ethics. It is when we cease to ask "Did Abraham do the right thing?" and engage, instead, with the shudder (*temblor, sollicitation*), the stupefied horror, the terror produced in us by what we cannot understand, that we embark on such a path.

While I recognize the value of Derrida's rhetorical gesture, in which sacrifice is rewritten as that which is necessarily surrendered for the sake of an aporetic ethics, I'll sacrifice the concept of *sacrifice* for the sake of binding. Ethics, after the binding of Isaac, can no longer be understood as the pursuit of the "good" but rather as the double bind of binding itself. Ethical responsibility takes form, in and through Abraham, in the (double, aporetic) act of binding: In binding his son (an act that seems unethical), Abraham binds himself to God (ethical). Like the act of circumcision, ethical binding cuts both ways: The ritual cutting of foreskin binds Jew to God (and to the rest of the Jewish community) through covenant and cuts the Jew off from the non-Jew. Of course, Abraham also binds himself to his son: This is counterintuitive, but Abraham's (potential) sacrifice is only a sacrifice because of his singular love for his son. This singular love is also terrifying: Terror, love, terrifying love, binds father to son.[5]

Hineni: Here I am. What does this mean today, then, for today's ethics? In one of the Jewish-Canadian songwriter and poet Leonard Cohen's final compositions, "You Want It Darker" (2016)—a song that, like David Bowie's "Blackstar," eerily positioned the semiautobiographical lyrical subject before God, or before death, just months before the artist's own death—we hear the words uttered by Abraham as he prepares to sacrifice his son, *Hineni, hineni*, here I am.

> If you are the dealer, I'm out of the game
> If you are the healer, it means I'm broken and lame
> If thine is the glory then mine must be the shame
> You want it darker
> We kill the flame
> Magnified, sanctified, be thy holy name
> Vilified, crucified, in the human frame
> A million candles burning for the help that never came

You want it darker
Hineni, hineni
I'm ready, my lord

In these verses that thematize brokenness and finitude, the lyrical subject situates himself before God with the same readiness as Abraham. His opening to God is not an opening to "light" or to the "good"; he is either unholy, or we must rethink holiness. Cohen was once asked, in an interview, why he had not carried on his family's Jewish tradition: "I did," he responded. "You became a 'priest'?" (The Kohanim, the Cohens, were the Israelites' priestly class.) "I became a bad priest" (Burger, *Leonard Cohen on Leonard Cohen*, 229).

Nearly fifty years earlier (amid the turmoil of the Vietnam War and in the wake of the Six Day War in Israel), Cohen penned the song "The Story of Isaac" (1969), another reference to the biblical story of binding and (non)sacrifice.[6] Narrated from the perspective of the son, the song teases out an aspect of the traditional tale that is often overlooked: the undecidable nature of Abraham's decision and of Abraham's status as ethical subject.

Cohen, an unorthodox heir to the writings of Kierkegaard, Levinas, and Derrida, offers a strange, rigorous *akedah*, a sung work of ethical philosophy in which decision guards a terrifying kernel of undecidability, in which the ethical scene is represented as violent at its very core.

"The Story of Isaac" has two parts. The first recounts the biblical tale from the perspective of Isaac. In the second part, the lyrical "I"—still Isaac—interpellates the present-day listener, demanding responsibility and threatening murder.

The door it opened slowly,
My father he came in,
I was nine years old.
And he stood so tall above me,
His blue eyes they were shining
And his voice was very cold.
He said, "I've had a vision
And you know I'm strong and holy,
I must do what I've been told."

The first part of Cohen's song recounts the intimate yet threatening relationship between a holy, murderous father and his son. The figure of the father entering the room of the son is menacing: "tall," "cold," "strong." He addresses his young child, a vulnerable nine-year-old, and demands that his son recognize his holiness and thus the validity of his vision, coupled with the injunction to obey ("I must do what I've been told"). After they climb the mountain toward Moriah, the father and son stop to drink from a wine bottle that Abraham then shatters, the shards of which anticipate the potential violence to come. Immediately following this moment, and right before Abraham builds the altar, the son recalls, "Thought I saw an eagle / But it might have been a vulture, / I never could decide." This pair of figures, the eagle-vulture, zoomorphically allows for the possibility that the father is at once strong, protective, *and* poised to kill. More significant, perhaps, is the son's inability to "decide": Here, the concept of decision, central to the thinking of both ethical and political subjectivities, is linked to the possibility of comprehension. The poetic, literary quality of the song holds together a contradiction or aporia that many readings of the biblical tale want to resolve. Rather than closure, it offers a radical undecidability that binds together ethics, politics, and literature.

In the second part of the song, Isaac turns to the listener/reader in a kind of musical apostrophe. Instead of referring to the murderous subject in the third person ("my father," "he"), the poetic voice now addresses the listener directly ("you") and makes her also potentially murderous. Echoing the altar his father built in the previous verse, Isaac imagines present-day altars: "You who build these altars now / To sacrifice these children, / You must not do it anymore." The "must" spoken by the father returns as an echo of the earlier injunction, now from the son to the implied listener, the present-day fathers who sacrifice their sons. (Remember the way that *hineni* echoes across the episode.) The Vietnam War is clearly on Cohen's mind, but the lyric's scope is broader, and its temporality violently binds together the present and an as-yet-unspecified future, a seemingly general future. "A scheme," Cohen-Isaac sings, "is not a vision / And you never have been tempted / By a demon or a god," he continues, asserting a distinction between the present-day will-to-sacrifice—a scheme—and the past will-to-sacrifice—the response to a vision. The lyrical subject Isaac then makes a second distinction: His father's vision may have come from a god, but it may just as well have come from a demon, recalling the unsettling undecidability of the eagle-vulture figure. In the final verses of the song, Isaac presents himself as this aporetic figure, at once responsible for the other and the other's potential murderer:

I will kill you if I must,
I will help you if I can.
When it all comes down to dust
I will help you if I must,
I will kill you if I can.
And mercy on our uniform,
Man of peace or man of war,
The peacock spreads his fan.

If Abraham's double, undecidable qualities confound Isaac in the first part, here Isaac appears as a perversely violent ethical subject, ready to take responsibility for the other but also poised to murder. The "I must" of the father returns once again, this time converted into the perverse promise of the son ("I will kill you if I must / I will help you if I can . . . I will help you if I must / I will kill you if I can"). Here, duty and responsibility are presented as both promise and threat—and ethics, if we can still call it that, is affirmed as constitutively violent.

What place does violent thinking have in the response to current crimes and ongoing global war? I imagine that if Levinas had listened to Cohen's verses, he would have responded as he did to Kierkegaard's gloss of the scene of binding ("It is Kierkegaard's violence that shocks me"). If, as Levinas insists with regard to Kierkegaard, who already anticipates the tradition of Nietzsche, one "philosophizes with a hammer," we must ask, now: When we claim an ostensibly nonviolent stance, when we absolve ourselves of the possibility that a murderer lurks within each of us, as well as the more terrifying possibility that in responding to the other we will never know whether we are saving or murdering him, in denying this, do we run the risk of committing violence of a *different* order, in which philosophy obscures and eclipses, rather than exposes, regimes of subjugation and oppression? Moralistic and moralizing philosophy, a practice that has as its most salient effect self-congratulation and self-soothing, a thought that trusts itself completely, would therefore act as the fiercest anvil.

Cohen does no such thing: He does not settle on a thesis that allows him to philosophize, violently and critically, upon the anvil of mere self-confident moralism. He is a strange kind of philosopher, a poet and a reader before anything else, even before he is a social activist (his critique of war is highly unorthodox),[7] and there is no moral to his story. I want to end with verses from yet another of his songs, this one a brave and brutal interpretation of liturgy from the Jewish Day of Repentance, Yom Kippur.

In the Jewish tradition, God writes in the Book of Life who will die, and by what means: "who shall live, and who shall die; who in his time, and who before his time; who by fire and who by water; who by sword and who by beast; who by hunger and who by thirst; who by storm and who by plague; who by choking and who by stoning . . ." In Cohen's modern rendition, "Who by Fire?" (1974), the mortal possibilities are updated, but the most radical shift is the reference to God, or to the possibility of an angel of death who comes calling at the end of each stanza:

> And who by fire, who by water,
> Who in the sunshine, who in the night time,
> Who by high ordeal, who by common trial,
>
> . . .
>
> And who shall I say is calling?
> And who in her lonely slip, who by barbiturate,
> Who in these realms of love, who by something blunt,
> And who by avalanche, who by powder,
> Who for his greed, who for his hunger,
> And who shall I say is calling?
>
> . . .
>
> Who by his lady's command, who by his own hand,
> Who in mortal chains, who in power,
> And who shall I say is calling?

"Who in her lonely slip, who by barbiturate / Who in these realms of love, who by something blunt, / . . . Who for his greed, who for his hunger, / And who shall I say is calling?" Cohen's "Who?" brings us back to Kierkegaard's naïve reader, the boy-turned-adult who sinks down with weariness and asks, "No one is so great as Abraham! Who is capable of understanding him?"

The question "Who?" emerges as an affirmation of the shudder of thought, that which exceeds our comprehension, that we have traced from the Hebrew Bible, through Kierkegaard, Levinas, and Derrida, to Cohen. It is the question asked by she who feels awe and dread, wonder and terror, facing what cannot be apprehended. It is what causes us to tremble where we stand, an event for which one cannot properly or fully prepare; it asks after the secret that the moralists and the moralizers aim to discover and reveal, while the violent ethicist remains fervent, even irresponsible, in her desire to pursue it.

Untimely Ethics

Deconstruction and Its Precursors

I've always found it difficult to read Derrida.
—Emir Rodríguez Monegal,
"Borges and Derrida: Apothecaries"

We've made, in "Violent Ethics," a turn to deconstructive reading that makes it constitutive of ethical and political thinking—or of the impossibility of such a task. As I turn now to deconstruction's anarchaeology, I will consider two possible "precursors" of deconstruction, from two quite different traditions: Emmanuel Levinas and Jorge Luis Borges. First I will trace the concept of the illegible demand (for reading)—the aporetic, haunting demand that returns again and again in the present book—in the thought of Levinas and Derrida, suggesting that the most significant consequences of Levinas's *oeuvre* can only begin to be traced "after" Derrida. ("After" here meaning, in the wake of Levinas's response to Derrida's reading of his work: a double mediation and a violent and violently seized inheritance.) I will then, through a reading of Borges's short essay "Kafka y sus precursores," argue that if literary and philosophical precursors can be determined retroactively and anachronically (Borges "after" Derrida), intempestive reading—reading after whatever is untimely in the work before it—might serve as the condition of possibility for a violent, indisciplinary, marrano thinking.

Marrano Ethics

Many scholars of deconstruction identify an ethico-political turn in Derrida's "late" work ("Racism's Last Word," *Altérités*, *Of Hospitality*, *Specters of Marx*, *The Politics of Friendship*, *Rogues*, *The Beast and the Sovereign*, *The Death Penalty* seminars, to give just a few examples). Patrick Dove warns against dividing Derrida's work into "late" and "early" periods, a gesture made, he says, intentionally or unintentionally, in the interest of "saving" deconstruction from criticism in the wake of the de Man affair. I've referred already to *Specters of Marx*, and this work strikes me as a particularly compelling example that might bridge what we think of as two distinct epochs (thus showing them to be related, not disparate at all). The ethico-political injunction from *Specters* to which I have referred repeatedly, in different contexts—the injunction, immediately brought into question, to "read me, will you ever be able to do so?"—appears unreadable while also, paradoxically, acting as a demand for *more* reading. I have been calling the opaque, secret ethics signaled by this demand and developed systematically in Derrida's work from the middle 1980s forward a marrano ethics, and the reading in question (the reading Derrida enjoins upon us, then draws into question) a marrano reading practice: a mode of reading that pursues what is untranslatable in a text, a reading that identifies the text's precursors, counterintuitively and anachronistically, in its future interpretations.

Where does this so-called ethical turn come from? Is it possible to identify Levinas as a precursor to Derrida's ethical concerns or even his thinking about politics? As a first step, let us turn to Levinas's concept of the ethical injunction, the demand of the other over the same. Martin Hägglund has convincingly argued in *Radical Atheism* that Simon Critchley and others misguidedly establish a relation of equivalence between the concepts of the ethical (and the related concepts of the trace, the other, and the infinite demand) in Levinas and Derrida—to produce what Critchley calls "an ethics of deconstruction." Hägglund is onto something important: It is a mistake to rush to forge Levinas into Derrida as we would metal into metal, as Drucilla Cornell, Robert Bernasconi, and Critchley have done (*Radical Atheism*, 76). He recalls Cornell's characterization of deconstruction as "aspiration to a nonviolent relationship to the Other" in *The Philosophy of the Limit* (61, qtd. in *Radical Atheism*, 76). Critchley, for his part, has become something of a sensation in the United States, especially following his appointment at the New School in 2008 (he is series moderator for the *New York Times* column "The Stone," and, in 2014, Edinburgh University Press issued the third edition of *The Ethics of Deconstruction: Derrida and Levinas*). He is perhaps the most widely read of the three and has most significantly shaped the idea that deconstruction is somehow *inherently* ethical.

Hägglund's critique of Critchley centers upon two principal issues: violence and temporality. He claims that Critchley is wrong to detect in Derrida's work a nonviolent ethical valence, to establish a conceptual parallel between ethics in Levinas and unconditional hospitality in Derrida:

"The ethical is . . . a matter of responding to alterity by making decisions and calculations, whereas the unconditional is the non-ethical opening of ethics, namely, the exposure to an undecidable other that makes it necessary to decide and calculate in the first place" (Hägglund, "The Non-Ethical Opening of Ethics," 301). This is of course a reference to Derrida's essay "The Violence of the Letter," in which he defines "arche-writing" as "the origin of morality as of immorality. The nonethical opening to ethics. A violent opening" (140). Hägglund's argument concerning the relation between unconditionality and the ethical nonviolence and violence in Levinas and Derrida is convincing but less important to our reading than the question of temporality. On this score, Hägglund insists that we must distinguish between a Levinasian concept of time (in which ethical responsibility is antecedent, comes prior, to everything else) and the Derridean notion of untimeliness. He reminds us that Derrida's reading of Hamlet, "The time is out of joint; O cursed spite, / That ever I was born to set it right!" (1.5.211–212), downplays the lines' more common interpretation—that Hamlet is complaining that he was born at an unjust time, or that it is unjust that he should have to bear the burden of the times—and proposes instead the concept of a time out of time with itself, an asynchronic time.

But I am not sure that Hägglund's argument concerning temporality is right. Temporality seems to belong to a cluster of concepts that Levinas revisits in response to Derrida's critique of his earlier work (in "Violence and Metaphysics"), so that when we read *Otherwise than Being* we are already reading Levinas-after-Derrida. Derrida's principal claim in "Violence and Metaphysics" is that while Levinas, in *Totality and Infinity*, aims to move beyond ontology, he does so within the confines of metaphysical language ("Violence and Metaphysics," 102). We thus find in *Otherwise than Being* that Levinas has undertaken a radical experimentation with language: We may recognize some of the key concepts of metaphysics, but they are rearranged, unsettled, through a proto-or paradeconstructive syntax. The concept of passivity would be one example. It does not appear to counter "activity," its ostensible opposite, but rather aims to evade this opposition altogether: "passivity more passive than all passivity" (*Otherwise than Being*, 15).

Allow me to underscore the strangeness of reading Levinas-after-Derrida, of offering an intempestive Levinas. I have been insisting throughout *Anarchaeologies* on the odd temporalities of ethical thought that refuses its classic constructions (the active decision an intending subject makes, foreseeing outcomes, according to grounded norms) and its traditional and recent adversaries (religion, faith, politics, moralism). In Levinas, there is a formal and rhetorical link between passivity and temporality: The philosopher experiments with these concepts in a similar way. Just as he is interested in a "passivity more passive than all passivity," Levinas experiments with the notion of "prior" to include the possibility of the "pre-original," that is, a before *before* the before. What at first appears as a chronological relation—saying (*le dire*) as "antecedent to the verbal signs it conjugates, to the linguistic systems and the semantic glimmerings, a foreword preceding languages" (5), a "pre-original language" (6), "the saying which signifies prior to essence, prior to identification" (45), "a *prior* signification proper to saying, which is neither ontological nor ontic" (46), "the very respiration of this skin *prior* to any intention" (49)—is explained to be other than a past moment locatable on a linear continuum. Rather, Levinas offers an anarchical past, a past-before-the-past, "a diachrony refractory to all synchronization, a transcending diachrony . . . a past more ancient than every representable origin, a pre-original and anarchical *passed*" (9)—hyperbolic formulas that serve as a kind of opening to the Derridean "always already." This is not to say that Levinas and Derrida describe identical concepts of time. We witness the beginnings of what will arguably acquire a more radical form in Derrida—but it becomes possible to read Levinas in this way only *after* having read Derrida. (This is not a strictly anachronistic reading since, as I have noted, we are already dealing with Levinas-after-Derrida.)

Of course, "prior" may not, or may not only, signify temporal precedence. If we say that "ethical responsibility is prior to everything else," we can mean prior in importance (the arrival of the other is a definitive moment for my ethical being; of all the moments that constitute me as an ethical being, it is the arrival of the other that is the most important, inasmuch as it alone is definitive: hence it has priority in respect to its importance, its definitiveness), prior in time (the other arrives and then I make a decision), or prior in terms of logical structure (the arrival of the other is the necessary condition for there to be an ethical response—if the other arrives then necessarily my response to the arrival of the other takes place in, even defines, the domain of the ethical). Hägglund perhaps confuses these senses of antecedence or priority: an axiological one (definitive importance), a temporal one (succession of moments), and a logical one (for x to be the case, y has to obtain). But the sort of metaphysics that Derrida is interested in dismantling (Levinas too, on this reading) depends upon this confusion, *is* at core this confusion. ("Beyond," in Levinas, poses this same problem.) Levinas's experimentation with language addresses frontally the confusion of axiology, temporality, and logic in order to come up with a way of thinking otherwise. When we arrive, in the next section, at the notion of the precursor, we can reconsider these differing senses of priority or priorness and suggest that a precursor text doesn't have to precede another chronologically: It can precede it logically or axiologically.

I may appear to be defending Critchley against Hägglund, when in fact I, too, want to avoid, even reject, the argument that deconstruction is somehow inherently ethical. My issue with Critchley is another—yet my critique would allow for the possibility that deconstruction is neither *reducible to* nor *incompatible with* a Levinasian ethics. To expose the differential compatibility of Levinas and Derrida (against both Critchley *and* Hägglund) I'd focus, instead, upon Critchley's treatment of what he calls the "infinite demand." In his 2007 book *Infinitely Demanding: Ethics of Commitment, Politics of Resistance*, Critchley draws a parallel between the Danish theologian Knud Ejler Løgstrup's idea of the "unfulfillable demand" and Levinas's "demand of a *Faktum*" (or a "fact of the other") in order to argue in favor of a politics that is motivated, at its heart, by the ethical demand. For Løgstrup, an exemplary instance of an unfulfillable demand is the Sermon on the Mount, the injunction that Christ's followers be perfect "even as your Father which is in heaven" (52). The impossibility of properly responding to the demand intrigues Løgstrup for its radicality: We understand the demand; it is legible, transparent, but we can never succeed in fulfilling it because we are human, we are unlike God, we are imperfect.

Critchley then turns to Levinas's own concept of the ethical demand, which he understands as similarly unfulfillable (and asymmetrical). Critchley makes only one distinction between the two: In Levinas, the demand is unfulfillable because of its incomprehensibility, which corresponds to an opacity at the core of the subject: "The ethical relation to the other is not one of comprehension . . . the relation to the other lives on as an imprint in the subject to which it responds but which it cannot comprehend" (62). Yet there remains a sense, on Critchley's account, that the ethical demand exhibits a positive quality: It is a buried secret to which we would be able to respond properly—or properly translate into what Critchley calls a "politics of resistance"—if only we could decipher or unearth it. (An archaeological principle of the sort on which I opened is in evidence again.) Whatever remains opaque about the demand is underemphasized or suppressed by Critchley in order to highlight the similarities between Løgstrup and Levinas (and, elsewhere, Badiou and Lacan). Critchley thus joins the legions of Levinasians and anti-Levinasians that see in his work an inescapably ontological quality, and Hägglund is right to take issue with Critchley's conflation of Levinas and Derrida.

But what do we lose in the attempt to divorce the work of Derrida from that of Levinas? If a "responsible" reading would aim to make salient the differences between the two thinkers—to demonstrate, as Hägglund has, the inherent, irreconcilable contradictions between the concepts of hospitality, violence, and temporality in Levinas and Derrida—wouldn't a responsible (deconstructive) critique also aim, irresponsibly, to read Levinas against the grain, to identify the seeds of concepts that will later appear in Derrida? In addition to the account of temporality that Levinas's syntactical experiments uneasily share with Derrida's discussion of untimeliness, we've already cited the Derridean notion of passive decision as the decision "of the absolute other in me, the other as the absolute that decides on me in me" (*The Politics of Friendship*, 68) as an echo of the Levinasian "command exercised by the other in me over me" (*Otherwise than Being*, 141). What would it mean, conversely, to read Levinas retroactively, intempestively, from Derrida, to read ideas, still latent, that can't quite break out of the ontological lexicon of the Lithuanian-French philosopher but that nevertheless find an afterlife in the work of Derrida?

It is only by reading Levinas through or from Derrida that we can begin to conceive of an ethical demand *not* as that which cannot be fulfilled because it is impossible, god-like, or impenetrable but because of its simultaneous call for and denial of interpretation. We know from *Specters of Marx* that "If the readability of a legacy were given, natural, transparent, univocal, if it did not call for and at the same time defy interpretation, we would never have anything to inherit from it" (18). Let us pretend, for a moment, that Derrida is *not* speaking of the specters of Hamlet's father, or of the specter of Marx, but the specter of Levinas: What would it mean to inherit from Levinas's ghost, to resist reaching consensus about what this legacy is? If the ethico-political, spectral demand, for Derrida, is aporetic in its simultaneous unreadability and demand to be read, if the demand does not communicate a positive content but rather guards a secret that exceeds the play of hiding and revelation, what kind of reading can we attempt today, what kind of anachronic, untimely readings are possible? How does one inherit from, respond to, the marrano specter? Is such an inheritance *violent*?

Borges after Derrida

Let's consider the relation between Borges and Derrida, two thinkers whose work has traversed, both thematically and performatively, the dangerous, murky border between literature and philosophy and whose readers see in them—not completely without justification—fertile ground for comparison. They are, we are told, intellectually alike, for better or worse, to the detriment or glory of one or the other. Before I begin, however, I want to alert you to two things and also to anticipate my conclusion, in the form of a suggestion. The comparison between Borges and Derrida is impossible; what's more, it's highly unoriginal. In the 1980s, the Latin American literary critics Roberto González Echevarría and Emir Rodríguez Monegal attempted to trace the textual and conceptual links between Borges and Derrida—and others have followed suit since then. What I'll be suggesting is that the notion of the *precursor* that each of them, Borges and Derrida, addresses and that is used by critics to place Derrida and Borges in relation to each other is tied to a range of undecidable questions that *because* they are undecidable make different forms of exteriority intrinsic to the work of Derrida and Borges. The demand that this undecidable, intrinsic exteriority makes alerts Borges's and Derrida's readers to the constitutive *unlikeness* of an author to himself, of a tradition to itself, of an archive to itself, of a discipline to itself. Coming to terms with this *unlikeness* is the task of Latinamericanism today, still.

Why should we read Borges and Derrida together? Why should we be interested in any of the concerns I've only begun to list—relations, grounds, comparisons, foundations, originality—when what we've learned from Borges and Derrida, in very different ways, is to be highly suspicious of claims to likeness, identity, foundations, origins? Can we read Borges as a precursor to Derrida, or to deconstruction more broadly, as some critics would have it? In what follows, I'll opt, instead, to dwell on the sites in which such inquisitions might fail or fall short, by proposing *other* inquisitions, such as why the question of the precursor, Latin America's violent inheritance, continues to haunt, unsettle, Latinamericanism.

I won't provide a comprehensive list of the studies comparing Borges and Derrida. Instead, I'll briefly consider González Echevarría's 1983 essay "BdeORridaGES (BORGES Y DERRIDA)" and Rodríguez Monegal's 1985 "Borges y Derrida: boticarios" not as representative studies but rather as readings that symptomatize a certain approach to literature, theory, and disciplinarity, as well as to the broader question of identity and origins in Latin American and Latinamericanist thought. I will then turn to Borges's 1951 "Kafka y sus precursores" in order to "unread" or "misread" Borges as a precursor to Derrida. I will argue that in drawing upon the example of Zeno's paradox of motion, Borges proposes a theory of precursors as retroactively determined: untimely, *intempestivo*, at once early and belated.

Jorge Luis Borges and Jacques Derrida

To relate Borges and Derrida, González Echevarría embarks upon an analysis of the three epigraphs of the third section of "Plato's Pharmacy," the first and last of which hail from Borges's work: the former from "La esfera de Pascal" and the latter from "Tlön, Uqbar, Orbis Tertius," both of which, the Yale professor would like us to know, were not easy to find. Citation, then, serves as the point of departure for the establishment of a textual relation between the two thinkers: "Given that Derrida has taught us to take seriously exterior, 'preliminary' elements such as epigraphs," he tells us, "I will reflect briefly upon the possible meaning of these . . . in order to make several indirect observations on the relation between Borges and Derrida" (207, translation mine).

Already from the title, "BdeORridaGES (BORGES Y DERRIDA)," we have a sense of what will follow. If at first glance the title appears to mimic the play with words, roots, phonemes, and graphemes characteristic of at least an early deconstructive tendency, it is followed by the parenthetical differ-entiation of the two writers in question, announced in caps and married by the Spanish conjunction *y*. While the graphic scrambling would, at first glance, seem to upend any thought tending to establish or flow from essen-tial identity or likeness (establishing the identity *of* Borges or *of* Derrida or the likeness of Borges *to* Derrida), the words or semiwords that jump out in fact do a very different kind of work, tending precisely to set in place what on the surface, in its play, it claims to unsettle. If we read from left to right, the first fully formed word in Spanish is *de*, evoking a sense of belonging, of pertinence or property, either in the sense of home, of national or local origins (*soy* de *California*), or of ownership (*este libro es* de *mi amiga Paola*). If I allow my eyes to be captured, instead, by the capital letters, they may be tricked into reading *orígenes*, again, signaling a desire to identify origins, beginnings, roots. Under the veneer of deconstruction (the essay turns on the idea of the supplement, it scrambles letters, it imagines literary and philosophical language as a tissue of citations), González Echevarría's essay reveals itself as most interested in establishing sources, influences, and origins: "Derrida ventures to indicate . . . that Borges is one of his sources" (212).

In the 1985 essay "Borges y Derrida: boticarios," González Echevarría's then colleague Emir Rodríguez Monegal takes up the question of the relation between the two by once again returning to "Plato's Pharmacy." The opening lines of the essay imply that it might not be *necessary* to read Derrida, since the philosopher merely repeats what Borges had already accomplished years before. "I've always found it difficult to read Derrida," the Uruguayan critic begins, in a statement sure to please a reader allergic to philosophy and critical theory. "Not so much for the density of his thought and the heavy, redundant, and repetitive style in which it is developed" (yes, Derrida's a bad writer, he seems to tell us, but I'm an agile reader),

> but for an entirely circumstantial reason. Educated in Borges's thought from the age of fifteen, I must admit that many of Derrida's novelties struck me as being rather **tautological**. I could not understand why he took so long in arriving at the **same** luminous perspectives which Borges had opened up years earlier. His famed "deconstruction" impressed me for its technical precision and the infinite seduction of its textual slights-of-hand, but it was all too **familiar** to me: I had **experienced** it in Borges *avant la lettre*. (128, emphasis my own)

The argument is rather straightforward, but it has a number of consequences I'd like to outline here. First, we don't need Derrida, because we have Borges. This might lead to a second, implicit point: We don't need philosophy, critical theory, etc., because we have literature. Third, deconstruction's origins are Latin American (echoing González Echevarría's point that Derrida places Borges, a "marginal" writer, into the "center" of European discourse). This reverses the center/periphery, original/copy formal relation pervasive in literary criticism at least until the Latin American avant-garde movements, but it does little to dismantle these oppositions (notice the reference to repetition, tautology, sameness, familiarity: Derrida as mere repetition of Borges). In addition to identifying a (Latin American) precursor of French (and later US) deconstruction, positing a rehierarchization of intellectual geopolitics, the essay affirms the same logic of identity, of origins and originality, that we witness in González Echevarría's piece and that is at the heart of the most commonly accepted understandings of what a "precursor" is, what work it does.

We see, here, that although González Echevarría's and Rodríguez Monegal's canon-expanding projects may seem antithetical to the identitarian impulse beginning in 1980s Latin American literary studies, in fact they are more intimately related than one might suspect: If the former emphasizes high culture over low, institutionality over marginality, both concern, first and foremost, the question of origins and an overdetermined, underthought affiliation between identity and origins, even when these origins are to be read through a cosmopolitan lens.

But what do we mean when we talk about a precursor, what is it that we seek, that we desire, when we search for such a thing? In the 1951 "Kafka y sus precursores," first published in the newspaper *La Nación* and later in *Otras Inquisiciones*, Borges reflects upon the question of influence by enumerating the works that anticipate—in theme, in tone, in spiritual affinity—the work of Franz Kafka in order to postulate an unorthodox theory of the relation between precursor and heir. Borges carries out his argument performatively rather than, or in addition to, constatively. As I hope to demonstrate, by thematizing the idea of the literary precursor, Borges proposes a method of reading that upsets our conventional notions of source and target, origin and heir, and alerts us to the untimely quality of inheritance and/as the demand for reading upon which Derrida will reflect decades later.

"Yo premedité alguna vez un examen de los precursores de Kafka" (I once premeditated making a study of Kafka's precursors) (88/199), Borges begins. The very first verb, the first signifier of action—*premeditar*—appears as a kind of reverse performative: Borges's "I" premeditates, or claims that he premeditates, as a counterintuitive entry into a meditation on the impossibility of premeditation, what we will come to see as the performative delinking of subject and effect. The introductory paragraph, however, still insists—if we are to read it at face value—upon the notion of authorial intention, not yet read as fiction, which can be understood in relation not only to the work of the essayist who "intends" to embark upon a study of *x* or *y* but also to a causal relation between precursor and heir, one that is rooted in time (Borges's narrative subject explains that he will list Kafka's precursors in chronological order). The "pre-" of the *premeditación*, which here signals, retroactively, that which shall not or cannot come to pass, alludes as well to the "pre-" of *precursor* (from the Latin *prae*, beforehand and *currere*, to run), so that even in this strange opening paragraph that would seem to propose a timely study of a chronological phenomenon, we begin to sense the untimely quality of the study and of the precursor itself.

The first—the "original"—precursor to Kafka, Borges tells us, is Zeno, whose paradox of motion parallels the problem of *The Castle*:

> El primero es la paradoja de Zenón contra el movimiento. Un móvil que está en A (declara Aristóteles) no podrá alcanzar el punto B, porque antes deberá recorrer la mitad del camino entre los dos, y antes la mitad de la mitad, y antes, la mitad de la mitad, y así hasta el infinito; la forma de este ilustre problema es, exactamente, la de *El Castillo*, y el móvil y la flecha y Aquiles son los primeros personajes kafkianos de la literatura. (88)

> (The first is Zeno's paradox against movement. A moving object at A (declares Aristotle) cannot reach point B, because it must first cover half the distance between the two points, and before that, half of the half, and before that, half of the half of the half, and so on to infinity; the form of this illustrious problem is, exactly, that of *The Castle*, and the moving object and the arrow and Achilles are the first Kafkian characters in literature.) (199)

In his discussion of Zeno's paradox, Borges not only provides an example of a thematic link between Zeno and Kafka; he allegorizes the very relation between precursor and heir and, consequently, between text and reader. But what, precisely, is allegorized here? How are we to understand the relation between a moving object and its destination (or its origin)? Suppose we think of the relation between the moving object and its destination (or its origin) as a figure for the relation between precursor and heir (or vice versa). Let us imagine, Borges seems to suggest, the infinite length of time it would take for the moving object to reach its destination (or conversely, the infinitely small distance the moving object would have to cover in order to begin to move) as an unsuturable gap between the so-called original and target texts. Could this not also serve as an allegory for reading more broadly?

Imagining Borges's story this way tends to make him a precursor not just of Derrida but of Paul de Man. (A dramatic and uncontainable proliferation of precursors is one consequence of reading Borges with Derrida: The closer we get to establishing the influence of *a* precursor, the more precursors we seem to discover, and the more a single precursor seems to have come before other figures as well. This, too, is a version of Zeno's paradox.) We know from de Man that "Allegories are always allegories of metaphor and, as such, they are always allegories of the impossibility of reading" (*Allegories of Reading*, 205). Such impossibility of reading, for de Man, has to do with the noncoincidence between allegory and its antecedent: "Allegory designates primarily a distance in relation to its own origin, and, renouncing the nostalgia and the desire to coincide, it establishes its language in the void of this temporal difference. In so doing, it prevents the self from an illusory identification with the non-self, which is now fully, though painfully, recognized as a non-self" (*Blindness and Insight*, 207). At the risk of echoing Rodríguez Monegal, hasn't that point already been made by Borges, if not constatively, then performatively? Isn't that precisely the problem that "Kafka y sus precursores" stages?

What, then, of the rapport between Borges and Derrida? When asked in an interview published in the blog "Outward from Nothingness" about Borges's influence upon his work, Derrida responds:

> What would be my spontaneous attitude to Borges? It's a pensive one. I am reminded of an interview with Borges, during a visit to Harvard in 1968. His father had a theory of forgetting that lingered with him. "I think if I recall something," his father said, "for example, if today I look back on this morning, then I get an image of what I saw this morning. But if tonight, I'm thinking back on this morning, then what I'm really recalling is not the first image, but the first image in memory. So that every time I recall something, I'm not recalling it really, I'm recalling the last time I recalled it, I'm recalling my last memory of it. So that really, I have no memories whatever, I have no images whatever, about my childhood, my youth." My relationship with Borges works precisely in this fashion; I have no relationship with him whatever. The only relationship I have with him, his writings, is his ghost—the traces of Borges.

A closer look at this interview reveals a Borgesian influence, but not upon Derrida himself: The interview was published in, and refers to, the year 2012, nearly a decade after the death of the so-called father of deconstruction.[1] The apocryphal quotation appears to hail not from Derrida but from Derrida's ghost, bringing together two crucial aspects of the work of Borges and Derrida: forgeries and specters, suggesting that literary inheritances—inheritances from a precursor—are only ever present hauntologically.

We are faced with the challenge of interpreting the link between precursor and heir, and, as such, we are heirs to the generations-old problem, in literary criticism, to establish an impossible relation: a problem that takes on an added cultural and political dimension in Latin American literary studies. An infinitely difficult problem that enjoins us to infinite reading, but what kind of infinity, what kind of reading? Such an injunction teases out the ethico-political quality of reading: In our encounter with what is unreadable in the text, in the other, we are called upon to venture a guess, to make a decision (an interpretation) about something fundamentally undecidable. Here, the ever-receding and ever-proliferating precursor resembles the ever-receding text: Whether we understand the chasm between precursor and heir, text and reader to be infinitely vast or infinitely small does not seem to matter. Rather, we are faced with the dizzying possibility of infinite choice (interpretation) within a given limit, an asymptote approaching a line it will never reach. The necessary decision that reading entails involves a kind of violence, perhaps the very violence upon which disciplines and disciplinarity are formed and which is never too far from ethics, however counterintuitive it may seem.

Let's turn to the final sentences of Borges's text, in which he makes the case for a kind of bidirectional relation between precursor and heir, one that complicates the chronological, causal relation announced in the opening lines of the essay. Browning's poem "Fears and Scruples," he argues, not only anticipates or foretells Kafka's work: Through Kafka's work, we can return to the poem and read what we could not have read at the moment of its composition, what Browning himself could not have anticipated. The uncanny bond between precursor and heir, then, comes about not only in our reading of Kafka through Browning but in our untimely, anachronic return to Browning *from* Kafka. "The fact is that every writer *creates* his own precursors. His work modifies our conception of the past, as it will modify the future," Borges offers, contradicting the Borges of the opening paragraph, the Borges that "premeditated," the Borges that would proceed in chronological order, the "introduction-Borges" that anticipated—and would be cancelled out by—"conclusion-Borges" (201).

It is this relation of unlikeness that Borges emphasizes in the final sentences of the essay: "The early Kafka of *Betrachtung* is less a precursor of the Kafka of somber myths and atrocious institutions than is Browning or Lord Dunsany" (201). Browning has more in common with late Kafka than early Kafka does, or, to put it another way, Browning has more in common with Kafka than *Kafka* has with Kafka. It is here that Borges gives the fatal twist to the significance—the meaning but also the importance—of a precursor. The precursor, we can now see, is that aspect of exteriority that alerts us to the constitutive *unlikeness* of an author to him- or herself. Borges is not

Borges, Kafka is not Kafka, Levinas is not Levinas, Derrida is not Derrida, the precursor arrives, belatedly, to tell us. And it is here that we can begin to imagine a rapport not only between Borges and Derrida but between literature and philosophy as two disciplines that, as they approach each other, never arriving, expose the principle of nonidentity at the heart of each (literature is not literature, philosophy is not philosophy, and—we could add—deconstruction is not deconstruction, Latinamericanism is not Latinamericanism). I suggested that the comparison between Borges and Derrida was impossible. It's now clear what that impossibility really means: not that we cannot compare them but that the point of the comparison is its undecidability. But it is an undecidability at the core of our notion of an author or his work: We never know which Borges is writing, early Borges or late Borges, we never know which Derrida we're reading, Derrida haunted by Borges or Derrida haunted by not-Derrida, "early" Derrida or "late" Derrida. Our search for precursors, then, insofar as it symptomatizes a desire for identity, for likeness, for origins, is doomed not to fail but to succeed. There are always enough precursors, narrowly understood, to go around, always enough fathers to kill anxiously, following yet another Yale critic.

The strange principle of intempestive unlikeness anticipates (again, retroactively) the words of Levinas, who characterizes ethical experience as the experience of noncoincidence with oneself in the splintering of time: "This being torn up from oneself in the core of one's unity, this absolute noncoinciding, this diachrony of the instant, signifies in the form of one-penetrated-by-the-other" (*Otherwise than Being*, 49).[2] When we rethink the idea of the precursor from and through Borges—as a moving object that never departs and never arrives, infinitely early, infinitely late—we find ourselves, writers and readers, torn up from ourselves, penetrated by the other. Our first act, perhaps taken defensively, with "no preceding political or ethical light to mark the path," to echo Moreiras's words, may be to invent a discipline in which to find shelter. But the discipline that we invent through and from Derrida, our Latinamericanism *after* deconstruction, "signifies in the form of one-penetrated-by-the-other." To read Latinamericanism in this light is to embark upon new, absolutely noncoinciding inquisitions, new interdisciplinary or *in*disciplinary inquiries that hold open the possibility of an outside or of an outside within: the unknown that structures every event of reading, a marrano discipline in which the practice of marrano ethics takes shape as first anarchaeological reading.

This means, concretely, that we need to revisit and challenge claims not only about Borges's antecedence but also the larger structures, logics, and vocabularies that have organized "our" disciplines. I'll open Part IV, "Political Thinking after Literature," with a critical appraisal of the allegorical readings that dominated Latin American literary studies in the 1980s and 1990s. The scholars I'll discuss insisted upon national allegory as the central narrative and—worse—critical-interpretative paradigm, echoing rather uncannily Fredric Jameson's hyperbolic and reductive claim about Third World literature. I'll suggest, finally, that by allowing Borges to guide us—not as precursor but precisely as the thinker who turned such relations (between precursors and heirs) upside down—we can pursue a Latinamericanism-after-deconstruction that can no longer be called Latinamericanism. This is, of course, logically impossible, but it does crucial work, and not only for Latinamericanists. Rather, it alerts us to the tautological structure of *any* discipline: Latinamericanism is that which defines its object of study as Latin American. Yet that does not mean we must do away with, say, reading Latin American literature: It simply means that a book—say, this book—that takes as its primary texts recent works from Argentina does not need to be defined as such. Its "identity" must be corrupted or surrendered through exposure and indisciplinarity (concepts to which I'll explore in more detail in Part V) and through the differential repetition we call reading.

Part IV. Political Thinking
after Literature

The Metapolitics of Allegory

> Whereas man is drawn towards the symbol, allegory emerges
> from the depths of being to intercept the intention, and to
> triumph over it.
>   —Walter Benjamin, "Allegory and Trauerspiel"

In his 1986 *Social Text* article "Third-World Literature in the Era of Multinational Capitalism," Fredric Jameson (in)famously proclaimed that "all
third world texts are . . . necessarily allegorical, and in a very specific way:
they are to be read as what I will call *national allegories*." This, predictably,
provoked strong reactions by scholars of this so-called Third World literature. Criticism of Jameson's troubling generalization focused upon his
grouping of *all* literary texts by African, Asian, and Latin American writers
together into one narrow category, a move that aside from being *literarily*
irresponsible was ethically and politically problematic as well. "It felt odd,"
Aijaz Ahmad wrote in "Jameson's Rhetoric of Otherness and the National
Allegory," his response to the piece. Jean Franco, for her part, took issue
not so much with Jameson's employment of the Three Worlds theory but
with the qualifier "national": "Not only is 'the nation' a complex and much
contested term," she wrote, "but in recent Latin American criticism it is
no longer the inevitable framework for either political or cultural projects"
(130). Of the many reactions elicited by Jameson's (surely deliberately)
provocative piece, however, few or none engaged with the question of
allegory itself.[1] Although "allegory" was a term much in dispute precisely
at that moment, Jameson's critics largely set it aside—as if its sense were
uncontroversial or as if its use represented a lapse in taste, an overliterari-
ness inappropriate to weightier political matters.

Around the same time that Jameson wrote his polemical essay, many
prominent US-based Latin American literary scholars were indeed engaging in precisely the kind of allegorical readings Jameson described—
"national allegories"—albeit from differing ideological and intellectual

positions: Doris Sommer's 1984 *Foundational Fictions* (which soon found a place on Spanish PhD comprehensive exam reading lists across the United States) made the case that nineteenth-century Latin American romances allegorized the trials and tribulations of nation building following the wars of independence in the region, while Roberto González Echevarría's 1985 *The Voice of the Masters* and, following him, Carlos Alonso's 1990 *The Spanish American Regional Novel* interpreted Rómulo Gallegos's *Doña Bárbara* as an allegory of the conflict between civilization and barbarism, prevalent in Latin American literary and political discourse since D. F. Sarmiento's 1845 *Facundo*. Each attempted to distance herself or himself from Jameson's rather reductive reading of allegory, in which there would be a one-to-one table of equivalences between the personal and the political, the literary and the national (a reading against which Jameson had warned), and, in particular, from Jameson's treatment of allegory as flowing from the intention of the author. Despite gesturing toward deconstructive arguments that would appear to open interpretative possibilities, their analyses remained rooted in the broader logic of intentionality, will, authority, mastery—that of the texts they read and, reciprocally, that of their *own* disciplinary authority, constituted through their analyses.

What conception of *allegory* is implied in Jameson's normative formulation, in the "national" literary-historical allegories told by Sommer, González Echevarría, and Alonso, and in the disciplining turn so many of Jameson's critics take in response to his essay? What sort of decision and what sort of allegory lie behind the coupled assertion of a *necessary* allegorical reading ("Third World texts" are "*necessarily* allegorical") and of a "very specific" content ("national" allegory)? And what to make of Jameson's strangely passive, impersonal formulation: "They *are to be read* . . .": by whom? To approach these questions, and to provide an account of allegory that turns the passivity of Jameson's formulation *against* its normative, mechanical frame—and thus against a notion of literature amenable to disciplinary capture—let me first consider these critical texts (Jameson's, Sommer's, González Echevarría's, Alonso's) as allegories themselves, allegories of certain practices of reading but also allegories of the constitution of disciplines and canons. (*Canon*, here, could be understood to refer to both primary texts as well as critical texts, to practices of reading as well as to their objects.)

Paul de Man, the critic whose work on allegory formed the acknowledged or unacknowledged center of each of these writers' engagement with allegory, wrote less than a decade earlier a phrase we have noted already: "Allegories are always allegories of metaphor and, as such, they are always allegories of the impossibility of reading" (*Allegories of Reading*, 205). Jameson, Sommer, González Echevarría, and Alonso specifically resist, in their formulations of allegory, the possibility of unreadability or undecidability. Why? With what consequences? Why can they not read, in de Man, what is so bleakly and clearly presented? Why do they find it *impossible* to read him? In what follows, I will address the following questions: What modes of reading were made possible or impossible (or *signaled* as possible or impossible) by these critical allegories, these allegories of criticism? What alternative critical practices in the field of Latin American literature were sidelined or eclipsed by these canon-forming gestures? I will then engage in a close reading of César Aira's 1997 *El congreso de literatura* (*The Literary Conference*, 2010), in order to propose an alternative politics of allegory, or allegory of politics, that would be based in the Derridean passive or unconscious decision, hearkening back, unintentionally, unconsciously, to Jameson's strange, passive grammar in his injunction "they are to be read." The problem of unconscious decision, which we have been developing throughout *Anarchaeologies*, is now treated literarily, allegorically.

Let us return to Jameson's article for a moment. "Third-World Literature," as Ahmad rightly points out, concerns itself first and foremost with the question of the Western literary canon or, more precisely, with the importance of the "radical difference of non-canonical texts" from Asia, Africa, and Latin America (65). Rather than arguing in favor of the inclusion of Third World texts on "great books" lists or "core course" curricula on the basis that these texts "are 'as great' as those of the canon," Jameson makes a case for reading them in their radical alterity: as, and only as, national allegories (specifically, "conscious" national allegories that may, in fact, allow First World readers to see the "unconscious" allegorical quality in their own tradition) (65). The radical split we see in First World texts, at least on the surface, between private and public realms, between aesthetics and politics, is absent in the literature from Asia, Africa, and Latin America, according to Jameson. Third World literature is faithful to, or is a faithful representation of, the events, broadly understood, of the history of the nation in which, and about which, it is written: This is what makes it "allegorical."[2] "National allegory" could just as easily be described as an allegory for *political* literature. Substitute "political" for "allegorical" in Jameson's essay, and you will see that the argument does not change significantly.

Let's say that the allegorical, for Jameson, is another name for the political, an allegory for the political. The concept of politics that Jameson's argument relies upon then seems violently normative—a matter of "necessary" interpretations or decisions to be performed voluntarily and intentionally by readers brought to realization of these "necessities." This is not, of course, the only way to imagine allegory—and with it, politics. How would our notion of politics change if we entertained different notions of allegory—say, ones based more openly in de Man's work or in Benjamin's, which have highly problematical relations to the concept of representation? What would it look like to recuperate the possibility of allegorical reading in light of de Man's argument that allegory always allegorizes the *impossibility* of reading? Minimally, such readings would have to alter our concept of politics or political representation more broadly—certainly they do not square with what appears to be Jameson's (and his critics') normative, even mechanical politics. Let us, then, argue in favor of a *metapolitics* of allegory (in the Rancièrian sense), one that performs, rather than thematizes, political and aesthetic representation as constitutively impossible.

For what, then, is "allegory" an allegory in Sommer, González Echevarría, and Alonso, if not for politics, or if not for Jameson's brand of politics?[3] Sommer argues that romantic dramas and dramatic romances allegorize the political challenges of the nineteenth century (Gertrudis Gómez de Avellaneda's *Sab* allegorizes a reigning patriarchal order in crisis in Cuba; Jorge Isaacs's eponymous María's Jewishness stands for unspeakable difference between black and white in Columbia, to give but two examples), while in González Echevarría and Alonso we witness another kind of literary politics: the politics of canon formation. Both González Echevarría and Alonso identify two types of allegory at work in *Doña Bárbara*: the first readable, explicit, *in* and *of* the text (which is to say, placed there *intentionally* by an author),[4] and a second, ostensibly more deconstructive type of allegory, which, in González Echevarría's words, "far from freezing meaning . . . sets other mechanisms of signification into motion by showing the radical separation between signifier and signified" (47). Alonso, following the lead of his mentor, argues that "allegory in *Doña Bárbara* is not *just* an interpretive intention projected into the text, but also a narrative technique extensively employed to construct the events depicted in the novel" (120, italics my own). He goes on to suggest that "the veritable proliferation of allegoresis in the novel brings implicit with it the understanding that in allegory anything can stand for anything else, provided there is a *discursive will* that suppresses the knowledge represented by that very insight" (130, italics my own).

This all seems well and good, until and unless we take note of several key concepts that accompany "allegory" in these arguments: authority, intention, will. The metapolitics of *this* reading of allegory, even as it distances itself from politics understood as ideological content, grounds itself in the related political concepts of sovereignty and decision, a rhetorical move that has far-reaching political consequences. Alonso allows for the possibility of interruption of authorial will, but it is only disrupted or suppressed by another will: the anthropomorphized text's "discursive will." The metapolitics of such an allegorical reading, then, still remains tied to the hegemonic concepts of sovereignty, intention, decision. Allegory, here, behaves as a kind of cloning machine, not unlike the cloning machine we'll see in Aira's *El congreso de literatura*. Yet Aira's machine, as I hope to demonstrate, allows for the possibility of error; in fact, error, in Aira, is shown to have always already annihilated the possibility of sovereign decision, of mastery. This possibility is not of interest to Alonso and especially not to González Echevarría, the title of whose book, *The Voice of the Masters: Writing and Authority in Latin American Literature*, seems to point to the authority of the voice of the critic. That is, by investing himself with the authority to identify the (literary) masters, González Echevarría constitutes *himself* as a critical master, as the voice of authority in the discipline, a discipline he has shaped through the establishment of a Latin American canon. Mastery, authority, will . . . the interpretative lexicon that seemed, at first, quite distant from the ostensibly democratizing literary politics of Jameson now reveals itself to be the flip side of the same critical-political coin. Allegories of *this* brand of politics, or the politics of *this* brand of allegory, by remaining tied to "master" concepts of mastery, work against the emancipatory possibilities of literature for which Jameson seemed to be advocating.

In response to this "boom" of allegorical criticism, the question of allegory began to be avoided by more theoretically oriented Latinamericanists, who largely missed the opportunity to read Latin American literature with and through a more Benjaminian or de Manian (or Derridean) concept of allegory. Yet I want to suggest that such a turn away from allegory is really a turn away from a *certain* politics of allegory. What might a turn, or return, to allegory mean now for Latin American literary studies? Let us consider alternative modes of allegorical reading that were sidelined in the discipline but that may, now, be finding an afterlife. Alberto Moreiras's 1993 "Pastiche Identity, and Allegory of Allegory"—a polemical afterword to a volume dedicated to the study of identity and difference in Latin America—argued in favor of a postsymbolic, melancholic allegorical approach to identity in Borges's "Tlön, Uqbar, Orbis Tertius." Borges's story, Moreiras claimed, "allegorize[d] the national allegory," exposing the way in which "the national allegory runs into its own impossibility" (227).

"To posit heterogeneity is to homogenize it; to project the unrepresentable is to represent it. To allegorize is then to authorize," Moreiras tells us (232). This subterranean strand—which we find treated directly in Moreiras as well as Idelber Avelar's book on allegory and postdictatorial mourning and in Kate Jenckes's writing on allegory as allography in Borges—could be said to relate, at least in spirit, to Bram Acosta's concept of illiteracy (as a practice of reading that takes into account the constitutive opacity at the heart of the opposition between writing and orality) as well as my own reflections on allegories of marranismo. We may not call this allegory: We may call it deconstruction, or we may call it, simply, reading, reading grounded in its own impossibility (de Man).

What would a politics, or metapolitics, of allegory, of allegory based in the impossibility of reading, look like? Returning to Rancière, perhaps *this* politics would be a politics of dissensus. Recall that, for Rancière, political disagreement, *la mésentente politique*, is formally related to literary misunderstanding, *le malentendu littéraire*. If what I've suggested here is that (to borrow from Raymond Carver) "what we talk about when we talk about allegory" is the question of politics, it is also always the debate over canon formation and disciplinary authority. If we were to extend the politics of discipline and canon formation to this subterranean strand, then, it would necessarily imply infinite disagreement over what texts would be considered canonical, which voices would be considered authorities over the others. Here, the sovereign voices of Latin American literary criticism who read texts that, in Moreiras's words, allegorize and thus authorize would recede in favor of postsovereign (Cabezas) critical practices, in which the authority of both literary and critical texts (including this one) would be called into question, masters (of texts, of departments, of fields) suspended, and allegory both wounded and wounding: infinite and infinitely impossible.

Allegories of Decision

> A decision, if there is one, disappears in its appearance.
> Jacques Derrida, "Nietzsche and the Machine"

Jameson proposes, in a strangely normative, passive voice, that Third World texts "are to be read as what I will call *national allegories*." I've just shown the way in which the masters of Latin American literary criticism fashioned their own authoritative voices in the 1980s according to a non–de Manian conception of allegoresis that excluded the possibility of unreadability, grounding their analyses instead in the concepts of sovereignty, will, and intentionality. In order to propose an allegorical reading of the *impossibility* of political subjectivity, of politics as sovereign decisionism, or of politics as intentional fidelity to an event, I will turn to César Aira's 1997 *El congreso de literatura*. The work of Aira, a veritable writing machine who publishes multiple novels a year, not only allows us to think the rapport between literature and the market (as Sandra Contreras, Phillip Penix-Tadsen, Héctor Hoyos, and others have argued) but also literature's relation to ethics and politics, specifically through the idea of the event as linked to the notion of passive or unconscious decision. I will suggest that the ethical and political ramifications of the literary are traced in *El congreso de literatura*, through a profound (and humorous) ambivalence toward the idea of the event as either the cause or effect of a decision. By inhabiting, exaggerating, parodying, trivializing, and ultimately eclipsing both event and decision, Aira's novel allegorizes the impossibility of political concepts such as sovereignty, decision, and event. In *El congreso de literatura*, as I hope to demonstrate, Aira simultaneously multiplies and subtracts from the idea of the event: There are either too many events, or not enough to go around, or one that has already happened but escapes narration.

How has the relationship between decision and event been thought? For Alain Badiou, the decision is central to the "truth-event": If the event is that which interrupts the situation or status quo, the subject's fidelity to the event (that which constitutes him as a subject) comes about through "the decision to relate henceforth to the situation *from the perspective of its eventual [événementiel] supplement*" (*Ethics*, 41). The rapport between decision and event in Badiou bears a formal compatibility with the concept of decision in Carl Schmitt, for whom the decision constitutes the sovereign ("Sovereign is he who decides on the exception" [5]). Yet as Gareth Williams has convincingly argued, drawing on Derrida's *The Politics of Friendship*, "Becoming subjected to the architecture of sovereign decisionism does not lay to rest, for once and forever more, the possible advent of reason's unconditional opening to the excessiveness (the incalculability) of the event" (151). That is, if there is decision in the Schmittian sense, decision taken by and proper only to the sovereign, it necessarily excludes the possibility of the event understood as the incalculable.

While Badiou's event heralds the arrival of what was previously unthinkable (the void of the situation) and, in this sense, might resonate with a more Derridean idea of a "democracy to come" or *a-vènir*, the key difference is that for Badiou the unthinkable *does* arrive and becomes nameable (the very concrete historical examples he cites are "the French Revolution of 1792, the meeting of Héloïse and Abelard, Galileo's creation of physics, Haydn's invention of the classical musical style [as well as] the Cultural Revolution in China (1965–67), a personal amorous passion," and so on [41]). The question I want to pursue has less to do with whether the event is thinkable or unthinkable and more with the status of the decision in relation to this event. Is the decision the condition of possibility of the event, or is the event the condition of possibility of the decision? How does the idea of unconscious decision allow us to imagine an event that would exceed chronology, causality, and calculability—in the way, for instance, that the notion of the "precursor" appears to do for both Borges and Derrida? Finally, what does literature or the literary have to tell us about such matters? How does allegory ("other writing") tell this story *otherwise*?

El congreso de literatura offers a possible avenue into this debate, if not as a representative example of the literary, then as one possible instance of a supplementary discourse to the philosophical. The novella relates the ambitious attempt of the narrator-protagonist, also named César Aira (a writer, translator, and mad scientist), to clone Carlos Fuentes in order to take over the world. The so-called genius Fuentes, who is in attendance at the same literary conference as Aira in Mérida, Venezuela, represents the best hope for world domination because, the narrator explains, high culture—philosophy, history, literature, classics—is the best way to distract the unsuspecting masses: "El disfraz de cosa anticuada y pasada de moda de la alta cultura era la estratagema perfecta para desorientar a las masas incautas" (high culture's disguise as something old fashioned and out-of-date was the perfect strategy to disorient the unsuspecting masses) (29/21–22). Aira's fantasy depends upon the reproduction of the same—totalitarian thinking in its most basic form—yet the fact that he will utilize a literary celebrity to do so exposes the potential pitfalls of literature as institution while at the same time introducing a necessary flaw to the plan through the motif of literature as translation.

After sending out a wasp to bring back a cell from Fuentes's body for cloning—and the cell comes back unexpectedly neon blue—he sets the cloning machine to work in the hills surrounding the city and proceeds to wait several days by the hotel swimming pool while the conference goes on without him. Aira spends the next two days poolside, attempting to slow or stop his hyperactive brain, which is never free of a thought, or a thousand thoughts, for a second. The tension between the automaticity of his thoughts and his attempt to halt them mirrors the relationship between "events" and Aira's narration of these events. He repeatedly, obsessively refers to the quantity of details he must leave out in order to stick to his

self-imposed page limit, an impossible task that requires multiple "translations," a motif that comes to stand for the task of writing more broadly:

> Creo que lo más conveniente será remontarme al comienzo. Pero no al
> comienzo de esta historia sino el anterior, el comienzo que hizo posible que
> hubiera una historia. Para lo cual es inevitable cambiar de nivel, y empezar
> por la Fábula que constituye la lógica del relato. Después tendré que hacer la
> 'traducción', pero como hacerlo completamente me llevaría más páginas de
> las que me he impuesto como máximo para este libro, iré 'traduciendo' sólo
> donde sea necesario; donde no sea así, quedarán fragmentos de Fábula en su
> lengua original. . . (25)

> (I deem it most appropriate to begin at the beginning. Not, however, at the
> beginning of this story but rather at the beginning of the previous one, the
> beginning that made it possible for there to be a story at all. Which in turn
> requires me to switch levels and begin with the Fable that provides the tale's
> logic. I will then have to do a "translation," which, if carried out in full,
> would take more pages than I have assigned as the maximum number for this
> book; thus I will "translate" only when necessary; all other fragments of the
> Fable will remain in the original language. . .) (17)

Appealing to a Benjaminian notion of translation as the fragment of an
unrecoverable whole, Aira embarks upon a kind of metacriticism as he
narrates, although the internal contradictions of such literary theory expose
an aporia at the heart of the novel: an unsuturable chasm between what the
narrator "does" and what he says he does.

Sunbathing at the pool, failing to stop the machinations of his brain,
Aira recalls the love of his life, his muse, whom he met at that very swimming pool on a trip to Mérida years earlier. The memory of Amelina is still
so clear—a direct contrast to the motif of amnesia that pervades the rest of
the novel—that he hallucinates her presence next to the water. Yet the
memory of Amelina, or the memory of his desire for Amelina, hearkens
back to an earlier memory, an earlier (originary?) desire, that of his first
love as an adolescent: "Al ver a Amelina, milagrosamente, reconocí en sus
rasgos, en su voz, en sus ojos, a una mujer que había sido la gran pasión de
mis veinte años. A la bella Florencia la había amado desesperadamente (lo
nuestro era imposible) con toda la locura de la adolescencia, y nunca dejé
de amarla" (when I saw Amelina, I miraculously recognized in her features,
her voice, her eyes, a woman who had been my great passion when I was
twenty. I had loved the beautiful Florencia to despair (ours was an

impossible love) with all the madness of adolescence, and I never stopped loving her) (49–50/44). Soon after this hallucination, Aira takes a new lover, a third link in the chain of equivalences that hearkens back to Florencia via Amelina: Nelly, Amelina's best friend and roommate.

It is Nelly (and thus also Amelina and Florencia) who accompanies César following a student performance of his play *En la corte de Adán y Eva*, a surreal interpretation that the narrator-protagonist describes as a monstrous adaptation of his original work: "¿Qué era todo eso? No lo reconocía, era demasiado dadaísta. Y sin embargo, yo lo había escrito" (What was all this about? I didn't recognize it, it was too Dadaist. Nevertheless, I had written that) (61/55). He experiences a doubling of the "self" as he observes the audience react with pleasure to the play: "Me entretuve espiando a la concurrencia. Todos volvían a parecerme autómatas surgidos del corazón de mis experimentos. Me poseía una especie de desdoblamiento" (I enjoyed spying on the audience. Everyone looked like automatons from the very heart of my experiments. I underwent some kind of doubling of the self) (59/54). This, too, allegorizes the rapport between machine and event that characterizes the act of writing, understood here as a kind of cloning experiment: The play is a reproduction gone awry, the audience members resemble automatons, Aira himself is "doubled." The monstrous play instantiates the horror of the uncanny—the unsettling presence of the familiar in the strange or the strange in the familiar—by alluding to the impossibility of reproduction without remainder.

Meanwhile, the main cloning experiment has taken on a life of its own, exceeding the plans of the mad scientist and exposing the machine-like quality of the event and the event-like quality of the machine. Instead of successfully reproducing Carlos Fuentes, the machine has instead cloned a fiber from Fuentes's bright blue tie. The next morning, an army of enormous neon-blue worms begin to descend from the hills surrounding Mérida, threatening to crush the entire city and its panicked inhabitants. Yet the catastrophe produces in Aira a certain optimism:

> Siempre he pensado que en una verdadera catástrofe colectiva podría encontrar la material de mis sueños, tomarla en las manos, darle forma, al fin; así fuera por un instante, todo me estaría permitido. Se necesitaría algo tan grande y general como un terremoto, una colisión planetaria, una Guerra, para que la circunstancia se hiciera genuinamente objetiva, y le diera espacio a mi subjetividad para tomar las riendas de la acción. (81)

> (I have always thought that in a real collective catastrophe I would find the material of my dreams, take it in hand, shape it, finally; then, even if only for

an instant, everything would be permitted. It would take something as grand and widespread as an earthquake, an interplanetary collision, or a war to make the circumstances genuinely objective and thus make room for my subjectivity to take hold of the reins of action.) (75–76)

This is the dream of the sovereign subject: Facing imminent disaster (event as radical interruption), subjectivation becomes possible. A sci-fi version of Badiou's ethical subject: In responding to an event of truth, the subject is constituted through his fidelity to this event.

Or is it? Just as Aira is set to ascend the mountain and reverse the cloning machine, he is confronted by a new event, which calls into question the pseudoevent that he thought was happening to him. Instead of rushing to stop the neon blobs, Nelly suggests that they return to her house to alert Amelina, who is sleeping:

Las palabras de Nelly transportaban una urgencia de realidad que me obligaba a tomar una perspectiva más práctica, como si Amelina realmente existiera. Y existía, sin dudas. . . . Pasó por mi cerebro la imagen de Florencia, mi amor juvenil, la Florencia joven y enamorada que yo había sentido renacer treinta años después en Amelina. . . . Los relevos fantasmales del amor que habían dado forma a mi vida giraban dando forma a un túnel de luz negra en el que me hundía. (89)

(Nelly's words carried with them an urgency of reality that forced me to adopt a more practical perspective, as if Amelina really did exist. And, undoubtedly, she did. . . . The image of Florencia, my childhood love, flitted through my mind, the young and enamored Florencia, whom I felt had been reborn in Amelina thirty years later. . . . Love's ghostly stand-ins, which had shaped my life, were spinning around me, forming a tunnel of black light that I was sinking into.) (84)

Now, this option not only will fail to save the city; it won't even rescue Amelina, who will perish along with the rest of them if Aira doesn't stop the psychedelic worms. Yet he cannot resist: The surprise of the event—the words that conjure the ghost of Amelina once again—forces him to make the ostensibly "unethical" decision of pursuing sentiment over duty, individual over collective good. After an initial euphoria—"En el momento de tomar la decisión, me poseía una euforia casi infantil" (the very instant I made the decision to go, I became possessed by an almost infantile euphoria) (90/84)—he immediately begins to feel ashamed for having abandoned his responsibility to the city in favor of his own selfish desires: "Me sentí un miserable. Todo lo que estaba pasando era culpa mía, y ahora, en lugar de jugarme el todo por el todo para aniquilar la amenaza (era el único que podía hacerlo), me dejaba llevar por un capricho íntimo, sentimental, con una irresponsabilidad que me avergonzaba" (I felt like a scoundrel. Everything that was happening was my fault, and now, instead of putting everything on the line to rid the world of this threat (I was the only one who could do it), I was allowing myself to be carried away by a private, sentimental whim; I was ashamed of my lack of responsibility) (91/86, trans. modified).

This (second) decision, too, *appears* to be consistent with the logic of the event in Badiou (we recall that for Badiou, a truth-event can pertain to one of four categories: politics, art, science, and love). Yet immediately after leaving for Amelina's house, he changes course once again, only this time we are not privy to what has derailed the hero: "Aquí hay un blanco en el relato. No sé lo que pasó en los minutos que siguieron. . . . Lo cierto es que de pronto me encontré treinta o cuarenta metros bajo el nivel de las calles" (Here there is a blank in the story. I don't know what happened in the following few minutes. . . . What I do know is that I suddenly found myself about a hundred feet below street level) (92/87). Instead of reuniting with his beloved muse, Aira finds himself face to face with one of the enormous silkworm clones and, together with Nelly, manages to absorb the worm using an "Exoscope," a prop from the monstrous production of Aira's play. The disappearance of the worm in question causes the elimination of all of the worms, and the public breaks into applause and cries of relief. "La gente lo tomaba por una especie de milagro, pero por supuesto yo sabía que con los clones es así: uno, son todos" (People took it as some kind of miracle, but I, of course, knew that clones were like that: one is all) (95/90).

Thus the narrator-protagonist Aira assumes the typical role of the hero: both literary and extraliterary. He confides to us that, while he has indeed become a kind of hero by taking action (rather than simply writing about it), the miracle is not his but belongs to the logic of cloning ("uno, son todos"). But what has motivated this change of course? And why locate such an event outside the bounds of the narrative (only to signal it *through* the narrative)? What relationship between decision and event is traced in this strange, climactic scene? There is no doubt that decisions are made in *El congreso de literatura*: If anything, there is an *excess* of decisions. But what is the nature of these decisions, who makes them, and what do they decide? Each supposed "event" that takes place in the novel seems briefly to correspond to a Badiouian event, but they each disappear almost as quickly as they appear, and each corresponding decision is displaced by another. Aira's events (and decisions) are simultaneously excessive and scarce, and what seems to be the decisive event happens in a kind of unconscious haze of amnesia.

The "decisive" episode resembles less an event in a Badiouian sense than Derrida's idea of passive, exposed, unconscious decision, an idea he develops as part of a broader critique of sovereign decisionism, exposing the paradoxical relation *between* and *within* decision and event:

> The aporia of the *event* intersects with, but also capitalizes or overdetermines, the aporia of *decision* with regard to the *perhaps*. There is no event, to be sure, that is not preceded and followed by its own perhaps, and that is not as unique, singular and irreplaceable as the decision with which it is frequently associated, notably in politics. But can one not suggest without a facile paradox, that the eventness of an event remains minimal, if not excluded, by a decision? Certainly the decision makes the event, but it also neutralizes this happening that must surprise both the freedom and the will of every subject—surprise, in a word, the very subjectivity of the subject, affecting it wherever the subject is exposed, sensitive, receptive, vulnerable and fundamentally passive, before and beyond any decision—indeed, before any subjectivation or objectivation. (*The Politics of Friendship*, 68)

The aporetic quality of the event is related to the paradoxical kind of decision we have been tracking at the point of mutual exposure of ethics and politics: a decision made *not* by an autonomous will, a conscious sovereign, but (as we have seen throughout *Anarchaeologies*) by the other in me. Decision is thus called a "condition of the event" at the same time that *passive* decision implies an unconditional opening to the demand of the other (the other as *arrivant, à venir*, the incalculable)—a demand that is *also* another name for the event. The passive decision is not made by a conscious ego, but this fact does not force us—or any ego, any responsible subject—to renounce responsibility and obligation: "*In sum, a decision is unconscious—* insane as that may seem, it involves the unconscious and nevertheless remains responsible" (69). In Aira, the moment that seems to determine everything is eclipsed by the protagonist's amnesia or loss of consciousness: As event, or condition of the event, or unconditional condition of the event, the unconscious decision exposes the eventual quality of the machine, the constitutive glitch or error of the cloning plot and thus also of literature, the incalculable that haunts every sovereign decision. I want to underscore, here, the *unconscious* quality of the passive decision we've been tracing throughout *Anarchaeologies*, a quality we can see best, or uniquely, in and through its (allegorical) literary representation.

The event, in Aira's fiction, in Aira's little allegory, neither subjectivizes nor desubjectivizes but rather exhibits a fundamental ambivalence. What is initially thought to be an event (the impending disaster) gives way to a new event (the mention of Amelina's name), which triggers what seems to be *another* event (Aira's decision to pursue her), followed by a final but ultimately evasive event: the moment of, one supposes, a decision that has been eclipsed by the amnesia that haunts the narrative. At the end, order is "restored," but symbolically it has been irreparably altered, or rather it is shown to have been always already altered, interrupted from within. In much the same way that the writer César Aira's complete surrender to the market (he has "a little something for everyone") is linked to an ostensible resistance to or withdrawal from the market (exemplified by the abundance of his novels published by small, independent presses), negating both alternatives (or at least the opposition between them), the slippage *between* and *within* decision and event creates the conditions of possibility *and* impossibility for ethico-political interruption in and from the literary. Like the uncanny adaptation of the narrator's play—indeed, like the cloning machine—allegory in Aira reveals itself to be nothing more (and nothing less) than a translation machine, a machine that bears an eventual quality at the same time that it reveals the machine-like quality of the event. It is here, in Aira's monstrous work, that we can begin to think the possibility of reading the machine—or the reading machine—as (returning to Derrida) a "monstrosity . . . an impossible event" and "therefore the *only* possible event" ("Typewriter Ribbon," 74).

The Aesthetics
and Politics of Error

Había una sola puerta, con un cartel encima que decía:
ERROR. Por ahí salí. No era como en los restaurantes o en los
cines, donde hay dos puertas vecinas, una de 'Damas' y otra de
'Caballeros', y uno elije la que le corresponde. Aquí había una
sola. No había elección. No sé qué palabra debería haber tenido
la otra puerta, cuál habría sido la alternativa de 'error', pero no
importa porque de todos modos no había más que una. Y no
estoy seguro de que yo hubiera elegido la otra, en caso de que la
hubiera. Sea como sea, tengo esa justificación: que era la única
puerta para salir, la que decía 'error'. Y yo tenía que salir. . .

(There was only one door, with a sign above it that read:
ERROR. I exited through there. It wasn't like in restaurants or
movie theaters, where there are two neighboring doors, one for
"Ladies" and the other for "Gentlemen," and one chooses the
door that corresponds. Here there was only one. There was no
choice. I don't know what word the other door should have
had, what the alternative to "error" would have been, but it
didn't matter because in any case there was only one. And I'm
not sure that I would have chosen the other, if there had been
one. Be as it may, I have the following justification: it was the
only door through which to exit, the one marked "error." And I
had to exit. . .)

—César Aira, *El error*[1]

Let us continue to mine Aira for political concepts. In what follows, I want
to consider "error" as a defective political concept, one that would accompany our thinking of defective *ethical* concepts and that would, finally,
contribute to the broader project of unsettling the disciplinary closure of
ethics, politics, and their relation. As I think through what "error" might
mean for a theory of aesthetics or a theory of politics (as a political concept
that we might imagine *through* or *from* the literary), I also want to reflect
upon what it is that we do when we turn to one discourse, practice, discipline, or method to think about another. We might rely upon literature,
or literary discourse, for clues on how to think about a particular concept,
political or otherwise. We might, alternatively, lean on philosophy,
theory, for guidance on how to think about this or that aesthetic practice.
Or we might look to political discourse to help us understand this or that

Andrea Mantegna, *St. Sebastian* (1480), Musée du
Louvre, Paris

philosophical concept. What I want to do is slightly different: I'll start with
an image, Mantegna's depiction of St. Sebastian after he's been pummeled
with arrows, which seem to arrive from all directions at once.

An inverosimile image: We'd expect a saint, a politician, to be crucified,
or to face a firing squad, or to be assassinated by a lone bullet or arrows

emanating from a single point of origin. I'm going to begin with a concept—error—and aim several arrows at it at once, from different directions and different moments. I'll ask how literature (César Aira's *El error*), critical theory (Paul de Man's *Blindness and Insight*), and art activism (the theatrical actions of the Internacional Errorista), can work against, with, and through one another to offer a working definition of error. I won't suggest that "error" is the same for each, nor will I argue that we can arrive at a consolidated definition of "error." Rather, I hope to demonstrate that the concept "error"—indeed, *every* concept—can be thought *only* at the point of mutual exposure or encounter between discourses, disciplines, fields.[2] An encounter between literature and philosophy (to give one example) would expose the constitutive flaw or lack in each (one could say the "error" of each).

Errant Narrative

What if we were to imagine error as something that is *not* chosen deliberately? One *means* to tell the truth, one *tries* to act correctly, but one errs, one "commits" an error (this is different from a mistake, which one "makes"). Is that what Aira's narrator-protagonist describes in this section's epigraph (our first arrow, if you will) when he describes an error-without-alternative, an error-without-truth, a universal error that one has no choice but to commit ("No había elección . . . era la única puerta . . . yo tenía que salir" [7])? What is the particular role of literature, of literary discourse, in the conceptualization of a strangely universal, compulsory (and thus not *decidable*) error?[3] Is the door described by Aira's narrator a door into the literary text, into literary language, a world that has error as its defining quality? Or is the literary text a door, a threshold, an entryway into the error that we all are?

"Había una sola puerta, con un cartel encima que decía: ERROR. Por ahí salí" (There was only one door, with a sign above it that read: ERROR. I exited through there) (7). This is how Aira's *El error* opens: The narrator *exits* through a door marked "error" *into* the novel itself. Not quite an exit into pure exteriority: Indeed, we are accustomed to exiting *out from* and entering *into*. Typically, we imagine *entering* a novel or a world of fiction or fantasy, although this figure might be compatible with the equally tired trope of fiction or fantasy as an *escape from* reality.[4] This will be the first of at least four strange *salidas* or, more precisely, deviations, *errancias*, for each plot abruptly pauses and gives way to another. I count at least four subplots: the story of the narrator and his spouse visiting El Salvador during a moment of crisis in their marriage; the adventure of a Salvadorean outlaw, Pepe Dueñas, the subject of a mural viewed by the married couple; the history of a woman on the run after having murdered her husband; and that of a woman in jail who enters into an epistolary relationship with a sculptor.

In the first of the four plots, the narrator enters/exits into a formal sculpture garden, which strikes him as out of place or senseless in a country as impoverished and unstable as El Salvador:

> Era un tanto incongruente, en un país tan pobre como El Salvador, un jardín formal de esas dimensiones, tan cuidado, tan lujoso. Aunque quizás tenía su razón de ser, en media de la miseria y el caos político: daba trabajo a una legión de empleados estatales, un trabajo que los distraía y les ocupaba la mente. Debía de cumplir también una función simbólica, al desplegar para sus visitantes un orbe de regularidades geométricas, en medio de las sucesivas catástrofes históricas que vivía el país. (10)

> (It was a bit incongruous, in a poor country like El Salvador, a formal garden of those dimensions, so manicured, so luxurious. Although perhaps it had its raison d'être, in the midst of the misery and political chaos: it provided employment to a legion of state workers, a job that distracted them and busied their minds. It must have fulfilled a symbolic function as well, unfurling for its visitors an orbit of geometrical regularities amid the successive historical catastrophes that the country suffered.)

We see already from this passage that aesthetics and politics, the symbolic and the real, exist in an unexpected and "incongruent" relation to each other. In addition to the uncomfortable contrast between luxury and poverty, national political catastrophes are compensated for by the "geometric regularities" of the garden, the luxury of which can perhaps be justified by the fact that it provides employment to numerous state workers. The narrator confesses that he, too, would benefit from the order imposed by the garden: "del orden de un regimen de signos que le diera algún sentido a mis actos" (from the order of a regime of signs that might imbue my acts with meaning) (10). Yet this wished-for symbolic order cannot be delivered by means of the present novel, the structure of which never comes full circle, the conflicts of which are never brought to a resolution but instead ceaselessly open up onto new problems, until the novel is abruptly and unsatisfactorily brought to a conclusion.[5]

The existence of the sculpture garden, the narrator's friend Óscar explains, has indeed drawn protests not for any matter related to the content of the works but rather for its placement: "Óscar se había puesto a nuestro lado y decía que esa instalación permanente de esculturas había levantado protestas en la ciudad. No por el contenido, sino por la ocupación de un lugar público, y el sesgo vanguardista de la obra" (Oscar had taken his place at our side and explained that the permanent installation had caused protests throughout the city. Not because of its content but rather because of its having occupied public space, and to the avant-garde bent of the work) (14–15). The works of art do not pose a threat for their aesthetic content or merit but rather for their misplaced or improper installation in a public space. What threatens about the garden is precisely the uncanny co-belonging of public (the realm of politics) and private (the realm of aesthetics).[6] The garden, which the narrator describes as resembling an abandoned factory full of machines to produce "cosas inimaginables" (unimaginable things) (16), therefore sets a curious scene of art that may be considered politically irresponsible (and thus, as I will argue, politically provocative) for its uselessness but, above all, for its eccentricity, its "out-of-placeness."

The formal displacements of plot in Aira's narrative to which I've alluded take place *within* as well as *between* each subplot, and the narrator and his friend find themselves suddenly facing a mural on the wall of a nearby café. The narrator struggles to interpret the painting, before which he'd hoped to confide in his friend the secret of his marital crisis. He thinks better of confessing (what if the story were to get out? stories are known to rebel against their authors and wander off, *errar* . . .), and instead they discuss the mural, which the narrator struggles to understand. It is only when they cease to speak about the mural that interpretation becomes possible: "Paradójicamente, fue cuando dejamos de hablar del mural y pasamos a otros temas cuando empecé a discernir las figuras y las historias que ilustraban" (Paradoxically, it was when we ceased to talk about the mural and shifted to other topics that I began to discern the figures and histories that it illustrated) (27). Interpretation-as-decision, here, can also be thought through the (defective) concept of passive or unconscious decision: As soon as the narrator ceases to *try* to make out the figures in the mural, he begins to detect a possible meaning.

The link between *historia* and image, narrative and painting, finds a curious echo in other recent works of Aira (I am thinking of "Picasso," and *Triano*, which I discuss further on), which ponder the strange rapport between genres and media. Here, as in "Picasso," Aira dwells upon the way the passage of time might be represented in painting: "La repetición de su figura indicaba una sucesión temporal" (The repetition of its figure indicated a temporal succession) (27). Yet if temporality is precisely what might

distinguish narrative from painting, and if the painting that could somehow represent time would prove "more" readable, here we find the opposite case: "Un cuadro así era difícil de contar, precisamente porque
intentaba reproducir la técnica de un cuento" (A painting like this was
difficult to recount, precisely because it sought to reproduce the technique
of a story) (28). Paradoxically, a painting that approximates narrative turns
out to be *more* difficult to interpret than one that eludes narrative coherence or linear time.

The difficulty does not hinder the narrator, however, who, using the
mural's alleged opacity as a point of departure for his analysis, explains that
"En este mural, Pepe Dueñas, Dante sin Virgilio, vengador solitario de las
injusticias sociales salvadoreñas, se repetía en un paisaje boscoso" (In this
mural, the figure of Pepe Dueñas, Dante without Virgil, solitary avenger
of Salvadorean social injustices, repeated itself in a wooded landscape) (30).
Faithful to the politically themed history of its genre, the mural tells the
story of the quest for social justice and, in an exceptional moment for the
novel, anticipates one of its future subplots: one of a handful of momentary
flashes of coherence and clarity of signification amid an otherwise enigmatic, wandering narrative. But aesthetic and political readability are ultimately avoided or eclipsed in *El error* in favor of an aesthetics and politics
of opacity, equivocation. The particular version of opacity, in Aira, is
through the image of the "paisaje boscoso"—a forest-like (or *Bosch*-like
landscape)—which, in addition to imagining a Virgil-less Dante, a poet
without his classical guide, ("En medio del camino de nuestra vida / me
encontré en un oscuro bosque, / ya que la vía recta estaba perdida" [Mid-
way upon the journey of our life / I found myself within a forest dark, / For
the straightforward pathway had been lost]) recalls Dante's words within
the setting of Hieronymus Bosch's fantastically perverse triptych *The Garden of Earthly Delights*.

Rather than account for the entire novel, the structure of which makes
accountability impossible, I'll jump to one last scene that allegorizes "error"
in order to consider its consequences for politics *through* or *from* literature
(as well as, we might add, literature *through* or *from* politics). The final
subplot, as I've mentioned, involves the imprisonment and subsequent
release of a woman accused of an unnamed crime. She can't imagine how
her minor, private offense can measure up to the massive, public crimes
taking place across the country:

No terminaba de convencerse, con una sensación de perpleja incredulidad,
de que su crimen privado y particular siguiera importando cuando arreciaban

los combates, las bajas se contaban por centenares cada día, menudeaban los
bombardeos, los fusilamientos ilegales y las degollinas. ¿Se habían encar-
nizado con ella? ¿O la estarían tomando como un caso testigo, para mantener
la fachada de una ficticia legalidad? (80–81)

(She didn't quite convince herself, with a feeling of perplexed disbelief, that
her private, individual crime would continue to matter when the fighting
intensified, the casualties were counted by the hundreds each day, the bomb-
ings, the illegal shootings, the slaughters were frequent. Were they attacking
her? Or were they making her case an example to maintain the façade of a
fictitious legality?)

After a month of captivity—carried out, she reasons, in order to uphold
the "fiction" of legality on a broader, national scale—the woman is inex-
plicably set free. Just as her arrest strikes her as senseless, asymmetrical, so
too does her release seem erroneous. "Su liberación había sido un error,"
the narrator writes: "El modo más vigoroso de pedirle perdón fue asegu-
rarle que no habría más errores y que se pasaría el resto de su vida presa"
(Her release had been an error. . . . The most vigorous way to ask for
forgiveness was to assure her that there would be no more errors and that
she'd spend the rest of her life in prison) (85).

After the woman's (possibly mistaken) release, however, the narrator
continues to recount the goings-on in jail, where the prisoners read defective books donated by publishers: "Las presas, leyendo a su paso lentísimo,
encontraban un día al volver una hoja, una página en blanco; su poca fre-
cuentación de libros las llevaba a creer que era lo normal y que así debía
ser" (The women prisoners, reading at a very slow pace, found one day
when they turned the page a blank page; their inexperience with books led
them to believe that this was normal and how it should be) (90). As
unlearned readers, the prisoners take the defective books to be the norm;
the crimes related in the books, consequently, seem "lighter" because of
the blank pages: "Los crímenes mismos, tan abundantes en las páginas de
esas novelas (al menos en las páginas que no habían quedado en blanco), se
volvían livianos y sin consecuencias (las páginas en blanco, justamente,
escamoteaban consecuencias, y muchas veces la falta quedaba sin castigo
gracias a ellas)" (The crimes themselves, so abundant in the pages of those
novels (at least on the pages that weren't blank), became light and without
consequences (the blank pages, as it happened, took away the consequences,
and often the crime was left without a punishment as a result)) (92). The
blank pages give the impression of a skewed justice—crimes appear to go
without punishment—but in fact this is precisely how the narrator has

characterized the political climate in El Salvador. The flawed pages of the crime novels—in addition to suggesting the spectral presence of murdered and disappeared insurgents—mirror the fiction of justice projected by the Salvadorean legal system (as well as, hauntologically, Argentina's). Error, therefore, serves not only as the constitutive trait of literature but of justice as well. Reading, or misreading, then, offers a possible avenue into political critique. Yet do we *need* literature, or literary theory, to alert us to the constitutive flaws of the law? Can literature or literary theory claim authority over politics or authorship of the concepts we fashion in order to understand politics? What would it mean to read political theory in the work of Paul de Man, the man who brought deconstruction from philosophy to the field of literary criticism? How can de Man be read as an unwitting political theorist, given that a redemptive ethico-political quality was attributed to deconstruction to exonerate it following the discovery of de Man's wartime journalism supporting the European fascist cultural program?

Error and Blindness

I claimed in the preceding section, somewhat clumsily, that "error" is a conceptual cousin of "misunderstanding"—and perhaps of marranismo, or marrano reading, as well. In his 1971 collection of essays *Blindness and Insight*, Paul de Man (slightly less clumsily) marshals a collection of concepts, if not interchangeably, as synonyms, then as a sort of rhetorical performance of differential repetition. This conceptual cluster, or cluster of concepts—blindness, error, misunderstanding, misreading, among others—serve, for de Man, as irreducible names for literature, and for the deconstructive reading of literature, and, later, of the literariness even of nonliterary texts: a reading practice that engages with the blind spots, errors, of the literary text in order to expose their relation to the text's (unwitting, unintentional) insights.[7] This will be our second scene, our second arrow. In one of *Blindness and Insight*'s most provocative essays, "The Rhetoric of Blindness: Jacques Derrida's Reading of Rousseau," de Man locates such errors at the core of the literary tradition: "The existence of a particularly rich aberrant tradition . . . is . . . no accident," he claims, "but a constitutive part of all literature, the basis, in fact, of literary history" (141). Several decades later, in "Literary Misunderstandings" (an essay that, as I have discussed, seeks to respond to the question "Does literature have a particular relationship with misunderstanding as a form?"), Jacques Rancière makes the slightly different but, in my view, compatible argument that gaps in understanding are in fact constitutive of language and thus of literature (and interpretation). Yet while Rancière draws a clear distinction between a concept of "misunderstanding" that implies and depends upon an opposing concept of "understanding" (which he critiques) and one that is constitutive of literary language and therefore a kind of strange universal, de Man uses "error" to refer *both* to "bad" readings, the readings that serve as the object of his critique, *and* to the insightful readings (often his own!) that he'll privilege.

Stanley Corngold addresses this ambivalence in his 1982 "Error in Paul de Man," in which he claims that de Man contrasts "error" with "mistake" or "mere error," and then seeks to correct several of de Man's mistakes. De Man responds that the effort to draw such a distinction is itself misguided, erroneous, and that he prefers to inhabit the undecidable territory between such false opposites:

> The refusal to decide between them, since it is itself a conceptual rather than a contingent decision, is always already a choice for error over mistake. Conversely, any decision one makes with regard to the absolute truth or falsehood value of a text always turns out to be a mistake. And it will remain one unless the perpetrator of the mistake becomes critically aware of the abusive schematization that caused his mistake and thus transforms the mistaking of error (for mistake) into the error of mistaking. ("Letter," 511)

It would seem that de Man *does* indeed draw a distinction between error (related to a *refusal* to decide) and mistake, here synonymous with a "decision." Here, he's characterizing two modes of reading: one that would insist upon its "truth" (or falsehood) and one that would remain undecidable, even though he makes such a distinction playfully, dancing with and juggling the concepts, performing the undecidability to which he refers constatively.

At the same time, a current of tension runs through "The Rhetoric of Blindness," for isn't de Man claiming authority to *decide* which critics have read blindly? Doesn't he carry out his critique of such blind readings as a sort of corrective, even if he does so in the service of guarding the blind, erroneous qualities of both text and reading? He describes contradictions internal to the literary text as nondialectical ("the one always lay hidden within the other as the sun lies hidden within a shadow, or truth within error") and then seems to invest *himself* with the authority to see:

> Their critical stance . . . is defeated by their own critical results. A penetrating but difficult insight into the nature of literary language ensues. It seems, however, that this insight could only be gained because the critics were in

the grip of this peculiar blindness: their language could grope toward a certain degree of insight only because their method remained oblivious to the
perception of this insight. . . . To write critically about critics thus becomes a
way to reflect on the paradoxical effectiveness of a blinded vision that has to
be rectified by means of insights that it unwittingly provides. (106)

In principle, this is a radical statement on the power of interpretation. It
can only be argued, or most powerfully argued, through the *multiplication*
of readings, through the critical readings of critical readings carried out by
de Man.

De Man concludes the essay with the following statement:

The existence of a particularly rich aberrant tradition in the case of the
writers who can legitimately be called the most enlightened, is therefore no
accident, but a constitutive part of all literature, the basis, in fact, of literary
history. And since interpretation is nothing but the possibility of error, by
claiming that a certain degree of blindness is part of the specificity of all literature we also reaffirm the absolute dependence of the interpretation on
the text and of the text on the interpretation. (141)

Here, de Man not only makes the claim that literature exhibits the constitutive quality of blindness, error, aberration; he makes the secondary
(really, primary) claim that literary criticism necessarily participates in this
aberrant tradition by reading for blind spots. Reading for the possibility of
error should be understood in a double sense: first, that error is always
possible, I may be proven wrong, and second, that error can also be a source
of possibility, error makes things possible.[8] Of course, we could also be
talking about the *impossibility* of error, if by error we mean a deliberately
chosen decision to make a mistake or to commit an error—in that sense
error is impossible, since my decision to err is necessarily not itself an error
when I make it (it may prove to be a mistake at some later point, but by
virtue of the fact that I am deciding now on this or that thing, I can't be
said to be in error yet, to be mistaken yet—error never coincides with
itself—it only reveals itself as error after the fact).[9]

What seems to be missing from de Man's account of error and/as blindness, however, is an allusion to the possibility of a critical reading of *de
Man's* critical reading (of critical readings). If there is *always* the possibility
of error, if, as de Man asserts, the work of interpretation is infinite, unend-
ing ("an endless process in which truth and falsehood are inextricably
intertwined" [ix]), more would need to be done, rhetorically, to guard a
structural opening in his *own* argument: a formal gap that would point to

the possibility of *de Manian* error. Is this merely a question of tone, or style? Surely de Man "knows" what he is doing.[10] The question then becomes, as I've already begun to suggest, the role of *intention* (and the related concept of *decision*) in the production of error, a problem that implies a series of consequences in the realm of literature and quite another set of problems in the field of politics.

Todos Somos Erroristas

This brings us to our third and final arrow, which seems to fly from and fall squarely in that field, the field of politics. In 2005, a group of activists formed in Buenos Aires under the name La Internacional Errorista. An offshoot of the Grupo Etcétera, a collective founded in 1997 by artists hailing from the areas of theater, visual arts, poetry, and music,[11] the Internacional carried out their first *acción teatral*[12] against George W. Bush during his visit to Mar del Plata in 2005.

Desembarco, Internacional Errorista, Mar del Plata (Operación B.A.N.G, Cumbre de las Americas, Mar del Plata, Argentina, 2005. Foto: Archivo Etcétera)

Protesting the US president's "War on Terror," the group thought to unite under the banner "Todos somos terroristas" (We are all terrorists), but—thanks to a typographic error—claimed to be *erroristas* instead.[13] The manifesto joins the long tradition of aesthetic-political manifestos from avant-garde movements on both sides of the Atlantic without grounding itself in the radical *break* that these *vanguardias* proposed.

Manifiesto Errorista

Internacional Errorista

1 – Todos somos Erroristas.
2 – El Errorismo basa su acción en el Error.
3 – El Errorismo es una posición filosófica equivocada. Ritual de la negación. Una organización desorganizada.
4 – El campo de acción del Errorismo abarca todas las prácticas que tiendan hacia la LIBERACIÓN del ser humano y del lenguaje.
5 – La falla como perfección, el error como acierto.
7 – El Errorismo: No Existe y Existe. Se acerca y se aleja. Se crea y se autodestruye. Se asume en viejas y nuevas formas. (a veces no da explicaciones y quizás, también es muy banal) (*Manifiesto Errorista*, 6)

Errorist International

1 – We are all Errorists.
2 – Errorism bases its action in Error.
3 – Errorism is a philosophically erroneous position. Ritual of negation. A disorganized organization.
4 – The field of action of Errorism contains all those practices that aim at the LIBERATION of the human being and language.
5 – Failure as perfection, error as delight.
7 – Errorism: Does Not Exist and Exists. One approximates and y [*sic*] one removes. One believes and one self-destroys. One assumes in old and new forms. (sometimes does not give explanations and perhaps, also is very banal.) (*Manifiesto Errorista*, 15–16, errors in original

Rather than a governing logic of rupture, there is, instead, a governing logic of spectrality, hauntology: The collective plays with—irreverently, parodically, and spectrally—the missing "t" that haunts their name, "una 't' no-teclada." "El errorismo nació por error," they recall, blaming or crediting contingency for their very existence. They go a step further to suggest that *all* existence has a great, haunting error at its core, its constitutive trait. "Todos somos erroristas," they write and chant, parroting and parodying past (and present) political slogans of solidarity based on identification (and on the consequent abolition of difference): "Nous *sommes* tous des *juifs allemands*," "Todos somos Ayotzinapa," "Je suis Charlie," etc. "Todos somos erroristas," it would seem, makes a universal, even identitarian claim while simultaneously alluding to the potential fallacy of the statement (if we are all *erroristas*, if error is what defines us, keeps us, this statement, too, may be an error or equivocation).

The *erroristas*, then, not only propose a new mode of activism; they critique what has often served as the ground for politics: identity, agreement, consensus. Employing humor to disrupt such a politics of consensus and sameness, the group proposes—and performs—a politics of *dissensus*. I am interested in the performative linguistic play of the movement, what the *erroristas* call *palabra-acción* (inseparable from their theatrical actions on the street), linking error to dissensus and, especially, to misunderstanding. We can begin to trace an unexpected but productive rapport between the *erroristas*, de Manian error, and Rancièrian misunderstanding and dissensus, the simultaneous, cross-arrowed reading of which makes possible a new way of thinking about the rapport between aesthetics and politics, a relation not grounded in recognition or readability but (un)grounded in disidentification, unreadability, and misrecognition.[14]

The gap, or error, at the core of *every* community, *every* collective, *every* universal that the *errorista* slogan seems to indicate can be traced back to the foundational linguistic or literary error of the group: an error whose intentionality we cannot determine. Was there a decision, a poetic-political intention, to omit the "t" of "terror," or was it left out by accident and then deliberately left uncorrected? In neither case is there a *lack* of intention, of political calculation; rather, we see that the intention can be interrupted, hijacked: Perhaps it is always interrupted. Sovereign decisionism begins to look very different once this possibility is granted. And if we grant it, the political force of error—indeed, what makes it utterly terrifying—is precisely its incalculability, its undecidability. Such undecidability reappears in the manifesto's anarchic oppositions ("organización desorganizada"), poetic antitheses ("error como acierto"), and logical impossibilities ("no existe y existe") as well as in the group's equivocal use of "error" more broadly: on the one hand, as object of critique and denunciation (on the bicentennial they celebrate "200 años de un error"), and as a defective universal, on the other.[15]

In this sense, the *erroristas* are not altogether unlike the de Man we see in his response to Corngold when they refuse to decide between different modes of error. This may be attributable to what we could call the poetic or literary quality of their discourse. We've seen that the collective, composed of artists hailing from different genres and media, employs aesthetic strategies such as antithesis, logical tactics like paradox or contradiction in their written texts, and theatrical elements in their *acciones*. While de Man talks about the specificity of literary language in *Blindness and Insight*, he does not restrict it to a particular discourse: Lukács, Blanchot, and Derrida can also be read as "literary," he argues, insofar as their writings exhibit the blindness we witness in literary texts (*Blindness and Insight*, 141). If we can assign a "literary" quality to political discourse (such as that of the *erroristas*), then, might we also be able to identify political theory in literature (such as Aira's) or literary criticism (de Man's)?

The errancy that takes a narrative form in Aira, the *salida* with which the novel opens, when coupled with the subsequent plot digressions, can be understood not as an exit to pure exteriority but as an errancy or exposure, a going off course that threatens to compromise the integrity or autonomy of what preceded it or to reveal the fact that it was never whole, autonomous to begin with. I began with the image of the arrows aimed at St. Sebastian from multiple, even unexpected angles and then "took aim" at the concept of "error" from multiple angles myself. I suggested that this model of imagining political concepts, by deviating from its classical "place" in philosophy, might offer a promising avenue for thinking not only because of its deviation or errancy into other, less "likely" fields—narrative, literary theory, activism—but also, more precisely, because none of these fields (genres, disciplines) becomes a stable, privileged mode of thought. I am not arguing that it is only through literature that we can conceive of new political concepts, thus reifying "literature" as a system and "literary criticism" as a discipline and offering one or both as the ground of (a new) politics. Nor am I claiming that literary theory, through the politically problematic figure of Paul de Man, can provide a more adequate method for political thought. Nor, finally, am I reversing, and thus reproducing, the theory/practice divide by claiming that "true" politics can only be theorized "outside," "on the street." I am claiming, rather, that it is only through the "possibility of error" that literature opens, through multiple erring and errancies, through the mutual exposure between genres, disciplines, fields, that the internal errors or flaws of each can be exposed, which then serve as the condition of possibility for thinking. "Error" can then be understood as a political concept, but it is a political concept that exposes the error or flaw within itself and therefore within all political concepts: If we imagine "error" politically, so, too, may we imagine politics to turn upon the possibility of *error*.

Where, exactly, does thinking, inasmuch as thinking means producing the "theory" of this "possibility of error," happen? Is the possibility for thought opened up in the university, on the street, in a novel or an artist's studio, or in the murky spaces in which they meet or clash? The exposure of one discipline to another, the turn from one discourse to another—a turn that implies a decision, even an erroneous decision, an errant, *wandering* decision—enables us to do more than unsettle the boundary between disciplines, languages, genres. It allows us, I want to suggest as a mode of conclusion, to (un)ground the politics of identification in, and by means of, "possibility," unreadability, and misrecognition. The aesthetic, logical, and performative paradoxes, antitheses, and overdetermined effects that the exposure of one discipline to another throw out allow us to confront the unsettled and unsettling error, the terrible and terrifying error—*(t)error*—within each discipline, which is also to say each expression of an interest or each way of making a claim, epistemological or political, and then to ask what kind of thought, what kind of thinking such exposure makes possible. If the richest translations carry within them the untranslatable qualities of the translated text, if the most astute critical readings include what is unreadable in the literary text, we can now imagine that in the realm of politics, the most promising—but also the riskiest—decisions might just be those that guard within them a fundamental undecidability, the possibility of error.[16]

Part V. Exposure and Indisciplinarity

Toward a Passive University

> Is a new type of university responsibility possible?
> —Jacques Derrida, "Mochlos; or, The Conflict of the Faculties"

> The passivity prior to the passivity-activity alternative, more passive than any inertia, is described by the ethical terms accusation, persecution, and responsibility for the others.
> —Emmanuel Levinas, *Otherwise than Being*

In their 2013 book *The Slow Professor: Challenging the Culture of Speed in the Academy*, two Canadian professors of English brought the "slow movement" from the culinary world to academia. Citing the relatively new pressures of the "corporate" or "managerial" university (the university of "excellence" or "quality") and noting that many faculty members find themselves spending a great part of their days evaluating their colleagues, preparing reports on "learning objectives" and "outcomes measurements," answering emails, writing memos, or becoming familiar with a new online system of evaluation or management, Maggie Berg and Barbara Seeber proposed, in a kind of manifesto, that we resist such pressures through the intentional incorporation of slowness into our professional lives.

They were not the first, of course, to take on the problem of the corporate university: Bill Readings outlines the possibility of critique of the discourse of "excellence" in *The University in Ruins*, although Gary Rolfe sees this approach as insufficiently critical, proposing instead the idea of the "paraversity," a "ghost within the machine of the University of Excellence," which would allow for a more radical critique of the contemporary institution. Ronald Barnett, for his part, proposes the "ungovernable" or "anarchic university" to counter the bureaucratic university, which forecloses the possibility of thought (93).[1] Fred Moten and Stefano Harney, finally—and, to my view, most convincingly—contend that most lamentations over the state of the university (Harold Bloom or Stanley Fish or Gerald Graff, who call for its restoration, or Derek Bok or Bill Readings or Cary Nelson, who prefer reform) take place in genteel, polite conversations among men around boardroom tables, and so Moten and Harney turn to what they imagine to be the underground university, "the downlow lowdown maroon community of the university . . . the Undercommons of Enlightenment, where the work gets done, where the work gets subverted, where the revolution is still black, still strong" (102). Berg and Seeber, in contrast, don't aim to revolutionize the university in any kind of collective way; they seem most concerned with the psychic health of its employees, so that *The Slow Professor* can be read as a kind of self-help book for individual university professors. Allowing time for "reflection, deliberation, and dialogue," they suggest, can create the conditions for deep thinking, pleasure in reading and teaching, and even the possibility of *doing nothing* every once in a while.

Many of us recognize ourselves in the picture painted by Berg and Seeber. If we are university professors today—either on the tenure track or in the more precarious categories of academic labor—we spend countless hours every semester evaluating ourselves and others, conforming to the quantitative machine that is the contemporary university. We are all caught up in the relentless pace of the machine described in *The Slow Professor*. It seems worthwhile asking, however, what we mean when we turn to the temporal metaphor of slowness to signify the possibility of resistance to (against, within) the corporate university. The same could be said about spatial metaphors: Those of us in the field of literary criticism continue to debate the merits of close reading (in Spanish, *lectura detenida*, "slow" or "halted" or "arrested reading") versus surface or distance reading. Yet beyond its metaphorical or rhetorical force, the discourse of temporality—in which slowness and speed are opposed—can be quite limiting. Is there any academic who has not had the experience of writing a conference paper, or essay, or even a book under pressure— perhaps internal pressure—which he or she can nevertheless stand behind? How do we know whether our work will be, or will always already have been, captured by the logic of the university "of excellence"? If I write furiously for ten years, have I worked more slowly than if I write calmly for one month?

While I imagine that most of us are in agreement with Berg and Seeber's diagnosis of the problem of the contemporary university, it seems worthwhile to consider other metaphors or defective concepts that would allow us to conceive of *another* university: the (im)possible university. In what follows, I'll return one last time to the related ideas of passivity and exposure, this time to think through the problem of the university. I'll pass quickly, or slowly, through Kant, Levinas, and Derrida, in order to imagine the possibility of an institution whose foundation is passive, anarchic,

What Derrida suggests in *Mochlos* is different, more specific perhaps, than what we find later in *The Politics of Friendship*. There, Derrida—exposed to Levinas, who is in turn exposing his argument to Derrida's critique of his work—offers not just an abstract notion of the ethical non-subject but the strange subject formed in and by (a particular inheritor of) the Kantian university. In "Mochlos" Derrida asks: "Is a new type of university responsibility possible?" (11). He means, we see through the later texts, through *The Politics of Friendship* and through *Rogues*, a passive, exposed responsibility. Is it possible, in, through, and for the university? Is a new type of university responsibility possible that is neither based upon the classical concepts of ethics and politics nor in the related concepts of subjectivity and recognition? I propose that we imagine, together, a university that would be grounded, or ungrounded, in misrecognition, in error, misunderstanding, and untranslatability. A university that would neither be divided into autonomous, sovereign, self-sufficient disciplines nor dissolved into that intellectual poverty called interdisciplinarity, a practice that—at least in its current forms—reproduces disciplinary boundaries and hierarchies while weakening thought and without destabilizing anything.

When we think, together, another (im)possible university, a responsible, passive, exposed university, we begin to respond to some of these questions, even when the response is negative, to form a kind of strange, eccentric community based in nonidentification and contingency, to expose ourselves to reading but also to read for exposure. In a sense, then, from within the university as currently constituted, asking after another university is to proceed both responsibly and irresponsibly according to the norms of the actually existing university. We read together after the defective, untranslatable qualities in texts, in concepts, in disciplines, and this endeavor might lead to the formation of another kind of university, or it might constitute that university, or a fold, a possible fold, in *this* university. An "exposed" university. We would mean by that not only the university's exposure to other institutions or to other ethico-political demands apparently exterior to the university—a recent image that comes to mind is the group of USC Law School faculty who rushed to the airport immediately following Trump's Muslim travel ban—but also, crucially, an *internal* exposure. Such internal exposure could take the form of internal ethical responsibility—I recall when USC faculty sat on the ground, listening passively to students of color shout and cry and recite poetry on the morning of November 10, 2016—but it could also be thought

Students of Color Teach-in, University of Southern California, November 10, 2016

institutionally, disciplinarily—as a circumstance in which the exposure of
one discipline to another would reveal the defective quality of the sovereignty or autonomy of each, the "points of untranslatability" that simultaneously constitute and unsettle disciplinary thinking.

An indisciplined or indisciplinary university in which literary studies,
moribund, would find an afterlife through its exposure to other practices
and discourses, such as philosophical discourse, and philosophy, moribund,
would find an afterlife through its exposure to aesthetic discourse.[2] An
exposed university, in which we would begin to think new concepts—
weak, erroneous concepts—of ethics and politics, in which we privilege
thought, thinking, over university knowledge (Villalobos-Ruminott,
"Genealogies of Difference"). "If there is a university responsibility, it at
least begins with the moment when a need to hear these questions, to take
them upon oneself and respond, is imposed," Derrida writes (3). Is it possible to imagine a university constituted by responsibility and radical hospitality, an institution based on, in the words of Emmanuel Biset that we
glossed earlier, "the always imperfect translation into laws of a radical
hospitality that is never identified with or identical to its laws" (39,

translation mine)? How do we begin to pursue, both performatively and constatively, the task of interdisciplinary and indisciplinary exposure, a task that would at once expose the wounded quality of political sovereignty as well as the sovereignty of the disciplines?

To conclude, let's return to the strange humor of César Aira for an example of what I'm calling indisciplinary thinking. As I've discussed, I'm interested in Aira's work not only because of his unorthodox, playful relation to writing and the market; because of his excessive publishing record (he averages three to four books per year; he is unquestionably a "fast," not a "slow," writer); because of his engagement with visual and digital cultural forms (his is a literature *of* and *against* neoliberalism, *of* and *after* literature); but also because his works theorize—obliquely, comically, unexpectedly—crucial political concepts such as sovereignty and decisionism, identity and singularity, repetition and event. His work is meta-political, in a sense I have borrowed from Rancière: As we have seen in my discussion of *El congreso de literatura* and *El error*, we cannot identify explicit political (ideological, "content-based") commitment in his work, nor should we. Rather, the overproductive Aira gives us clues to political concepts through *exposure*, both performative and constative; specifically, through the performance and articulation of a strange, aporetic bond between exposure and secrecy, providing a way into the thinking of an in-disciplined or indisciplinary university.

Let's turn, together, to two recent works of short fiction by Aira— "Picasso" (2006) and *Triano* (2010)—both of which dwell within and thematize the strange zone of contact between distinct artistic genres. In each work, visual arts, specifically, cubist painting, and narrative confront each other in a humorous, shocking encounter in which the traits and limits of each are exposed in its relation to the other, so that narrative discovers its cubist asymmetries and cubism encounters its poetic and narrative secrets. This unsettling of genres, which takes place at a moment of crisis or "emergency" for the "book," the "novel," or "literature" more broadly, sheds crucial light upon the related concepts of identity, sovereignty, and decisionism, and it allows us to think newly, again, about politics *after* literature. Cubism, or literary cubism, serves as a kind of *topos* through which to imagine these new possibilities of thinking.

The short story or fable "Picasso," which appears in Aira's *Relatos reunidos* as well as, more recently, in translation in the *New Yorker*, recounts the humorous tale of a visitor to the Picasso Museum who is visited by a genie from his Magic Milk bottle in the museum café. The genie grants him a wish in the form of a decision: to have a Picasso or to *be* Picasso. A dicey

Pablo Picasso, *Portrait of a Woman* (1910) (© 2018 Estate of Pablo Picasso / Artists Rights Society (ARS), New York)

dilemma, for which the narrator finds himself wholly unprepared: "No hay bibliografía ni antecedentes serios en los que basarse para decidir porque esas cosas sólo pasan en cuentos o chistes, no en la realidad" (There are no records or reliable precedents on which to base a decision, because this sort of thing happens only in stories or jokes) (23), he writes, recalling that he had only ever considered the three-wishes scenario, "el clásico" (23). He carefully considers the pros and cons: On the one hand, the latter would encompass the former, given that if he were to *be* Picasso he would also *have* a Picasso, *many* Picassos, in fact. He contemplates becoming a kind of über-Picasso, which he imagines to be more appealing than the fate of any other individual, even kings or presidents, because "éstos estaban amenazados por la política o la Guerra, mientras que el poder de Picasso, sublimando el de cualquier presidente o rey, estaba libre de problemas" (they can be removed by political events or wars, while the power of Picasso, transcending that of any president or king, was invulnerable) (24). This idea of transcendent, aesthetic sovereignty ultimately horrifies him, however, and besides, he reasons, it might be difficult to become someone else, to have to learn how to deal with an entirely new set of manias and neuroses when he only just barely copes with his own. This leads to a further problem, which is the problem of identity:

En el fondo, la situación era un caso extremo del problema de la identificación, que va más allá del maestro ya que se plantea ante cada artista admi-
rado o venerado o estudiado. Va más allá, pero al mismo tiempo se queda en
Picasso. La identificación es una de esas cosas que no se pueden generalizar.
No hay identificación en general, como concepto, sino que la hay en particular con esta o aquella figura. Y si esa figura es Picasso, como lo es,
entonces no hay ninguna otra. El concepto se invierte sobre sí mismo como
si dijéramos . . . que no se trata de "la identificación con Picasso" sino de
"el Picasso de la identificación." (25)

(Fundamentally, this was an extreme case of the problem of identification,
which is raised not only by the master of Málaga but by every artist one
admires or venerates or studies. The problem goes beyond Picasso, and yet
remains within him, too. Identification is one of those things which can't be
generalized. There is no identification in general, as a concept, only identification with this or that figure in particular. And if the figure is Picasso, as in
this case, there can be no other. The concept turns itself inside out, as if we
were to say . . . that it's not about "identifying with Picasso" but about
"Picassifying identification.")

For the narrator, Picasso represents both radical alterity (becoming Picasso
would entail a renunciation of his "self") and the possibility of shared traits,
of shared particularity, in this case a tendency toward overproduction to
compensate for a paralysis of the will when it comes to small tasks such as
picking up a loose sheet of paper that's fallen to the ground. (We'll see, as
the story develops, that this contradictory understanding of singularity and
universality, of autonomy and heteronomy, can be thought through using
the question of genre.)

The narrator finally makes a decision, or rather, the decision is made for
him: "Mi decisión estaba tomada" (My mind was made up), he declares
using the passive voice, "Quería un Picasso" (I wanted a Picasso) (26).
These two sentences, in which decision is the subject of the first and the
narrator, through his desire, the subject of the second, establishes from the
outset an ambivalent account of autonomy. On the one hand, the narrator
knows, or states that he knows, what he wants; on the other, the decision
seems to be made passively. As soon as the narrator articulates this strange,
desirous, passive decision—"Mi decisión estaba tomada. Quería un Picasso," a decision against übersovereignty made by a passive sovereign—a
Picasso appears in his hands. The images in the painting accost him
delightfully, a chaotic mix of shapes he describes as at once wild and har-
monious, shapes that continually emerge and then return into hiding.

It is here that Aira begins to anticipate the eponymous painter-maestro of his 2010 novel *Triano*, who lectures the teenage poet-narrator César and his friend Arturo on the significance of cubism for theology, physics, and, above all, literature. Triano—whose cubist paintings are exhibited accompanied by César and Arturo's poetry in a small, hidden back room of the local library—explains the introduction of time into painting by cubism: "Elimina lo simultáneo. Es como si hiciera un relato visual" (Cubism eliminates simultaneity. As if it were creating a visual story) (33). In "Picasso," the narrator insists that the formal qualities of the painting "no hacían más que invitar a una exploración del contenido narrativo" (were merely an invitation to explore its narrative content) (26), the details of which reveal themselves to the narrator little by little, like hieroglyphics:

> El primero fue una flor, una rosa carmesí, asomando de la multiplicación de sus propios planos cubistas, que eran los pétalos; enfrentado, en espejo, un jazmín en blancos virginals, renancentista salvo por las volutas en ángulos rectos de sus zarcillos. En la habitual colisión picassiana de figura y fondo, hombrecitos moluscos y hombrecitos chivos llenaban el espacio, con sombreros emplumados, jubones, calzas, o bien armaduras gorros de cascabeles de bufón, también alguno desnudo, enanos y barbudos; era una escena de corte, y la figura que la presidia tenía que ser la reina, a juzgar por la corona, la reina monstruosa y desvencijada como un juguete roto; pocas veces la torsión del cuerpo femenino, uno de los rasgos más característicos de Picasso, había sido llevada a semejante extremo. Piernas y brazos le salían por la espalda, los rasos multicolores del vestido se le incrustaban en el molinete del torso, un pie calzado en un zapatón de taco saltaba al cielo . . . (27)

> (First, there was a flower, a crimson rose, emerging from the multiple cubist planes of its petals; facing it, like a mirror image, was a jasmine in virginal whites, painted in Renaissance style, except for the right-angled spirals of its tendrils. In a collision of figure and ground, typical of Picasso, the space between was filled with little snail-men and goat-men, wearing plumed hats, doublets and breeches, or armor; one wore a fool's cap and bells; there were nude figures, too, dwarflike and bearded. Over this court scene presided a figure who must have been the queen, to judge by her crown: a monstrous broken-down queen, like a damaged toy. Rarely had the distortion of the female body, one of Picasso's trademarks, been taken to such an extreme. Legs and arms stuck out of her any old way, her navel and her nose were chasing each other across her back, the windmill of her torso was inlaid with the multicolored satins of her dress, and one foot, encased in an enormous high-heeled shoe, shot up skyward . . .)

He soon recognizes in the mess of horticulture and monarchy a traditional Spanish tale or joke (recall that the premise of this very story, the story of the genie in the museum, *also* struck the narrator as a scenario only possible in tales or jokes). The tale, or joke, a version of which is attributed to Quevedo, goes like this in Aira's version: There is a queen who is lame, but none of her subjects dare to reveal this awful truth to her, until the minister of the Interior comes up with a plan. (We might ask, if we had more time, why the queen's subjects fear revealing her secret to her or, more curiously, what sadistic subjection compels them to reveal her secret to her, to subject her to this exposure and shame. Who is subject and who subjected?) Upon the minister's suggestion, they organize a flower contest, in which the greatest botanists of the kingdom present their bounty to the queen, who serves as judge. After a series of rounds, two flowers remain—a rose and a jasmine—which are displayed to the queen so that she may choose a winner. The minister approaches the queen, places the two flowers before her and states: "Su majestad, escoja" (Your Majesty, choose).

This pun, or *calambur* (a play of words based in polysemy, homonymy, or paronymy), detectable only in the Spanish, offers a double reading of sovereignty. On the first account—the explicit, and also the classical, account—the sovereign is she who decides (on the exception, Schmitt would add). The second reading, the hidden message *of* (and *in*) the story, is that *su majestad es coja*, "Your Majesty is lame." Read as political philosophy—admittedly, a clumsy, irresponsible, even violent gesture—this double account of sovereignty speaks to both the deciding power *and* the constitutive flaw of the sovereign. Derrida tells us, ambivalently, in "Provocation: Forewords" and *Rogues*, that "pure sovereignty is indivisible or it is not," which, as Jacques Lezra has pointed out, can be interpreted in at least three ways: pure sovereignty is indivisible or it is not (sovereignty), pure sovereignty is indivisible or it is not (pure), pure sovereignty is indivisible or it is not (indivisible) (*Wild Materialism*, 70). Geoffrey Bennington reminds us that in "The Beast and the Sovereign," Derrida asserts that "Sovereignty . . . is posited as immortal and indivisible precisely because it is mortal, and divisible" (463, qtd. in Bennington, "Sovereign Stupidity" 110n7). "A sovereign that remained merely itself, purely sovereign, in its defining self-sufficiency, indivisibility, inalienabilty, and perfection," argues Bennington, "would not even be sovereign." "In order to 'be' sovereign at all," he tells us, "the sovereign has to descend a little from the sovereign heights, from the summit of its most-highness (as Bataille or Nancy might say), and give itself an executive, an *arm* or *branch*" (or, we can add with Aira, a lame foot) (99). A sovereign is only sovereign—and therefore indivisible—on the condition that it (he, she) is *not* (sovereign *or* indivisible).

Aira's parodic recovery of the apparent contradiction at the heart of the sovereign—an undecidable relation between decision and wound and the consequently undecidable relations *between* these possibilities (the sovereign decides *or* she is lame, the sovereign decides *and* she is lame, the sovereign decides *because* she is lame)—is accompanied by another layer of meaning that has to do with the strange rapport between what is hidden and what is revealed in this tale, itself related to the question of translatability. Why would Picasso choose to include this joke, Aira's narrator wonders, which only makes sense in Spanish, in a painting created after three decades of residence in and assimilation into French culture? (He leaves aside, in a glaring absence, the fact that the narrative pun is by definition untranslatable into the language of painting.)

The facetious play between translatability and untranslatability, visibility and invisibility, secrecy and exposure, relates not only to borders *between* languages, between artistic genres—here, narrative and painting—but also to a dynamic proper to *each* genre, an improper dynamic that becomes evident only in its exposure to the other. The painter-maestro of *Triano* defines the work of cubism as making visible the hither side of a cube. "Imagínense un cubo," he tells César and Arturo: "Se lo imaginarán, es inevitable, en perspectiva: verán tres caras nada más" (Imagine a cube. You'll imagine it, inevitably, in perspective: You'll see three faces, nothing more) (34, translation mine). The primary operation of cubism, he explains, is to disassemble the cube, to make the three invisible sides visible, to *expose* the hidden faces: The cubist painter doubles the three visible faces of the cube, making six. Triano goes on to link the six-faced cube, in his hallucinatory monologue, with the sestina, the six-verse stanza found in Argentina's epic poem *Martín Fierro*. He then makes a proposition to the young poets:

> Ustedes que están en el métier, prueben esto: fabriquen trescientos noventa y siete cubos, que es la cantidad de estrofas que tiene la Ida. Un cubo contiene una estrofa, con un verso escrito en cada una de sus caras. Revoleen los cubos y arrójenlos como si fueran dados, pónganlos en fila tal como cayeron, y transcriban en ese orden los versos que queden en la cara superior. Les dará un poema de trescientos noventa y siete versos, derivado del original pero distinto. . . . Pueden repetir la operación cuantas veces quieran y siempre les va a dar un poema distinto. Las ganas que tengo de leer uno de esos poemas me hacen pensar que la literatura cubista todavía no ha nacido. (37–38)

(You two, who are in that line of work, try this: Assemble three-hundred ninety-seven cubes, the number of stanzas in [the first part of *Martín Fierro*], the *Ida*. Each cube contains one stanza, with a verse inscribed on each of its six faces. Shake up the cubes and throw them as if they were dice, then place them in a line exactly how they fall, and transcribe in that order the verses that appear on the top. It'll give you a poem of three hundred ninety-seven verses, derived from the original but different. . . . You can repeat the operation however many times you like, and it'll always give you a different poem. How I long to read a poem like that! It makes me think that cubist literature hasn't yet been born.)

Cubist literature—and, we could add, cubist thinking, a thinking of exposure—has yet to be born, Triano laments. Surely he can't mean that there has never been literary experimentation, that the avant-garde has not yet arrived (avant-garde gestures and pronouncements abound, above all in this postliterary moment, in which we don't stop hearing about the death of the book, the death of literature, the death of reading . . .). Perhaps the desire—the *ganas*—to read cubist poetry that Triano expresses points to a broader and also more urgent desire to read, period: a desire to read works that guard the possibility of unceasing or limitless interpretation, a possibility exemplified by the hypothetical cubist poem that at once subverts and breathes new life into Argentina's lyrical origins.

   Why do we need cubist painting to think about literature or about reading, and, conversely, why do we need narrative (Aira's story) to think about visual arts or about indisciplinary exposure more broadly? Why do we need literature to think about political philosophy, to fashion or advance political concepts? It's easy, tempting, simply to impose, or *over*-read, the political concepts I've discussed (divisible sovereignty, sovereign decisionism) onto or into Aira's work, but I'm not entirely convinced by such a move, especially because the most compelling political concepts, I'm arguing, are those that we can think in their impaired, lame sovereignty, *la soberanía coja*, that also tells us about wounded, broken genres, disciplines (and also because, simply put, literature fashions these concepts differently, obliquely—in Aira's case, depending very heavily on humor and wordplay). These are problems that beg for what Aira might call *cubist thinking* but that we could call exposed, indisciplined thinking: a thinking that at once exposes the invisible faces of a cube and fashions new secrets from the play between hiding and disclosure. Narrative, I've suggested, discovers its cubist asymmetries when it is exposed (or exposes itself) to another form, and cubism encounters its poetic and narrative secrets when it exposes itself (or is exposed) to linguistic forms. Can the untranslatable, singular, secret wounds of philosophical discourse be exposed in and by literary discourse? Conversely, we could ask, what is literature's wound? How might philosophy disclose it? The performative exposure I've been tracing reveals the identity of each discourse (genre, discipline) as a nonidentity: the secret flaw or defect that resides at the core of *every* genre, every discipline, every concept, that also stands as its single and singular condition of possibility.

What kind of university does such indisciplinary interpretative work make possible? Might we imagine an indisciplined institution that would simultaneously expose *and* guard[3] the maroon undercommons described by Moten and Harney, strangely related to the eclipsed, opaque, or marrano intellectual labor I've described in this book? Derrida suggests, in "Mochlos," that "every text, every element of a corpus reproduces or bequeaths, in a prescriptive or normative mode, one of several injunctions: . . . form this or that type of institution so as to read me and write about me, organize this or that type of exchange of hierarchy to interpret me, evaluate me, preserve me, translate me, inherit from me, make me live on." Yet he points out that every text also reproduces or bequeaths the *inverse* injunction: "If you interpret me . . . you shall have to assume one or another institutional form." The passive, exposed university responds to a radical demand to read. It enjoins upon us to pursue a reading, an interpretation or decision, that guards within it the possibility of illegibility, opacity, untranslatability . . . a reading, or misreading, that bears witness to the impossibility of testimony, of reading, of responsibility. Or rather, and more concretely: In this university, faculties, departments, objects of study, and styles of instruction enter into conflict and expose themselves in one another, as legible-illegible *to* one another, and turn that point of exposing legibility-illegibility into the university's nonsovereign or postsovereign duty. The indisciplined university, constituted by passivity and exposure, *this* university is made possible in the precise moment in which we gather together to bear witness to and seek to interpret "divisible sovereignty," "passive decision," "error," and "exposure" in a literary text but also when we form a reading community that bears witness to and guards the "divisible sovereignty," "passive decision," the "error" and "exposure" that constitute it.

Afterword

Truth and Error in the Age of Trump

> The Party told you to reject the evidence of your eyes and ears.
> It was their final, most essential command.
>
> —George Orwell, *1984*

> The single, irreplaceable Truth (about deconstruction, but also
> about "absolutely anything"), supposed to stand at an infinite
> remove from the movement of substitution—which is to say,
> of writing—cannot but be overtaken by the movement of its
> own inscription. And with that movement, places shift, reverse,
> collapse, but also something else gets inscribed: a displacement
> of the Truth in writing and by writing. And this displacement is
> anything but a destruction or a disappearance; on the contrary,
> it represents an altogether unprecedented demand for the
> written "truth," the literal "truth," the "truth" of "literature."
> And for its teaching.
>
> —Peggy Kamuf, *The Division of Literature,*
> *or the University in Deconstruction*

What is the role of the university in the age of Trump, in the so-called post-truth era? What must be imagined, created, produced, and nourished, defended, guarded, protected, now that we find ourselves not only in the midst of a neoliberal, corporate institution, which was of course already the case before November 2016, but also drowning in a sea of what we can easily identify as untruths, as falsehoods, as lies—having to do with everything from "fake news" to climate-change denial, a tendency that has rapidly moved from willing or unwilling blindness to fascist inventions of reality reminiscent of the Ministry of Truth in George Orwell's *1984*? Sales of the novel surged 9,500 percent on the Friday following Trump's poorly attended inauguration, returning to the bestseller lists, after the new leader of the free world boasted about "the largest audience ever to witness an inauguration." Trump's spokeswoman Kellyanne Conway excused this as an "alternate fact," reminding many Americans of the novel's Ministry of Truth, a government institution that manufactured new truths and discarded those that threatened its hegemony. How do we, in the university, approach truth today?

Since November 2016, we watch as some university campuses become, or are turned into, a battlefield between so-called defenders of free speech and protesters who challenge the right of neo-Nazis and white supremacists to speak on campus. We watch as right-wing media figures and provocateurs cast what is quickly becoming a civil war between racists and anti-racists as a constitutional issue and as the president draws a false equivalence between violence and "fine people" on both sides. Increasingly we realize that the very appeal to free speech is a veil, a lie, barely covering assaults on the most vulnerable among us. Can a university campus offer sanctuary to undocumented students at risk of deportation, or to the objects of racial violence, or to professors targeted for controversial political positions? If universities in Chile, in Argentina, in Brazil, the areas I research, are legally considered autonomous, in response to police attacks under the civic-military dictatorships of the 1970s and 1980s, to protect students from disappearance and murder, how can we think about the autonomy of the university in the increasingly neofascist climate of our own country? What kind of autonomy, what kind of sanctuary?

Here I want to pursue several distinct but related problems that face us today in the university. The first, the possibility of a defense against inventions and untruths that do not, or do not only, rely upon scientific or legal, proof-based knowledge—knowledge for which I confess to feeling immensely grateful, as I watch scientists take to the streets to shout the truth about climate change and attorneys rushing to the airport immediately upon the announcement of the Muslim travel ban in January 2017—but also, crucially, perhaps even more crucially than I ever could have imagined, upon knowledge, truths that pertain to the logic of testimony and witnessing but that are themselves unprovable in an empirical sense. It may seem a strange moment to turn, or return, to figures such as Jacques Derrida or Paul de Man, thinkers that have been wrongly accused of relativizing truth or of doing away with truth altogether.

Yet I think that this is *precisely* the moment to turn, to return, to the work of deconstruction, to *rethink* truth, not—as I might have said before November 2016—to defend the humanities "against" or within a university that privileges discourses of truth in a legal or scientific sense, a logic of provable truths. I find myself—perhaps this will change, I hope it will change—grateful for, as I've said, the voices of legal scholars and scientists who resist attacks on vulnerable communities and a burning planet. The election and its aftermath have created, at least for me, a relation of strange or at the very least unexpected bedfellows. I never expected to end up in bed with lawyers and biologists.

But neither did I expect to be thrown into bed, against my will, with Steven Bannon after he called for the "deconstruction" of the administrative state. This conflation of "deconstruction" and "destruction" did not surprise those of us who are, by now, accustomed to nonacademics or nonphilosophers using the two interchangeably. What was much more disturbing—or disturbing in a completely different way—was when the newly elected president (not, this time, of the United States but of the Modern Language Association) wrote, in her "inaugural" blog entry, entitled "Becoming We," about Bannon's deconstructive project. Taking issue with the dismantling of the Department of Education as one branch of the administrative state, Diana Taylor parroted Bannon's use of deconstruction, although in quotation marks, and even went so far as to characterize members of the administration as de Manian! She wrote:

> Apparent followers of Paul de Man, administration leaders aim to delink speech from meaning, lauding the virtues of education while placing the Department of Education in the hands of a person who has long attacked the public school system. Those of us in the MLA can't sit on the sidelines while the educational system is being "deconstructed." The MLA is part of a larger WE, a community of scholars and academics across the spectrum that also understands the need for action. WE can link up with others to pursue broader, shared goals. It is not an exaggeration to say that the future of education in the United States is playing out right now. WE need to have a part in shaping that future.

The president of the MLA—perhaps the most significant institution in the critical humanities—paints with a broad brush the work of deconstruction and links it to the catastrophic vision of a white supremacist. Here, to "deconstruct" means to delink signifier and signified in a complete divorce from the truth, and this is likened to the hypocrisy of a lying administration that feigns interest in education while dismantling the public school system. The MLA president then posits a WE, a collective subject, that will oppose the Trump administration's attack on education. This WE, according to her, will bring together "scholars and academics across the spectrum"—the spectrum of *what* is not entirely clear to me—in order to form a community that can defend "our" shared goals.[1] I worry, however, that "our" shared goals do not include the work of deconstruction, which for me has less to do with an insistence that our students read de Man or Derrida (whom she curiously does not mention: de Man is the "bad" deconstructor, after all, whose anti-Semitic writings were published in the pro-Nazi Belgian newspaper *Le Soir* and who fits more comfortably into the analogy to Bannon) and more to do with the demands that decon-struction (now I am thinking of Derrida) placed on our work in the university.

Far from doing away with truth, as Derrida's detractors claimed when they sought to protest the award of an honorary doctorate at Cambridge University ("Academic status based on what seems to us to be little more than semi-intelligible attacks upon the values of reason, truth, and scholar-ship is not, we submit, sufficient grounds for the awarding of an honorary degree in a distinguished university," they wrote, in a letter to the *Times* of London signed by a group of philosophers led by Barry Smith), the university is *precisely* the place where truth must be pursued, debated, questioned. Describing a, or the, "University without Condition," Der-rida writes:

> This university demands and ought to be granted in principle, besides what is called academic freedom, an *unconditional* freedom to question and to assert, or even, going still further, the right to say publicly all that is required by research, knowledge, and thought concerning the *truth*. How-ever enigmatic it may be, the reference to truth remains fundamental enough to be found, along with light (*lux*), on the symbolic insignias of more than one university. The university *professes* the truth, and that is its profession. It declares and promises an unlimited commitment to the truth. No doubt the status of and the changes in the value of truth can be discussed ad infinitum (truth as adequation or truth as revelation, truth as the object of theoretico-constative discourses or as poetico-performative events, and so forth). But these are discussed, precisely, in the university and in depart-ments that belong to the Humanities. (202–3)

For Derrida, then, far from something to be relativized or discarded, truth is at the *center* of the university's mission.

Let's return to George Orwell's *1984*. I'm not sure how many read, or reread, the dystopic novel, or how many bought it in a kind of hysterical panic, but I realized, when I purchased my first copy several months later, that I'd never read it. Strange: I'd thought I'd read it—hasn't everyone?—I knew all about Big Brother, the Ministry of Truth, had forgotten, or had never known, about the enemy-Jew Goldstein. I never knew about the haunting figure of the Jewish mother hiding her baby from the Nazis in one of the films shown to the citizens, and I certainly never knew that it was one of the most stirring, erotic, love stories I've had the chance to read. The scene in which the protagonist, desperately seeking an outside to the all-encompassing system dominated by the Party, is brought to a room above Charrington's antique shop in the prole sector of the city is quite moving:

> The thought flitted through Winston's mind that it would probably be quite easy to rent the room for a few dollars a week, if he dared to take the risk. It was a wild, impossible notion, to be abandoned as soon as thought of; but the room had awakened in him a sort of nostalgia, a sort of ancestral memory. It seemed to him that he knew exactly what it felt like to sit in a room like this, in an armchair beside an open fire with your feet in the fender and a kettle on the hob: utterly alone, utterly secure, with nobody watching you, no voice pursuing you, no sound except the singing of the kettle and the friendly ticking of the clock. "There's no telescreen!" he could not help murmuring.

The passage is one of the most breathtaking I've read in quite a while, which makes it all the more devastating when Winston and Julia, who adopt that space as their lovers' alcove, ostensibly escaping the eyes and ears of the Party, discover that the painting on the wall is in reality the screen that occupies the living room of every non-prole citizen, transmitting propaganda and surveilling every word, every gesture. There is no outside—or, really, inside—there is no escape, there is no sanctuary.

These are the scenes that surprised me, and then devastated me, in the fullest sense of these words. What follows, of course, is the imprisonment and torture, or reeducation, of Winston. He guards, until the end, the hope that he'll preserve the ability to rebel, or resist, in the second before his inevitable death at the hands of the Party (the ability of persecuted crypto-Jews to recite the Shema moments before the Inquisitorial flames consume them). The protagonist harbors a fervent desire—more fervent, even, than his desire for Julia, and even more fervent than his desire never to betray her (he does)—to preserve the ability to say NO in those final seconds. He fails. His last thought is not of his mother, nor of his first wife, nor of his former lover, wrenched from his arms in their alcove, but of his new, his *only* beloved: Big Brother. The possibility of resistance—the possibility of thought—is extinguished.

Of course, Orwell's novel can be read on two levels: constative and performative. If what is described, in painful detail, is the extinction of the possibility of thought (what Spinoza called the "freedom to philosophize"), what the book *performs* is something rather extraordinary. We accompany Winston on his road to total surrender, bearing witness to the process whereby the Party eliminates, step by step, his ability to question, to take a distance from the simulated reality represented by Newspeak. As O'Brien tortures the last shred of doubt out of Winston, we are privy to the final moments in which the protagonist is able to point to a "real" world where "real" things happen. He then realizes that such a thought (the word "thought" does not exist in Newspeak) should never have occurred to him in the first place: "The mind should develop a blind spot whenever a dangerous thought presented itself," Winston tells himself. His final unconscious cries for Julia are beaten out of him, yet these unconscious, dangerous thoughts eclipsed by protective blind spots still exist for the reader, for us. It is through literary language, through reading, that we are able, first, to bear witness to the construction of a false reality (alternative facts) and then to alert ourselves to the blind spots that will signal these wild, rebellious truths.

Literature, or aesthetics more broadly—coupled with the possibility of thought, or thinking—emerges as the only sanctuary against or within totalitarianism. Even when the Party's work is complete, even when there seems to be no outside, literature, *thought*, can point us in this direction. While it may seem counterintuitive, *1984* stands as a novel that affirms beauty in its ruins, the possibility of writing in its extinction, imagination in its destruction, lovemaking in its disappearance—privileged acts, gestures, or practices through which it becomes possible to upset the false truth-error dichotomy held up by the State. So yes, environmental scientists: Tell the truth about climate change! Immigration lawyers: Demand sanctuary for refugees and dreamers! Sociologists: Teach us about institutionalized racism in the NFL! Historians: Instruct us about the slow creep of fascism and alert us about the early stages of concentration camps and genocide! But also, literary scholars: Teach us how to read for blind spots and errors, where Paul de Man once found insight—this flickering light of the university, the light that may hide in shadows, and may *be* those shadows, is in your hands. *This* is the politics of truth in, and *after*, the age of Trump.

Acknowledgments

This book marks a period in which I decided to take intellectual risks that I hadn't had the courage to take before, to take positions I preferred to downplay in previous work. I would not have been able to compose these pages without the sense that there were others—friends, colleagues, students, interlocutors in the best sense—ready to invite, welcome, debate, question, and even *reject* the arguments I advance here. In this sense, I can now see, the history of one's intellectual trajectory can be understood as the history of one's interlocutors.

An invitation by Sam Steinberg to write a response to John Beverley's *Latinamericanism after 9/11* first inspired me to engage with Latinamericanist polemics, to which, until that point, I'd remained a somewhat passive bystander. The following year, David Johnson's invitation to the "Literature and the Secret of the World" symposium at the University of Buffalo and Alberto Moreiras and José Luis Villacañas's invitation to participate in the summer course on "Posthegemony" at the Universidad Complutense de Madrid in El Escorial enabled me to formulate the two concepts that lie at the heart of this book: misunderstanding literature and anarchaeological thinking.

Subsequent opportunities to share my work at Harvard; New York University; Princeton; Stanford; the University of Michigan; the University of California–Irvine; Yeshiva University; Indiana University; Temple University; Arizona State University; the University of Illinois, Chicago; Universidad Metropolitana de Ciencias de la Educación; Universidad ARCIS; Pontificia Universidad Católica de Valparaíso, Chile; Universidad de Buenos Aires; Universidad Nacional de Córdoba; Universidade Nacional de Brasilia, Brazil; and the Università degli Studi di Salerno, Italy, were vital to the composition and revision of a great deal of this book. I want to thank the following people for their generous invitations: Emmanuel Biset, Valeria Campos Salvaterra, Willie Chase, Jaime Donoso, Patrick Dove, Tatjana Gajic, Charles Hatfield, Héctor Hoyos, Kate Jenckes, Horacio Legrás, Steven Marsh, Anna More, Gabriela Nouzeilles, Ronnie Perelis, Adam Joseph Shellhorse, Mariano Siskind, Willy Thayer, Francesco Vitale, and the graduate students of Indiana University's and Arizona State University's departments of Spanish and Portuguese.

During the past decade or so I have drifted more and more into the fields of comparative literature and continental philosophy. The influence of new friends and interlocutors, many of whose own books stand as stunning examples of scholarship and imagination, have provoked, challenged, and inspired me. I look forward to ongoing plotting and planning, collaborations and coffees with Geoff Bennington, Rebecca Comay, Miriam Jerade, Elissa Marder, Tracy McNulty, Andrew Parker, Marc Redfield, Rei Terada, and Dimitris Vardoulakis. I would not have written about Leonard Cohen had it not been for Jonathan Freedman's persistence and passion. Jonathan's presence in these pages is at once significant and difficult to describe adequately.

At the University of Southern California, I am surrounded by graduate students and colleagues whose curiosity and intelligence sustain me. In particular, the wonderful students from the seminars "After the Death of Reading: Error, Blindness, Misunderstanding" and "Violent Ethics" generously and patiently allowed me to test out some of the ideas in this book: thank you. The most recent arrivals to the faculty of Latin American and Iberian Cultures and Comparative Literature—Natalie Belisle, Ronald Mendoza-de Jesús, and Veli Yashin—push me in new directions, constantly.

Living in Southern California is a gift, and not only because I can walk on the beach in January. Colleagues from neighboring universities have joined forces to form the Southern California Working Group "Hispanism/Critical Thought," which means that I get to see, read, and listen to Matías Beverinotti, Alessandro Fornazzari, Marta Hernández Salván, Adriana Johnson, Horacio Legrás, Jacques Lezra, Jaime Rodríguez Matos, and Freya Schiwy more often.

The Seminario Crítico-Político Transnacional, which has met every summer in Madrid for the past six years, has contributed not only to the drafting of sections of this book but to my general intellectual well-being. Thank you to the co-directors, Jacques Lezra, Alberto Moreiras, and José Luis Villacañas, and to the wonderful colleagues who have participated: Angel Octavio Álvarez Solis, Jorge Álvarez Yagüéz, Peter Baker, Jon Beasley-Murray, Rodrigo Castro Orellana, Emma Ingala Gómez, John Kraniauskas, Brett Levinson, Cristina Moreiras, Antonio Rivera, César Pérez Sánchez, Teresa Vilarós, Gareth Williams, and many, many more.

The annual meeting of the Grupo chileno-argentino on "Filosofía, arte y política" has not only been a source of stimulating conversations but the origin of lasting friendships, both of which imbue this book with greater meaning. Gisela Cantanzaro, Alejandra Castillo, Elizabeth Collingwood-Selby, Mary Luz Estupiñán, Roque Farrán, Federico Galende, Luis García, Daniel Groisman, Alejandro Kaufman, Manuel Moyano, raúl rodríguez freire, María Stegmayer, Willy Thayer, Miguel Valderrama: Here's to many more years of anarchic debate and discussion!

Colleagues and friends in Argentina who accompanied me as I drafted the final pages of this manuscript cannot go unmentioned. Even those whose work did not directly enter this book are present spectrally, as our coffee dates in Palermo, Belgrano, and Chacarita, conversations on the streets of Colegiales, Villa Crespo, and San Telmo, and of course late-night dinner parties in apartments and restaurants across the city nourished me and made possible this and future books, still unknown: *fuerte abrazo* a Gonzalo Aguilar, Albertina Carri, Álvaro Fernández Bravo, Paola Cortés Rocca, Marta Dillon, Pablo Dreizik, Alejandro Dujovne, Ricardo Forster, Verónica Gago, Loreto Garín Guzmán, Florencia Garramuño, Luz Horne, Alejandra Laera, Ana Paula Penchazadeh, Fermín Rodríguez, Claudia Soria, Jorge Stamadianos, Diego Tatián, Federico Zukerfeld, and the Internacional Errorista.

As soon as I saw the description of Fordham University Press's Lit Z series, edited by Sara Guyer and Brian McGrath, I knew I *had* to publish this book there. I want to express my sincere appreciation to Brian and Sara, as well as to Tom Lay (editor extraordinaire), the anonymous readers of this manuscript (whose generous readings and prodding suggestions greatly improved the book), Eric Newman, and the entire editorial staff for their support and professionalism, as well as Andrew Ascherl for his work on this book's index.

I would like to express appreciation to the editors of journals and books in which earlier versions of parts of this book were published. Sections of Part I were originally published as "Marrano Secrets, Or, Misunderstanding Literature," in *CR: The New Centennial Review* 14, no. 3 (2014); and "Beyond Inquisitional Logic, or, Toward an An-archaeological Latin Americanism," *CR: The New Centennial Review* 14, no. 1 (2014). In Part II, "Politics Against Ethics" was first published in *Política Común. A Journal of Thought* 4 (2013). An earlier version of "Levinas in Latin America" was published as "The Ethical Turn" and is republished with permission of Routledge, from *New Approaches to Latin American Studies: Culture and Power*, ed. Juan Poblete (2017) (permission conveyed through Copyright Clearance Center, Inc.). "Untimely Ethics: Deconstruction and Its Precursors" originally appeared as "Deconstruction and Its Precursors: Levinas and Borges after Derrida," in *The Marrano Specter: Derrida and Hispanism*, ed. Erin Graff Zivin (New York: Fordham University Press, 2017). In Part IV, "Beyond Jameson: The Metapolitics of Allegory" originally appeared in *Yearbook of Comparative Literature* 41 (2017), and an earlier version of "The Aesthetics and Politics of Error" was published in *Política Común. A Journal of Thought* 10 (2016). I also want to acknowledge the USC Dornsife Office of the Dean, which contributed to the publication of this book.

My deepest gratitude goes to Josh, Simon, Miles, and Eli: my family, travel partners, food tasters, conversationalists, cuddlers, and of course members of the Lola the Puppy fan club.

This book is dedicated to the memory of my dear friend Erin Williams Hyman: Her laughter, and all of her books, written and unwritten, are with me always.

Notes

Introduction: Ethical and Political Thinking after Literature

1. In the first part of *Reading Capital*, Louis Althusser distinguishes between "innocent" and "guilty" readings: "A philosophical reading of *Capital* is quite the opposite of an innocent reading. It is a guilty reading, but not one that absolves its crime on confessing it. On the contrary, it takes the responsibility for its crime as a 'justified crime' and defends it by proving its necessity. It is therefore a special reading which exculpates itself as a reading by posing every guilty reading the very question that unmasks its innocence, the mere question of its innocence: *what is it to read*?" (15).

2. In *Of Hospitality: Anne Dufourmantelle Invites Jacques Derrida to Respond* (26–28).

3. There are exceptions. In Latin American studies alone, Brett Levinson's *The Ends of Literature*, Abraham Acosta's *Thresholds of Illiteracy*, Kate Jenckes's *Witnessing Beyond the Human*, Patrick Dove's *Literature and Interregnum*, Adam Joseph Shellhorse's *Anti-Literature*, Jaime Rodríguez Matos's *Writing of the Formless*, Samuel Steinberg's *Photopoetics of Tlatelolco*, and Mariano Siskind's unpublished "About the End of the World: Towards a Cosmopolitanism of Loss" exemplify—performatively and constatively—a renewed engagement with aesthetics that eschews understanding or comprehension, the unsettling of disciplinary boundaries, the insubordination of signs, to borrow from Nelly Richard.

4. In his essay "The Ethics of Criticism and the International Division of Intellectual Labor," Idelber Avelar details the "asymmetrical and hierarchical distribution of cognitive positions among different countries and regions of the globe" (80).

5. When Piglia does establish a connection between the (passive, indecisive) scene of reading and the (active, decisive) space of politics, he does so through the acti-passive figure of Ernesto "Che" Guevara. By considering Guevara as one of the last readers, it becomes possible to think through the "end" of revolutionary politics together with the "end" of reading.

6. I borrow the compelling idea of "defective concept" from Jacques Lezra's *Wild Materialism* (110–12).

Misunderstanding Literature

1. The English translation of this essay was published in 2011 as "Literary Misunderstanding" in *The Politics of Literature*.

2. This is tricky because Rancière's *La mésentente: politique et philosophie* has been translated into English as *Disagreement: Politics and Philosophy*. Gabriel Rockhill argues that disagreement is not same as misunderstanding, but he uses misunderstanding

here to refer to "a general lack of comprehension", rather than as that which is constitutive of language itself. Really, though, the problem has less to do with translation, or between a different interpretation of the correct "meanings" of *mésentente* in French and "misunderstanding" in English, and more to do with competing meanings of these terms within each language.

3. In "Rancière's Leftism, Or, Politics and Its Discontents," Bruno Bosteels challenges the equivalence between Rancière's treatment of art and politics: "if art is treated according to the vaguely historical order of three regimes of identification (the ethical regime, the representative regime, and the aesthetic regime), without there being any essence proper to art in itself," the same is not true for his discussion of politics. While he outlines an historical triad for politics (archi-politics, para-politics, and meta-politics), there exists "an essence or a rational kernel of politics, which subsequently would have been covered up, denied, repressed, or obscurely designated in those three dominant forms of political philosophy" (162).

4. Rancière continues: "Literary dissensus works on changes in the scale and nature of individualities, on deconstruction of the relationships between things and meanings. In this, it differentiates itself from the work of political subjectification which configures new collectives by means of words. Political dissensus operates in the form of subjectification procedures that identify the declaration by the anonymous that they are a collective, an *us*, with reconfiguration of the field of political objects and actors. Literature goes in the opposite direction to this organization of the perceptual field around a subject of utterance. It dissolves the subjects of utterance in the fabric of the percepts and affects of anonymous life. Literary 'misunderstanding,' then, tends to oppose the staging of a speech peculiar to political disagreement with a different staging, one that deploys other relationships between meanings and states of things that come along and invalidate the markers of political subjectification" (43–44).

5. "In the recent history of politicized art, two forms are readily identifiable. The first form, which might be referred to as content-based commitment, is founded on the representation of politicized subject matter. The second form, which might be called formal commitment, locates the political dimension of works of art in their mode of representation or expression, rather than in the subject matter represented" (Rockhill, "The Politics of Aesthetics," 195).

6. "This turning toward the voice of the law is a sign of a certain desire to be beheld by and perhaps also to behold the face of authority, a visual rendering of an auditory scene—a mirror stage or, perhaps more appropriately, an 'acoustic mirror'—that permits the misrecognition without which the sociality of the subject cannot be achieved. This subjectivation is, according to Althusser, a misrecognition, a false and provisional totalization; what precipitates this desire for the law, this lure of misrecognition offered in the reprimand that establishes subordination as the price of subjectivation?" (Butler, *The Psychic Life of Power*, 112).

7. In the "Translator's Introduction" to *The Politics of Aesthetics*, Gabriel Rockhill outlines Rancière's concept of an "aesthetic regime of art" (or literature) and the notion of "literarity" as "the status of a written word that freely circulates outside any system of legitimation" (5).

8. As I have argued in *Figurative Inquisitions*, representations of the marrano (beginning in the fourteenth century) betray a tension, an ambivalence, between two very different conceptions of marranismo, which correspond to two competing logics of the idea of the secret, or of truth itself. In the first version, the marrano embodies a hidden truth: She is either a faithful Christian or a clandestine Jew, the truth of which can only be determined through the pain of torture and Inquisitional interrogation. Such a use for torture within the early modern world draws upon the ancient Athenian practice, which the Greek scholar Page duBois has linked to classical Athenian conceptions of truth, specifically, the idea of *alêtheia* as a buried truth brought to light, as unconcealment (in contrast to *nêmertes*, the unfailing, accurate truth of the underworld). A second interpretation of marranismo would move away from the idea of the secret as positive content in favor of a notion of secrecy that would resist the logic of *alêtheia*, that would exceed the play of hiding and revealing, forgetting and remembering, as Derrida has argued in "Passions: An Oblique Offering" (26).

9. "Es la desproporción entre lo que Solís y sus hombres pensaban de sí mismos y la función que le atribuyeron los indios al comérselos . . . caricatura del relativismo cultural, lo que vuelve al hecho impensable en su desmesura y vagamente cómico a causa del malentendido brutal de dos sistemas de pensamiento" (Saer, *El río sin orillas*, 56; quoted in Copertari, "La invención de la identidad en *El entenado*," 226).

10. Gabriela Copertari, who argues that in *El entenado* Saer theorizes a "deconstructed" or decentered Western subject, rightly perceives in this paragraph the anticipation of the captain's death (like the hare caught in the hunter's trap) (230), but I want to insist that the more significant death here is the symbolic death: that of the person he'd convinced himself he was.

11. "Is the need for self-exposure a rhetorical need? But no: It conditions all rhetoric, but in doing so it also expresses its distance from all rhetoric. It is perhaps from the incalculable abyss of this need—we want to expose ourselves, and we want to expose ourselves to others, without calculation, without interest, in our truth, in our pathology, and that is so, according to Kant, not out of our human character as insociable or antisocial, but out of our deepest and most intimate relation with the *socius*, with the other—that there can be something like an infrapolitical position, which is in itself neither properly ethical nor properly political, but which nevertheless abhors moralist betrayal. We should wonder whether this need, which I am calling the infrapolitical position, condition, or determination, is not the reason why there should be literature. And, if there should be literature, is it also the reason for why there should be a reflection on the literary, and for instance, the reflection on the literary and on other things as well that we call Hispanism" (Moreiras, "Infrapolitical Literature," 192).

Toward an Anarchaeological Latinamericanism

1. See my *Figurative Inquisitions*, esp. xii–xiv.

2. In 2013, I defined "inquisitional logic" as "the violent face of the dominant concepts of modernity: identity as reflexivity or self-presence (and difference as its

corresponding mirror image), sovereignty, and the idea of the political as the Schmittian divide between friend and enemy," a logic that "grounds itself in the violent conversion of others (Jews and Muslims in the Iberian Peninsula and indigenous peoples in the Americas), in the representation of the Americas as a new and eminently "convertible" world, and in the subsequent "reconversion" of these subjects through interrogation and torture" (*Figurative Inquisitions*, xii). Together with the confessions of victims accused of heresy, interrogation serves as the foundational discursive act of the Inquisition. In this way, we can understand religious conversion (as well as a secondary conversion carried out through the act of torture itself) as what makes possible the Inquisition but also—conversely—understand the Inquisition as what makes conversion possible, as Brett Levinson ("On Netanyahu's *The Origins of the Inquisition in Fifteenth-Century Spain*") argues and as Oscar Cabezas takes up in his book *Postsoberanía*: "El converso en tanto sujeto desfigurado respecto de una identidad estable desata el terror de la Inquisición permitiéndole operar, ocupar y desplegarse, bajo sospecha delictual, sobre todo el cuerpo de la comunidad" (The converso—a subject disfigured with respect to a stable identity—unleashes the terror of the Inquisition, allowing it to operate, occupy and unfold, under delictual suspicion, across the entire body of the community) (78).

3. See José Luis Villacañas (who emphasizes the double exclusion of Spinoza's marranismo), Ricardo Forster (who reads the marrano as the alter ego of the modern, autonomous subject), and Jacques Derrida, who relates the marrano secret to the right to resist the order of the political ("History of the Lie," 64).

4. Stathis Gourgouris identifies *archē*, playfully and seriously, as the first political concept.

Part II. The Ethical Turn

1. See, for example, Garber, Hanssen, and Walkowitz, eds., *The Turn to Ethics* (2000); and Davis and Womack, eds., *Mapping the Ethical Turn* (2001).

Ethics against Politics

1. I am indebted to Kate Jenckes's *Reading Borges after Benjamin* for this reference.

2. In *Totality and Infinity* one can find sentences such as: "[God's] very epiphany consists in soliciting us by his destitution in the face of the Stranger, the widow, and the orphan" (78).

3. This is Dussel's response to the French dedication of *Autrement qu'être*, which is dedicated "A la mémoire des êtres les plus proches parmi les six millions d'assassinés par les nationaux-socialistes, à côté des millions et des millions d'humains de toutes confessions et de toutes nations, victimes de la même haine de l'autre homme, du même antisémitisme." Below the French, however, is a dedication in Hebrew to the actual relatives and friends who were closest of the millions of millions; that is, Levinas enacts a necessary but improper translation of the proper name, which is then (mis)read by Dussel. When Dussel asks Levinas, "So, what about *our* victims?" Levinas responds, "That's something for you to think about." This is a brilliant

response, which I read not as "That's your problem!" but "That is an unanswerable question that should serve as the birth, not the death, of thought." For more on the Dussel-Levinas exchange, see Slabodsky, *Decolonial Judaism*, chap. 4.

4. Beverley: "The appeal to Levinas is itself symptomatic of one aspect of what I am calling the neoconservative turn. That is because it reduces the problem of difference or subalternity, which is both a political and cultural problem, to an ethical one, a question of exercising choice" (83).

5. In her book *Altered Reading*, Jill Robbins suggests "misreading" Levinas's examples of the ethical encounter with the other as metaphorical, arguing that the figurative nature of Levinas's characterization of ethical experience is more compatible with aesthetic discourse than Levinas himself would have it.

6. Hallward, in the translator's introduction to the English version of Badiou's *L'ethique: essai sur la conscience du Mal*, forcefully argues for an abandonment of any ethics predicated on the other, quoting Badiou: "'All ethical predication based on recognition of the other should be purely and simply abandoned.' Why? Because the real practical and philosophical question concerns the status of the Same" (xv). Bosteels follows Hallward's lead in his 2007 essay "The Ethical Superstition."

7. While he has always acknowledged a reading of the subaltern as that which escapes all representation (Spivak's position, among others), he is never fully convinced, dismissing it instead as too rooted in deconstruction.

8. Bosteels: "Almost nothing major is lost in Badiou's overall philosophy if we take away his tiny book *Ethics*, which in any case was written over the time span of barely a few weeks for an audience of mostly high school students" (15).

9. "Events are irreducible singularities, the 'beyond-the-law' of situations" (Badiou, *Ethics*, 44).

10. Badiou lists "love, art, science and politics" as the four categories of truth within which, and against which, an event could potentially erupt: "An evental fidelity is a real break (both thought and practised) in the specific order within which the event took place (be it political, loving, artistic or scientific . . .)" (*Ethics*, 42).

11. See José Rabasa on Zapatismo and Benjamin Arditi on the Arab Spring and student movements in Chile.

12. "At the heart of politics lies a double wrong, a fundamental conflict, never conducted as such, over the relationship between the capacity of the speaking being who is without qualification and political capacity" (Rancière, *Disagreement*, 22).

13. I do not have time, here, to explore Beverley's indictment of literature, represented metonymically by Borges. Suffice it to say that it follows the identitarian logic of his discussion of ethics and politics, specifically, that a writer's ideological affiliation (if it can be determined) determines the disruptive potential of their work. It seems to me to be a mistake to discount or disregard all texts that, while hailing from writers who could be identified as "elite" or "letrado" (in Rama's sense) or "reactionary" (in Borges's case), might offer the possibility of radical interruption. Isn't the author dead anymore?

14. Here I refer to Steven Corcoran's argument, in his discussion of Rancière, that "every political moment involves the incalculable leap of those who decide to

demonstrate their equality and organize their refusal against the injustices that promote the status quo" (10). Pursuing a similar line, Gareth Williams and Jon Beasley-Murray (following Williams) elegantly argue in favor of the Derridean "perhaps."

Levinas in Latin America

1. Written in 1973 and published in Dussel and Guillot, *Liberación latinoamericana y Emmanuel Levinas*, 8–9. Cited in Dussel, "Lo político en Levinas," 115.

2. See Castro Arellana, "Foucault y la post-hegemonía," in which he argues that "la teoría *decolonial* reproduce el mismo error epistemológico que denuncia" (228).

3. Alberto Moreiras has called this almost-but-not-quite deconstructive approach an "auratic practice of the postauratic" (*The Exhaustion of Difference*, 222).

4. These interventions have been published in a two-volume collection called *No matar: sobre la responsabilidad*, and a selection has been translated and published in the *Journal of Latin American Cultural Studies*. I am using the English translations here.

5. Dove: "While the debate between del Barco and his opponents has been characterized as a polemic between mutually exclusive points of view . . . militant reason and its critique in fact resemble one another in a way that neither position is prepared to acknowledge" (289).

6. The del Barco debate thus becomes, for Dove, a pretext: a case study though which it is possible to rethink the opposition between ethics and politics. Of course, this dynamic is already at work in del Barco and his respondents, for if they are sparring over the politics of memory, over past "decisions" between ethics and politics, they are also speaking above all about the present: "If the Left is to reconstitute itself as a viable social force in a contemporary setting—in which ideological conflict has been thoroughly stigmatized and the reigning assumption for some time has been that the end of history as progression and development is now in sight—this Left must first learn to reckon with its own past, not by judging the past as past but rather by interrogating the ways in which the past appears in the present, or how the historical present has been shaped by the past and its decisions" (292).

7. Nicole Anderson reads the "nonethical opening of ethics" as "ethics under erasure" (25).

8. Moreiras has since revised this paper and now includes the reference to Derrida's "Violence of the Letter." The essay has been published as "Infrapolitical Derrida: The Ontic Determination of Politics beyond Empiricism."

Abraham's Double Bind

1. Ettinger explores the idea of Isaac's compassion for his father, a "primary compassion [that] could be a kind of psycho-aesthetical and psycho-ethical archaic unconscious basis for the Levinasian 'an-archic' and feminine kernel of the ethical sphere," tracing it to the womb (רחם, *rekhem*) and the compassion (רחמים, *rakhamim*) of Sarah (100–1).

2. הנני, *hineni*, or "Here am I": "Such is the answer of the pious: it is an expression of meekness and readiness" (Midrash Tanchuma 1:4:22).

3. "Harshness and aggressivity in thought, which until then characterized the least scrupulous and most realist action, henceforth justify this violence and terrorism. It is not just a question of literary form. Violence emerges in Kierkegaard at the precise moment when, moving beyond the esthetic stage, existence can no longer limit itself to what it takes to be an ethical stage and enters the religious one, the domain of belief. This latter is no longer justified in the outer world. Even within, it is at once communication and solitude, and hence violence and passion. Thus begins the disdain for the ethical basis of being, the somehow secondary nature of all ethical phenomena that, through Nietzsche, has led us to the amoralism of the most recent philosophers" (*Proper Names*, 72). And later: "It is Kierkegaard's violence that shocks me. The manner of the strong and the violent, who fear neither scandal nor destruction, has become, since Kierkegaard and before Nietzsche, a manner of philosophy. One philosophizes with a hammer. In that permanent scandal, in that opposition to everything, I perceive by anticipation the echoes of certain cases of verbal violence that claimed to be schools of thought, and pure ones at that. I am thinking not only of National Socialism, but of all the sorts of thought it exalted. That harshness of Kierkegaard emerges at the exact moment when he 'transcends ethics'" (76).

4. After writing this, I came across a wonderful gloss of the biblical scene and its readings by Kierkegaard, Levinas, and Derrida in an essay by the Mexican philosopher Miriam Jerade. She, too, is interested in the violence of ethics, what she calls "la violencia de la irresponsabilidad de la responsabilidad" (the violence of the irresponsibility of responsibility) (115).

5. There is also the question of what would have happened had Abraham refused God's command: In a short piece called "Abraham," Franz Kafka imagines an alternative Abraham, one who could not, or would not, respond to God's call out of shame. "It couldn't possibly be for me; surely I am not that man." Derrida will follow this thread in "Abraham, the Other," the essay that perhaps most forcefully rejects an identitarian tie between Derrida and Jewishness (surely that's not me of whom you speak). Derrida doubts this other Abraham is possible yet himself hesitates before responding to a call, a call to respond to the idea of "judeities"—a misrecognition and misunderstanding (4). Jewishness, for Derrida, the possibility of Derrida's Jewishness is, like Kafka's other Abraham, a "laughable misunderstanding"—or is it? (8).

6. Full lyrics to Leonard Cohen, "The Story of Isaac" (1969):

The door it opened slowly,
My father he came in,
I was nine years old.
And he stood so tall above me,
His blue eyes they were shining
And his voice was very cold.

He said, "I've had a vision
And you know I'm strong and holy,
I must do what I've been told."
So he started up the mountain,
I was running, he was walking,
And his axe was made of gold.
Well, the trees they got much smaller,
The lake a lady's mirror,
We stopped to drink some wine.
Then he threw the bottle over.
Broke a minute later
And he put his hand on mine.
Thought I saw an eagle
But it might have been a vulture,
I never could decide.
Then my father built an altar,
He looked once behind his shoulder,
He knew I would not hide.
You who build these altars now
To sacrifice these children,
You must not do it anymore.
A scheme is not a vision
And you never have been tempted
By a demon or a god.
You who stand above them now,
Your hatchets blunt and bloody,
You were not there before,
When I lay upon a mountain
And my father's hand was trembling
With the beauty of the word.
And if you call me brother now,
Forgive me if I inquire,
"just according to whose plan?"
When it all comes down to dust
I will kill you if I must,
I will help you if I can.
When it all comes down to dust
I will help you if I must,
I will kill you if I can.
And mercy on our uniform,
Man of peace or man of war,
The peacock spreads his fan.

7. "War is wonderful. They'll never stamp it out. It's one of the few times people can act their best. It's so economical in terms of gesture and motion, every single

gesture is precise, every effort is at its maximum. Nobody goofs off. Everybody is responsible for his brother" (Burger, *Leonard Cohen on Leonard Cohen*, 62).

Untimely Ethics: Deconstruction and Its Precursors

1. "Outward from Nothingness" also includes apocryphal interviews with Kierkegaard and Benjamin.

2. I want to thank Ronald Mendoza-de Jesús for pointing me in the direction of this breathtaking passage from Levinas in a public lecture at the University of Southern California on February 3, 2016, "Time Fails: Reading Ethics in Two Poems of Borges."

The Metapolitics of Allegory

1. If Franco discounted the idea of national allegory as "genre" in light of the many hybrid texts produced by Latin American writers, there was a dearth of criticism that engaged with allegory as *mode of signification* (in the Benjaminian sense).

2. The hypothesis is not as reductive as it can be made to appear. These events are not only historical facts—the dates of this or that revolution, colonial expedition, etc.—they are also ideologies and dynamic networks of situations. First World literature may also be faithful to these sorts of events, they may also faithfully represent them, but in First World literature the relation between the work and what it represents is unavoidably expressed in language mediated by post- or non-national figures (bourgeois interiority, the overdeterminations of a literary tradition tied to an international market). First World literature, by implication, has lost a direct relation to the event.

3. Jameson's politics is a politics of transparency or, more specifically, of concealment and revelation: "In distinction to the unconscious allegories of our own cultural texts," he tells us, "third-world national allegories are conscious and overt" (79–80). This is perhaps a logical extension of the argument in his 1981 *The Political Unconscious*, in which ideological reading, or reading *for* ideology, relies upon the classical concept of *alêtheia* as a buried truth brought to light. Taken to its ultimate consequences, this would imply a politics of totalitarianism (or Inquisitional logic) or a totalitarian, totalizing practice of reading: one that demands complete transparency, one that—through political or hermeneutic interrogation—aims to extract the buried truth from the text or the slave. The political turn, in *Jameson's* practice of reading, is a turn toward complete readability or translatability, so that his well-meaning "inclusion" of Third World texts "in their radical alterity" within First World criticism presumes that we know who "Third World intellectuals" are, what they do, etc.

4. Alonso: "The doctrinaire allegorical intention of the novel dictates that there must be a struggle between Santos Luzardo and doña Bárbara, which in turn must be interpreted as alluding to the conflict between the abstract concepts of Civilization and Barbarism; I have already remarked on some of the strategies used by the text to guarantee such an interpretation. And yet, one can further establish that

allegory is simultaneously used by Gallegos also as a means of depicting the very struggle between doña Bárbara and Santos Luzardo that constitutes the novel's argument. Consequently, allegory in *Doña Bárbara* is not just an interpretive intention projected into the text, but also a narrative technique extensively employed to construct the events depicted in the novel" (120).

The Aesthetics and Politics of Error

1. All translations my own.

2. What is a concept? Adi Ophir argues that a concept "is neither given nor created but rather performed or played in the act of conceptualization. This play both invents and discovers the concept, both lets it appear and gives it existence, and in doing all this it also blurs the distinction between what is given and revealed, and what is invented and created."

3. There is a difference between undecidability and compulsion but still a certain relation: Undecidability is not synonymous with free will, for example. Yet the non-coincidence between undecidability and free will is significant: For Derrida, undecidability always involves a decision.

4. Recall that in "El sur," Borges already plays with such clichés, as the protagonist Juan Dahlmann enters/exits *A Thousand and One Nights* as well as the fantasy of autochthony through the figure of the *gaucho* in the south of Argentina.

5. This "orbe de regularidades geométricas" recalls the description of the garden and the house in Borges's "La muerte y la brújula," also about the "danger" of looking for "el orden de un regimen de signos que le diera algún sentido a mis actos":

> Lönnrot avanzó entre los eucaliptos, pisando confundidas generaciones de rotas hojas rígidas. Vista de cerca, la casa de la quinta de Triste-le-Roy abundaba en inútiles simetrías y en repeticiones maniáticas: a una Diana glacial en un nicho lóbrego correspondía en un segundo nicho otra Diana; un balcón se reflejaba en otro balcón; dobles escalinatas se abrían en doble balaustrada. Un Hermes de dos caras proyectaba una sombra monstruosa. Lönnrot rodeó la casa como había rodeado la quinta. Todo lo examinó; bajo el nivel de la terraza vio una estrecha persiana. La empujó: unos pocos escalones de mármol descendían a un sótano. Lönnrot, que ya intuía las preferencias del arquitecto, adivinó que en el opuesto muro del sótano había otros escalones. Los encontró, subió, alzó las manos y abrió la trampa de salida. Un resplandor lo guió a una ventana. La abrió: una luna amarilla y circular definía en el triste jardín dos fuentes cegadas. Lönnrot exploró la casa. Por antecomedores y galerías salió a patios iguales y repetidas veces al mismo patio. Subió por escaleras polvorientas a antecámaras circulares; infinitamente se multiplicó en espejos opuestos; se cansó de abrir o entreabrir ventanas que le revelaban, afuera, el mismo desolado jardín desde varias alturas y varios ángulos; adentro, muebles con fundas amarillas y arañas embaladas en tarlatán. Un dormitorio lo detuvo; en ese dormitorio, una sola flor en una copa de porcelana; al primer roce los pétalos antiguos se deshicieron. En el segundo piso, en el último, la casa le

parecio infinita y creciente. «La casa no es tan grande —pensó—. La agrandan la penumbra, la simetría, los espejos, los muchos años, mi desconocimiento, la soledad.»

6. The *sesgo vanguardista*, or "avant-garde slant," recalls the scientific concept of an *error de sesgo* (bias error), which is contrasted to *error aleatorio* (accidental error).

7. De Man's work, of course, goes against an exegetical tradition that would privilege a hidden meaning (archaeological reading). Yet, as I argue here, I'm not sure that he's fully moved beyond it. He's able to show how, in the literary text as well as its critical readings, blindness and insight, truth and falsehood are always intertwined, but he doesn't sufficiently manage to allow for that possibility in his *own* critical reading.

8. This opens onto what we might call a politics of possibility that depends on what I intend and what I judge to be true or the case not because such judgments are true or accurate but because they may possibly be wrong: politics grounded on the possibility of error, in both senses of the genitive "of."

9. Such a reading finds a kind of strange precursor in what Louis Althusser calls symptomatic reading, as Warren Montag describes in *Althusser and His Contemporaries*: "[Althusser] argued that to read *en matérialiste* or in a materialist way is thus not to accept or reject a philosophical doctrine in toto as if it were homogenous but instead 'to trace lines of demarcation within it,' to make visible and palpable the presence of conflicting forces within even the most apparently coherent text and to heighten and intensify its contradictions. To do so is to take the side of a text against itself" (5–6). Montag links Althusserian symptomatic reading, in turn—in what *itself* is an against-the-grain reading of Althusser—with Derrida, who, in *Of Grammatology*, characterizes deconstructive reading in the following way: "The movements of deconstruction do not address [or perhaps 'shake'—Derrida uses the verb 'solliciter'] structures from the outside. They are only possible and effective, they only aim their blows by inhabiting these structures. By inhabiting them in a certain way, for one inhabits always and especially when one does not suspect it. Operating necessarily from the interior, borrowing from the former structure all the strategic and economic resources of subversion, borrowing them structurally, that is, without being able to isolate their elements and atoms, the enterprise of deconstruction is always in a certain way led astray by its own labor" (*Of Grammatology*, 24, qtd. in Montag, *Althusser and His Contemporaries*, 6).

10. This is the introduction to the second edition of *Blindness and Insight*, at a time in which de Man is reflecting on his career already and thinking about the errors in the first edition.

11. Members of the collective include Eluney Caputto, Cristian Forte, Loreto Garín, Nancy Garín, Federico Langir, Ariel Martínez Dericenzo, Antonio O'Higgins, Luciana Romano, Leopoldo Tiseira, and Federico Zukerfeld.

12. *Acción teatral*, or theatrical action: according to Diana Taylor, "'acción' brings together both the aesthetic and political dimensions of 'perform.' . . . 'Acción' seems more directed and intentional, and thus less socially and politically embroiled than 'perform' which evokes both the prohibition and the potential for

transgression. We may, for example, be performing multiple socially constructed roles at once, even while engaged in one clearly defined anti-military 'acción.'" http://scalar.usc.edu/nehvectors/wips/acts-of-transfer-1.

13. "Un día, un compañero nuestro estaba escribiendo un texto en la computadora y cometió un error. En vez de escribir 'Teatro y Terrorismo', olvidó la 'T'. Cuando apretó el corrector F7 la primera palabra que apareció marcada como incorrecta fue 'errorismo'. El corrector decía 'errorismo no existe', usted quiso decir 'erotismo' o 'terrorismo'. De ahí surgió el nombre. Por un lado, como oposición y denuncia al estereotipo. Pero por otro, hallamos la palabra justa, que tiene su propia discusión filosófica sobre el tema del error." http://www.unidiver sidad.com.ar/el-error-como-alegoria-de-la-contracultura.

14. We recall that in *Disagreement*, Rancière writes that "Politics begins with a major wrong: the gap created by the empty freedom of the people between the arithmetical order and the geometric order. . . . It is the introduction of an incommensurable at the heart of the distribution of speaking bodies. This incommensurable breaks not only with the equality of profits and losses; it also ruins in advance the project of the city ordered according to the proportion of the cosmos and based on the arkhê of the community" (19). What Rancière will call a foundational "wrong" of politics, that constitutive disturbance in the archē of the community, its anarchic core, is slightly distinct from the concept of "error."

15. The longer version of the *manifiesto* defines "erroristas" as "*multitudes, sujetos o grupos que practican el Errorismo*" (7).

16. It is also worth considering the concept of political error in the work of Spinoza, "those views which, simply by being put forward, *dissolve the agreement* by which each person surrenders their right to *act according to their own judgment*" (Spinoza, *TTP*, XX, 254; qtd. in Biareishyk, "Spinoza's Politics of Error," 8). Siarhei Biareishyk argues that, for Spinoza, "Because a political error threatens to undermine sovereign's monopoly on interpretation, it aims at the very essence of singular sovereignty" (8).

Toward a Passive University

1. In neoliberal Chile, Willy Thayer, Elizabeth Collingwood-Selby, and raúl rodríguez freire have written on the problem of the (non)modern university and the university of excellence.

2. Jacques Rancière begins to think through this possibility when he considers the constitution of disciplines in a short essay called "Thinking between Disciplines: An Aesthetics of Knowledge." "A discipline," he writes, "is always much more than an ensemble of procedures which permit the thought of a given territory of objects. It is first the constitution of this territory itself, and therefore the establishment of a certain distribution of the thinkable" (8). Indisciplined thought, he argues, ignores disciplinary boundaries, lifting an object of thought from its defined territory in order to reflect upon it out of place, make it "strange," emancipate it. Such thinking would expose the very process of disciplinary foundation. I would propose a more radical version of this, in which indisciplinarity would expose not only the constructed

nature of disciplines and disciplinary objects but also the wounded, untranslatable points within each discipline. Infinite, permanent exposure.

3. The aporetic link between exposure and guarding, or protecting, might be thought of as a variation on Derrida's "Unconditionality or Sovereignty," in which sovereignty paradoxically protects the right to ask anything in the university, even including the right to question and deconstruct sovereignty.

Afterword: Truth and Error in the Age of Trump

1. Taylor emphasizes the importance of the first-person plural in other work as well. Once again, scare quotes seem to indicate a distancing from such identitary logic, but no alternative is provided. I am thinking, for example, of her essay "Trauma in the Archive," in which she details a visit to the former torture and extermination camp Villa Grimaldi in Santiago, Chile. After the tour guide, a former prisoner, mistakenly addresses her in English because of her last name, Taylor assures him that although she is from Mexico, they speak the same language. She then goes on to assert that Villa Grimaldi is "'our' responsibility" (240). The "truth" of what transpired at Villa Grimaldi, too, is placed in quotation marks: Surely Taylor is not "Demanian"?

Bibliography

Acosta, Abraham. *Thresholds of Illiteracy: Theory, Latin America, and the Crisis of Resistance.* New York: Fordham University Press, 2014.

Ahmad, Aijaz. "Jameson's Rhetoric of Otherness and the National Allegory." *Social Text* 15 (1986): 3–25.

Aira, César. *El congreso de literatura.* 1997. Mérida, Venezuela: Editorial Venezolana, 2007.

———. *El error.* Barcelona: Mondadori, 2010.

———. *The Literary Conference.* Trans. Katherine Silver. New York: New Directions, 2010.

———. "Picasso." In *Relatos reunidos,* 23–30. Barcelona: Mondadori, 2013.

———. "Picasso." Trans. Chris Andrews. *New Yorker,* August 11, 18, 2014. http://www.newyorker.com/magazine/2014/08/11/picasso.

———. *Triano.* Buenos Aires: Milena Caserola, 2014.

Alonso, Carlos. *The Spanish American Regional Novel.* Cambridge: Cambridge University Press, 1990.

Althusser, Louis, and Étienne Balibar. *Reading Capital.* 1968. Trans. Ben Brewster. London: Verso, 2009.

Andermann, Jens. *New Argentine Cinema.* London: I. B. Tauris, 2012.

Anderson, Nicole. *Derrida: Ethics under Erasure.* London: Bloomsbury, 2012.

Andrade, Oswald de. "Cannibalist Manifesto." Trans. Leslie Bary. *Latin American Literary Review* 19, no. 38 (1991): 38–47.

Arditi, Benjamin. "Insurgencies Don't Have a Plan—They *Are* the Plan: Political Performatives and Vanishing Mediators in 2011." *JOMEC Journal: Journalism, Media, and Cultural Studies* 1 (2012). http://www.cardiff.ac.uk/jomec/jomec journal/1-june2012/arditi_insurgencies.pdf.

Avelar, Idelber. "The Ethics of Interpretation and the International Division of Intellectual Labor." *SubStance* 29, no. 1 (2000): 80–103.

———. *The Untimely Present: Postdictatorial Latin American Fiction and the Task of Mourning.* Durham, NC: Duke University Press, 1999.

Badiou, Alain. *Ethics: An Essay on the Understanding of Evil.* Trans. Peter Hallward. London: Verso, 2002.

Barnett, Ronald. *Being a University.* Oxford: Routledge, 2010.

Basterra, Gabriela. *Seductions of Fate: Tragic Subjectivity, Ethics, Politics.* London: Palgrave Macmillan, 2004.

Beasley-Murray, Jon. *Posthegemony: Political Theory and Latin America.* Minneapolis: University of Minnesota Press, 2010.

Belzagui, Pablo René, ed. *No matar: sobre la responsabilidad.* Vol. 1. Córdoba, Argentina: Ediciones del Cíclope–Editorial de la Universidad Nacional de Córdoba, 2007.

Benjamin, Walter. "Allegory and Trauerspiel." In *The Origin of German Tragic Drama,* trans. John Osborne. London: Verso, 2003.

Bennington, Geoffrey. "Sovereign Stupidity and Autoimmunity." In *Derrida and the Time of the Political,* ed. Pheng Cheah and Suzanne Guerlac, 97–113. Durham, NC: Duke University Press, 2009.

Berg, Maggie, and Barbara Seeber. *The Slow Professor: Challenging the Culture of Speed in the Academy.* Toronto: University of Toronto Press, 2016.

Beverley, John. *Against Literature.* Minneapolis: University of Minnesota Press, 1993.

———. *Latinamericanism After 9/11.* Durham, NC: Duke University Press, 2011.

Biareishyk, Siarhei. "Spinoza's Politics of Error." In *Spinoza's Authority,* vol. 2: *Resistance and Power,* ed. A. Kiarina Kordela and Dimitris Vardoulakis, 101–24. London: Bloomsbury, 2017.

Biset, Emmanuel. *El signo y la hiedra. Escritos sobre Jacques Derrida.* Córdoba, Argentina: Alción Editora, 2013.

Boddeke, Saskia, and Peter Greenaway. *Obedience / Gehorsam.* May–November 2015, Jüdisches Museum Berlin, Germany.

Borges, Jorge Luis. "El etnógrafo." In *Elogio de la sombra,* 58–61. Buenos Aires: Emecé, 1969.

———. "The Ethnographer." In *Collected Fictions,* trans. Andrew Hurley, 334–35. New York: Penguin, 1998.

———. "Kafka and His Precursors" (1962). In *Labyrinths: Selected Stories and Other Writings,* ed. Donald A. Yates and James E. Irby, trans. James E. Irby, 199–201. New York: New Directions, 2007.

———. "Kafka y sus precursores" (1951). In *Obras completas,* vol. 2: *1952–1972,* 88–90. Buenos Aires: Emecé, 1989.

———. "La muerte y la brújula." In *Ficciones.* Buenos Aires: Ediciones Sur, 1944.

Bosteels, Bruno. "The Ethical Superstition." In *The Ethics of Latin American Literary Criticism: Reading Otherwise,* ed. Erin Graff Zivin, 11–23. New York: Palgrave Macmillan, 2007.

———. *Marx and Freud in Latin America: Politics, Psychoanalysis, and Religion in Times of Terror.* London: Verso, 2012.

———. "Rancière's Leftism, or, Politics and Its Discontents." In *Jacques Rancière: History, Politics, Aesthetics,* ed. Gabriel Rockhill and Philip Watts, 158–75. Durham, NC: Duke University Press, 2009.

———. "Una arqueología del porvenir: acto, memoria, dialéctica." *La Palabra y el Hombre: Revista de la Universidad Veracruzana* 134 (2005): 161–71.

Burger, Jeff. *Leonard Cohen on Leonard Cohen: Interviews and Encounters.* Chicago: Chicago Review Press, 2015.

Butler, Judith. *The Psychic Life of Power: Theories in Subjection.* Stanford, CA: Stanford University Press, 1997.

Cabezas Villalobos, Oscar. "Edicto de 1492: el registro marrano entre la errancia, la identidad y el exilio." In *Exilio e identidad en el mundo hispánico: reflexiones y representaciones*, ed. Laura López Fernández and Beatriz Caballero Rodríguez. Madrid: Biblioteca Virtual Miguel de Cervantes, 2012.

———. *Postsoberanía: literatura, política y trabajo*. Buenos Aires: La Cebra, 2013.

Carri, Albertina, dir. *Cuatreros*. 2017.

———. *Los Rubios*. 2003.

Carri, Roberto. *Isidro Velázquez: formas prerrevolucionarias de la violencia*. 1968. Buenos Aires: Ediciones Colihue, 2005.

Castro Arellana, Rodrigo. "Foucault y la post-hegemonía. Tres episodios de una recepción: Said, Spivak y Mignolo." In *Post-hegemonía. El final de un paradigma de la filosofía política contemporánea en América Latina*, ed. Rodrigo Castro Orellana, 217–32. Madrid: Biblioteca Nueva, 2015.

Cervantes Saavedra, Miguel de. *Don Quijote de la Mancha*. 1605. Ed. Francisco Rico et al. Instituto Cervantes. Barcelona: Crítica (Biblioteca Clásica), 1998.

———. *Don Quixote*. Trans. Edith Grossman. New York: Harper Collins, 2003.

Clark, T. J. "For a Left with No Future." *New Left Review* 74 (2012): 53–75.

Cohen, Leonard. "The Story of Isaac." *Songs from a Room*. Columbia Records, 1969.

———. "Who by Fire?" *New Skin for the Old Ceremony*. Columbia Records, 1974.

———. "You Want It Darker." *You Want It Darker*. Columbia Records, 2016.

Collingwood-Selby, Elizabeth. "Post-hegemonía y universidad." In *Post-hegemonía. El final de un paradigma de la filosofía política en América Latina*, 205–16. Madrid: Biblioteca Nueva, 2015.

Contreras, Sandra. *Las vueltas de César Aira*. Rosario, Argentina: Beatriz Viterbo Editora, 2002.

Copertari, Gabriela. "La invención de la identidad en *El entenado* de J. J. Saer." *Latin American Literary Review* 26, no. 52 (1998): 225–40.

Corcoran, Steven. "Editor's Introduction." In *Dissensus: On Politics and Aesthetics*, by Jacques Rancière, ed. and trans. Steven Corcoran, 1–24. London: Continuum, 2010.

Cornell, Drucilla. *The Philosophy of the Limit*. New York: Routledge, 1992.

Corngold, Stanley. "Error in Paul de Man." *Critical Inquiry* 8, no. 3 (1982): 489–507.

Coste Lewis, Robin. "Pleasure and Understanding." In *Voyage of the Sable Venus and Other Poems*, 129–31. New York: Knopf, 2015.

Critchley, Simon. *Infinitely Demanding: Ethics of Commitment, Politics of Resistance*. London: Verso, 2012.

Davis, Todd F., and Kenneth Womack, eds. *Mapping the Ethical Turn: A Reader in Ethics, Culture, and Literary Theory*. Charlottesville: University Press of Virginia, 2001.

de Grandis, Rita. "The First Colonial Encounter in *El entenado* by Juan Jose Saer: Paratextuality and History in Postmodern Fiction." *Latin American Literary Review* 21, no. 41 (1993): 30–38.

de Man, Paul. *Allegories of Reading: Figural Language in Rousseau, Nietzsche, Rilke, and Proust*. New Haven, CT: Yale University Press, 1979.

———. *Blindness and Insight: Essays in the Rhetoric of Contemporary Criticism*. 2nd ed. Minneapolis: University of Minnesota Press, 1983.

———. "A Letter from Paul de Man." *Critical Inquiry* 8, no. 3 (1982): 509–13.

Del Barco, Oscar. "No matarás: Thou shalt not kill." *Journal of Latin American Cultural Studies* 16, no. 2 (2007): 115–17.

Derrida, Jacques. "Abraham, the Other." In *Judeities: Questions for Jacques Derrida*, trans. Gil Anidjar, ed. Bettina Bergo, Joseph Cohen, and Raphael Zagury-Orly, 1–35. New York: Fordham University Press, 2007.

———. "History of the Lie: Prolegomena." In *Without Alibi*, ed. and trans. Peggy Kamuf, 28–70. Stanford, CA: Stanford University Press, 2002.

———. Interview with Jacques Derrida. *Out of Nothing*. http://outwardfromnothingness.com/interview-with-jacques-derrida.

———. "Mochlos; or, The Conflict of the Faculties." In *Logomachia: The Conflict of the Faculties*, ed. Richard Rand, trans. Richard Rand and Amy Wygant, 1–34. Lincoln: University of Nebraska Press, 1992.

———. "Nietzsche and the Machine." In *Negotiations: Interventions and Interviews, 1971–2001*, ed. and trans. Elizabeth Rottenberg, 215–56. Stanford, CA: Stanford University Press, 2002.

———. "Passions: An Oblique Offering." In *On the Name*, ed. Thomas Detoit, trans. David Wood, John P. Leavey Jr., and Ian McLeod, 3–31. Stanford, CA: Stanford University Press, 1995.

———. "Plato's Pharmacy" (1972). In *Dissemination*, trans. Barbara Johnson, 61–172. Chicago: University of Chicago Press, 1981.

———. *The Politics of Friendship*. Trans. George Collins. London: Verso, 2005.

———. "Provocation: Forewords." In *Without Alibi*, ed. and trans. Peggy Kamuf, xv–xxv. Stanford, CA: Stanford University Press, 2002.

———. *Rogues. Two Essays on Reason*. Trans. Pascale-Anne Brault and Michael Naas. Stanford, CA: Stanford University Press, 2005.

———. *Specters of Marx: The State of Debt, the Work of Mourning, and the New International*. Trans. Peggy Kamuf. New York: Routledge, 1994.

———. "Typewriter Ribbon: Limited Ink (2)." In *Without Alibi*, ed. and trans. Peggy Kamuf, 71–160. Stanford, CA: Stanford University Press, 2002.

———. "Unconditionality or Sovereignty: The University at the Frontiers of Europe." Trans. Peggy Kamuf. *Oxford Literary Review* 31 (2011): 115–31.

———. "The University without Condition." In *Without Alibi*, ed. and trans. Peggy Kamuf, 202–37. Stanford, CA: Stanford University Press, 2002.

———. "Violence and Metaphysics: An Essay on the Thought of Emmanuel Levinas" (1967). In *Writing and Difference*, trans. Alan Bass, 97–192. Chicago: University of Chicago Press, 1978.

———. "Violence of the Letter. From Lévi-Strauss to Rousseau" (1967). In *Of Grammatology*, trans. Gayatri Chakravorty Spivak, 101–40. Baltimore: Johns Hopkins University Press, 1997.

———. "Whom to Give to (Knowing Not to Know)" (1999). In *The Gift of Death*, trans. David Wills, 54–81. Chicago: University of Chicago Press, 2008.

Derrida, Jacques, and Anne Dufourmantelle. *Of Hospitality: Anne Dufourmantelle Invites Jacques Derrida to Respond*. Trans. Rachel Bowlby. Stanford, CA: Stanford University Press, 2000.

Dove, Patrick. "Critique of Critique." *Política Común* 4 (2013). http://dx.doi.org/10
.3998/pc.12322227.0004.008.

———. "Memory between Politics and Ethics: Del Barco's Letter." *Journal of Latin American Cultural Studies* 17 (2008): 179–97.

———. "Two Sides of the Same Coin? Form, Matter, and Secrecy in Derrida, de Man, and Borges." In *The Marrano Specter: Derrida and Hispanism*, ed. Erin Graff Zivin, 81–99. New York: Fordham University Press, 2017.

Draper, Susana. "Fragmentos de futuro en los abismos del pasado: *Amuleto*, 1968–1998." In *Fuera de quicio: Bolaño en el tiempo de sus espectros*, ed. Raúl Freire. Santiago, Chile: Editorial Ripio, 2012.

duBois, Page. *Torture and Truth.* New York: Routledge, 1991.

Dussel, Enrique. *Liberación latinoamericana y Emmanuel Levinas.* Buenos Aires: Editorial Bonum, 1975.

———. "Lo político en Levinas: hacia una filosofía política *crítica.*" *Signos filosóficos* 9 (2003): 111–32.

———. "'Sensibility' and 'Otherness' in Emmanuel Levinas." Trans. John Browning and Joyce Bellous. *Philosophy Today* (1999): 126–34.

Dussel, Enrique, and Enrique Guillot. *Liberación latinoamericana y Emmanuel Levinas.* Buenos Aires: Editorial Bonum, 1975.

Epplin, Craig. *Late Book Culture in Argentina.* New York: Bloomsbury, 2014.

Esposito, Roberto. 1999. *Categories of the Impolitical.* Trans. Connal Parsley. New York: Fordham University Press, 2015.

Ettinger, Bracha. "From Proto-Ethical Compassion to Responsibility: Besideness and the Three Primal Mother-Phantasies of Not-enoughness, Devouring, and Abandonment." *Athena: Philosophical Studies* 2 (2007): 100–45.

Forster, Ricardo. "La aventura marrana en la constitución del sujeto moderno: claves para comprender la entrada del judaísmo en la época de la secularización." In *Mesianismo, nihilismo y redención: de Abraham a Spinoza, de Marx a Benjamin*, by Ricardo Forster and Diego Tatián, 143–203. Buenos Aires: Altamira, 2005.

Franco, Jean. "The Nation as Imagined Community." In *Dangerous Liaisons: Gender, Nation, and Postcolonial Perspectives*, ed. Anne McClintock, Aamir Mufti, and Ella Shohat, 130–37. Minneapolis: University of Minnesota Press, 1997.

Gallix, Andrew. "In Theory: The Death of Literature." *Guardian*, January 10, 2012, https://www.theguardian.com/books/2012/jan/10/
in-theory-death-of-literature.

Garber, Marjorie, Beatrice Hanssen, and Rebecca L. Walkowitz, eds. *The Turn to Ethics.* New York: Routledge, 2000.

Gnutzmann, Rita. "*El entenado* o la respuesta de Saer a las crónicas." *Revista de Estudios Hispánicos* 20 (1993): 199–206.

Gollnick, Brian. "El color justo de la patria: agencias discursivas en *El entenado* de Juan José Saer." *Revista de Crítica Literaria Latinoamericana* 29, no. 57 (2003): 107–24.

González Echevarría, Roberto. "BdeORridaGES (BORGES Y DERRIDA)." In *Isla a su vuelo fugitivo: ensayos críticos sobre literatura hispanoamericana*, 205–15. Madrid: José Porrúa Turanzas, 1983.

————. *The Voice of the Masters: Writing and Authority in Latin American Literature.* Austin: University of Texas Press, 1985.

González, Eduardo. "Caliban; or, Flesh-Eating and Ghost Text in Saer's *El entenado.*" *Dispositio* 23, no. 50 (1998): 1–18.

González, Horacio. "El cuatrerismo de las imágenes." *La Tecl//www.lateclaene.com/horacio-gonzlez-cuatreros.*

Gourgouris, Stathis. "Archē." *Political Concepts* 3, no. 5 (2016). https://www.political concepts.org/arche-stathis-gourgouris/.

Graf, Eric C. "When an Arab Laughs in Toledo: Cervantes's Interpellation of Early Modern Spanish Orientalism." *Diacritics* 29, no. 2 (1999): 68–85.

Graff Zivin, Erin. *Figurative Inquisitions: Conversion, Torture, and Truth in the Luso-Hispanic Atlantic.* Evanston, IL: Northwestern University Press, 2014.

Hägglund, Martin. "The Non-Ethical Opening of Ethics: A Response to Derek Attridge." *Derrida Today* 3, no. 2 (2010): 295–305.

————. *Radical Atheism: Derrida and the Time of Life.* Stanford, CA: Stanford University Press, 2008.

Hallward, Peter. "Translator's Introduction." In *Ethics: An Essay on the Understanding of Evil,* by Alain Badiou, trans. Peter Hallward. London: Verso, 2002.

Hoyos, Héctor. *Beyond Bolaño: The Global Latin American Novel.* New York: Columbia University Press, 2015.

Internacional Errorista. *Manifiesto errorista.* Buenos Aires: Milena Caserola, 2009.

Jameson, Fredric. "Third-World Literature in the Era of Multinational Capitalism." *Social Text* 15 (1986): 65–88.

Jenckes, Kate. *Reading Borges after Benjamin: Allegory, Afterlife, and the Writing of History.* Albany: SUNY Press, 2007.

Jerade Dana, Miriam. "Violencia y responsabilidad: releer el silencio de Abraham." *Acta Poética* 31, no. 1 (2010): 101–34.

Jinkis, Jorge. "A Reply to Oscar del Barco." *Journal of Latin American Cultural Studies* 16, no. 2 (2007): 119–25.

Juárez, Enrique, dir. *Ya es tiempo de violencia.* 1969.

Kafka, Franz. "Abraham." In *Parables and Paradoxes in German and English,* trans. Clement Greenberg, 36–41. New York: Schocken, 1946.

Kamuf, Peggy. *The Division of Literature, or the University in Deconstruction.* Chicago: University of Chicago Press, 1997.

Kant, Immanuel. *The Conflict of the Faculties,* trans. Mary J. Gregor. Lincoln: University of Nebraska Press, 1992.

Kaufman, Alejandro. "The Paradoxical Legacy of a Lost Treasure." *Journal of Latin American Cultural Studies* 16, no. 2 (2007): 145–53.

Kierkegaard, Søren. (Johannes de Silentio). *Fear and Trembling.* 1843. Trans. Alistair Hannay. London: Penguin, 1985.

Kohan, Martín. "La apariencia celebrada." *Punto de Vista* 78 (2004): 24–30.

Legrás, Horacio. *Literature and Subjection: The Economy of Writing and Marginality in Latin America.* Pittsburgh: University of Pittsburgh Press, 2008.

Levinas, Emmanuel. *Otherwise than Being, or Beyond Essence.* 1974. Trans. Alphonso Lingis. Pittsburgh: Duquesne University Press, 1998.

————. *Proper Names*. 1975. Trans. Michael B. Smith. Stanford, CA: Stanford University Press, 1996.

————. *Totality and Infinity: An Essay on Exteriority*. 1961. Trans. Alphonso Lingis. Pittsburgh: Duquesne University Press, 1969.

Levinson, Brett. *The Ends of Literature: The Latin American "Boom" in the Neoliberal Marketplace*. Stanford, CA: Stanford University Press, 2002.

————. "On Netanyahu's *The Origins of the Inquisition in Fifteenth-Century Spain*: Does the Inquisition Justify Zionism?" *Journal of Spanish Cultural Studies* 4, no. 2 (2005): 18–36.

Lezra, Jacques. "On Contingency in Translation." In *Early Modern Cultures of Translation*, ed. Karen Newman and Jane Tylus, 153–74. Philadelphia: University of Pennsylvania Press, 2015.

————. *Wild Materialism: The Ethic of Terror and the Modern Republic*. New York: Fordham University Press, 2010.

Link, Daniel. "Hay guerra." *Perfil*, February 28, 2017. http://www.perfil.com/columnistas/hay-guerra.phtml.

Liu, Catherine. *American Idyll: Academic Antielitism as Cultural Critique*. Iowa City: University of Iowa Press, 2011.

Macherey, Pierre. *A Theory of Literary Production*. New York, Routledge, 1978.

Markell, Patchen. *Bound by Recognition*. Princeton: Princeton University Press, 2003.

Medina Molera, Antonio. *Cervantes y el Islam: el Quijote a cielo abierto*. Barcelona: Ediciones Carena, 2005.

Menocal, Maria Rosa. *The Ornament of the World: How Muslims, Jews, and Christians Created a Culture of Tolerance in Medieval Spain*. Boston: Little, Brown, 2002.

Miller, Karina. "No todo lo que reluce es oro: realidad y representación en *El entenado* de Saer." *Dissidences* 3, no. 6 (2012). http://digitalcommons.bowdoin.edu/dissidences/vol3/iss6/7/.

Montag, Warren. *Althusser and His Contemporaries: Philosophy's Perpetual War*. Durham, NC: Duke University Press, 2013.

Moreiras, Alberto. "Common Political Democracy: The *Marrano* Register." In *Impasses of the Post-Global: Theory in the Era of Climate Change*, ed. Henry Sussman, 2:175–193. Ann Arbor, MI: Open Humanities Press, 2012.

————. *The Exhaustion of Difference: The Politics of Latin American Cultural Studies*. Durham, NC: Duke University Press, 2001.

————. "Infrapolitical Derrida: The Ontic Determination of Politics beyond Empiricism." In *The Marrano Specter: Derrida and Hispanism*, ed. Erin Graff Zivin, 116–37. New York: Fordham University Press, 2017.

————. "Infrapolitical Literature: Hispanism and the Border." *CR: The New Centennial Review* 10, no. 2 (2010): 183–203.

————. "Infrapolitics and the Thriller: A Prolegomenon to Every Possible Form of Antimoralist Literary Criticism. On Héctor Aguilar Camín's *La guerra de Galio* and *Morir en el golfo*." In *The Ethics of Latin American Literary Criticism: Reading Otherwise*, ed. Erin Graff Zivin, 147–179. New York: Palgrave Macmillan, 2007.

————. *Línea de sombra. El no sujeto de lo político*. Santiago, Chile: Palinodia, 2006.

———. "Pastiche Identity, and Allegory of Allegory." In *Latin American Identity and Constructions of Difference*, ed. Amaryll Beatrice Chanady, 204–38. Minneapolis: University of Minnesota Press, 1994.

Morris, David. "Gothic Sublimity." *New Literary History* 16 (1985): 299–319.

Morrison, Toni. *Beloved*. New York: Knopf, 1987.

Moten, Fred, and Stefano Harney. "The University and the Undercommons." *Social Text* 79 (2004): 101–15.

Newfield, Christopher. *Unmaking the Public University: The Forty-Year Assault on the Middle Class*. Cambridge, MA: Harvard University Press, 2011.

Ophir, Adi. "Concept." Trans. Naveh Frumer. *Political Concepts: A Critical Lexicon* 1 (2011). http://www.politicalconcepts.org/issue1/concept/.

Orwell, George. *1984*. London: Penguin, 1950.

Penix-Tadsen, Phillip. "Marketing Marginality: Resistance and Commodification in Contemporary Latin American Cultural Production." PhD diss., Columbia University, 2009.

Piglia, Ricardo. *El último lector*. Barcelona: Editorial Anagrama, 2005.

Pound, Ezra. *The Cantos of Ezra Pound*. 1942. New York: New Directions, 1996.

———. *Make It New*. Essays. London: Faber & Faber, 1934.

Rabasa, José. *Without History: Subaltern Studies, the Zapatista Insurgency, and the Specter of History*. Pittsburgh: University of Pittsburgh Press, 2010.

Rancière, Jacques. *Disagreement: Politics and Philosophy*, trans. Julie Rose. Minneapolis: University of Minnesota Press, 1999.

———. *The Politics of Aesthetics*. 2000. Trans. Gabriel Rockhill. New York: Continuum, 2004.

———. *The Politics of Literature*. 2007. Trans. Julie Rose. Cambridge: Polity, 2011.

———. "Thinking between Disciplines: An Aesthetics of Knowledge." *Parrhesia* 1 (2006): 1–12.

Rappaport, Joanne, and Tom Cummins. *Beyond the Lettered City*. Durham, NC: Duke University Press, 2011.

Readings, Bill. *The University in Ruins*. Cambridge, MA: Harvard University Press, 1997.

Richard, Nelly. *La insubordinación de los signos. Cambio político, transformaciones culturales y poéticas de la crisis*. Santiago, Chile: Editorial Cuarto Propio, 1994.

Riera, Gabriel. *Littoral of the Letter: Saer's Art of Narration*. Lewisburg, PA: Bucknell University Press, 2006.

Robbins, Jill. *Altered Reading: Lévinas and Literature*. Chicago: University of Chicago Press, 1999.

Rockhill, Gabriel. "The Politics of Aesthetics: Political History and the Hermeneutics of Art." In *Jacques Rancière: History, Politics, Aesthetics*, by Gabriel Rockhill and Philip Watts, 195–215. Durham, NC: Duke University Press, 2009.

———. "Translator's Introduction: Jacques Rancière's Politics of Perception." In *The Politics of Aesthetics*, by Jacques Rancière, trans. Gabriel Rockhill, 1–6. London: Continuum, 2004.

rodríguez freire, raúl. "Arte, trabajo, universidad." In *Archivos de frontera*, ed. Iván Pincheira, 161–92. Concepción, Chile: Escaparate, 2012.

Rodríguez Monegal, Emir. "Borges and Derrida: Apothecaries." In *Borges and His Successors: The Borgesian Impact on Literature and the Arts*, ed. Edna Aizenberg, 128–54. Columbia: University of Missouri Press, 1990.

———. "Borges y Derrida: boticarios." *Maldoror* (Montevideo) 21 (1985): 123–32.

Rolfe, Gary. *The University in Dissent: Scholarship in the Corporate University*. New York: Routledge, 2013.

Romano Thuesen, Evelia. "*El entenado*: relación contemporánea de las memorias de Francisco del Puerto." *Latin American Literary Review* 23, no. 45 (1995): 43–63.

Saccavino, Emma. "El error como alegoría de la contracultura." *Unidiversidad*, November 29, 2013. http://www.unidiversidad.com.ar/el-error-como-alegoria -de-la-contracultura.

Saer, Juan José. *El entenado*. Mexico: Folios Ediciones, 1983.

———. *El río sin orillas. Tratado imaginario*. Buenos Aires: Alianza, 1991.

———. *The Witness*. Trans. Margaret Jull Costa. London: Serpent's Tail, 2009.

Safran Foer, Jonathan. *Here I Am*. New York: Farrar, Straus and Giroux, 2016.

Salomon, Frank, and Mercedes Niño-Murcia. *The Lettered Mountain*. Durham, NC: Duke University Press, 2011.

Sarlo, Beatriz. *Tiempo pasado. Cultura de la memoria y giro subjetivo: una discusión*. Buenos Aires: Siglo Veintiuno, 2005.

Schmitt, Carl. *Political Theology: Four Chapters on the Concept of Sovereignty*. 1922. Trans. George Schwab. Chicago: University of Chicago Press, 1985.

Self, Will. "The Novel Is Dead (This Time It's for Real)." *Guardian*, May 2, 2014. https://www.theguardian.com/books/2014/may/02/ will-self-novel-dead-literary-fiction.

Slabodsky, Santiago. *Decolonial Judaism: Triumphal Failures of Barbaric Thinking*. New York: Palgrave Macmillan, 2014.

Smith, Barry, et al. "Letter to the *Times* (London)." *Times* (London), May 9, 1992.

Sommer, Doris. "About-Face: The Talker Turns." *boundary 2* 23 (1996): 91–133.

———. *Foundational Fictions: The National Romances of Latin America*. Berkeley: University of California Press, 1991.

———. *Proceed with Caution, When Engaged by Minority Writing in the Americas*. Cambridge, MA: Harvard University Press, 1999.

Spinoza, Benedict de. *Theological-Political Treatise*. Ed. Jonathan Israel, trans. Michael Silverthorne and Jonathan Israel. Cambridge: Cambridge University Press, 2007.

Steinberg, Samuel. *Photopoetics at Tlatelolco: Afterimages of Mexico, 1968*. Austin: University of Texas Press, 2016.

Tatián, Diego. "Letter from Diego Tatián." *Journal of Latin American Cultural Studies* 16, no. 2 (2007): 141–43.

Taylor, Diana. "Becoming We." *MLA Newsletter* (Summer 2017). https://president .mla.hcommons.org/2017/04/19/becoming-we/.

———. "The Act of Transfer." In *What Is Performance Studies?*, ed. Diana Taylor and Marcos Steuernagel. Durham, NC: Duke University Press, 2015. http://scalar.usc .edu/nehvectors/wips/acts-of-transfer-1.

———. "Trauma in the Archive." In *Feeling Photography*, ed. Elspeth H. Brown and Thy Phu, 239–51. Durham, NC: Duke University Press, 2014.

Thayer, Willy. *La crisis no moderna de la universidad moderna*. Santiago, Chile: Cuarto Propio, 1996.

Ulin, David. "Notes on the (Non-)Death of the Book." *Los Angeles Times*, May 5, 2014. http://www.latimes.com/books/jacketcopy/la-et-jc-notes-on-the-nondeath-of-the-book-20140505-story.html.

Vargas Llosa, Mario. *El hablador*. Barcelona: Editorial Seix Barral, 1987.

———. *The Storyteller*. Trans. Helen Lane. New York: Farrar, Straus, and Giroux, 1989.

Villacañas, José Luis. "Spinoza: democracia y subjetividad marrana." *Política Común. A Journal of Thought* 1 (2011): 55–86.

Villalobos-Ruminott, Sergio. "Genealogies of Difference: Marranism and Indigenism in Marchant and Ajens." Paper presented at "The Marrano Spirit: Derrida and Hispanism" colloquium, University of Southern California, 2014.

Watkins, Susan. "Presentism? A Reply to T. J. Clark." *New Left Review* 74 (2012): 77–102.

Weber, Samuel. *Theatricality as Medium*. New York: Fordham University Press, 2004.

Williams, Gareth. *The Mexican Exception: Sovereignty, Police, and Democracy*. New York: Palgrave Macmillan, 2011.

———. *The Other Side of the Popular: Neoliberalism and Subalternity in Latin America*. Durham, NC: Duke University Press, 2002.

Index

48; of Inquisitional logic, 32, 43; Kierkegaard's, 87, 169n3; militant acts of, 40; political, 44, 70, 78; to come, 86; totalitarian state, 33–34
violent thinking, 84, 87

wandering, 126, 136. *See also* errancy
Williams, Gareth, 36–37, 41, 43, 113, 168n14

writing, 112, 115–16, 153, 158; the market and, 145; minority, 62, 64; other, 55, 58, 114. *See also* allography; arche-writing; reading
will, 12, 108, 110–12, 119; free, 172n3; paralysis of, 147; to sacrifice, 86. *See also* intentionality; sovereignty

Zeno's paradox, 95, 99–100

Erin Graff Zivin is Professor of Spanish and Portuguese and Comparative Literature and Chair of the Department of Comparative Literature at the University of Southern California. She is the author of *Figurative Inquisitions: Conversion, Torture, and Truth in the Luso-Hispanic Atlantic* (Northwestern University Press, 2014, winner of the 2015 Award for Best Book, Latin American Jewish Studies Association) and *The Wandering Signifier: Rhetoric of Jewishness in the Latin American Imaginary* (Duke University Press, 2008), and the editor of *The Ethics of Latin American Literary Criticism: Reading Otherwise* (Palgrave Macmillan, 2007) and *The Marrano Specter: Derrida and Hispanism* (Fordham University Press, 2017).

Sara Guyer and Brian McGrath, series editors